BUILDING BLOCKS
OF
FAITH

JOHN MARK CATON, PH.D

AUSTIN
BROTHERS PUBLISHING

Building Blocks of Faith
John Mark Caton

Published by Austin Brothers Publishing, Fort Worth, Texas

www.abpbooks.com

ISBN 978-0-9996328-6-4

Printed in the United States of America
2018 -- First Edition

I dedicate this book to my beloved church, and the people who live and work out their faith day by day outside the walls of a seminary or local church. I wrote out of a passion for making doctrinal building blocks of the faith both accessible and readable to anyone and everyone.

It seems like much theological writing is not easily understood by those not familiar with certain ideas and terms. However, I believe the best theology is taken straight from the pages of Scripture and delivered directly to the lives of people in the congregation.

One of my favorite verses in all of Scripture is "For everything that was written in the past was written to teach us, so that through the endurance taught in the Scriptures and the encouragement they provide we might have hope" (Romans 15:4).

My desire is that by reading **Building Blocks of Faith**, every reader will grow in the knowledge of Scripture as well as receive new hope for the days ahead.

THE BUILDING BLOCKS

THE DOCTRINE OF THE BIBLE

The Bible is the written word of God's will to man. The word "Bible" has Greek and Latin origins and simply means *book*. The Bible, as one unified book, contains 66 smaller books written by over 40 different authors over the course of approximately 1,600 years. The central theme of the Bible is that God the Father's eternal plan is to provide redemption for all His people in His Son, Jesus Christ by the power of the Holy Spirit.

> *2 Timothy 3:16-17,* *All Scripture is God-breathed and is useful for teaching, rebuking, correcting and training in righteousness, so that the servant of God may be thoroughly equipped for every good work.*

Since the Bible is the only book that reveals God's saving grace for fallen mankind, it is to be considered the most important book in the world. Because the Bible is God's inspired and authoritative revelation to man, it is a unique book and is in a class of its own.

Other books have been written by men, but the Bible was authored by God. Books written by men reveal to us the thoughts and wisdom of mankind, but only the Bible reveals the thoughts and wisdom of God.

The Old Testament was written mostly in Hebrew with a few short passages in Aramaic. The New Testament was written in Greek. Our English Bibles are translations from Hebrew, Aramaic, and Greek manuscripts. The word "testament" means covenant or agreement. The Old Testament is God's covenant or agreement with mankind before Jesus Christ came. The New Testament is God's covenant or agreement with mankind after Jesus Christ came. In the Old Testament, we see the Covenant of the Law, while in the New Testament, we see the Covenant of Grace through Jesus Christ.

> _Romans 3:21-26,_ But now the righteousness of God has been manifested apart from the law, although the Law and the Prophets bear witness to it—the righteousness of God through faith in Jesus Christ for all who believe. For there is no distinction: for all have sinned and fall short of the glory of God, and are justified by his grace as a gift, through the redemption that is in Christ Jesus, whom God put forward as a propitiation by his blood, to be received by faith. This was to show God's righteousness, because in his divine forbearance he had passed over former sins. It was to show his righteousness at the present time, so that he might be just and the justifier of the one who has faith in Jesus.

In the New Testament, Jesus Christ quoted from 22 of the 39 Old Testament books. He quoted from the Old Testament in Matthew 19 times, Mark 15 times, Luke 25 times, and John 11 times. The Bible contains 1,189 chapters, and 31,373 verses. The longest chapter in the Bible is Psalm 119, while the shortest chapter in the bible is Psalm 117. The longest book in the Old Testament is Psalms, and the longest book in the New Testament is the Gospel of Luke.

The Bible is not only the sole reliable source on God, but also on human life and its origin. The true and ultimate purpose of mankind is found in the pages of the Bible. All that is known about sin and man's true spiritual condition is revealed to us in the Bible. Only in the pages of the Bible can the truth concerning God's love in sending His Son into the world be found. All that we know about salvation and how man can have right standing with God comes from the Bible.

Therefore, in order to know truth about anything related to God, the world, or ourselves we must diligently study the Word of God.

Divine Revelation

In spite of the mountains of scientific advancements and the proliferation of knowledge in our time, some of life's greatest questions still remain unanswered scientifically. The structure of the universe clearly points to a divine Creator, but no purely scientific endeavor has been or ever will be able to reveal to us the divine mind. Scientists can carefully catalog the stars and even identify the materials that exist and measure their heat, size, and distance from the earth, but the efforts of scientists are limited to the known physical world. However, the scientist's work will always come up short when trying to explain the material universe's origin.

Scientists may be able to grow in knowledge about human anatomy, promote healing, and even extend the length of life upon earth, but scientists will never be able to explain man's true origin, purpose, and meaning apart from the Bible. Scientists will also never be able to explain the human soul, the mystery of death, and what, if anything occurs afterward. Those answers are only found in God's infallible word: the Bible.

This brings up four important questions. Has the great God and Creator of heaven and earth chosen to communicate Himself to creatures? If so, in what form has God chosen to communicate? Is this communication source still relevant? If so, has God made provisions for finite minds to receive and understand this profound knowledge? We can be confident in this study with the remarkable, true knowledge that God has chosen to reveal Himself to us, and we have this revelation preserved in our Bibles.

Christianity is a revealed religion in the sense that its claims are founded upon revelation from God. It is not the product of man's own thinking or reaching out for a better life. Christianity is neither folklore nor folk tale—an idea passed down through generations or a quaint story from a particular culture. Rather, the claims and confessions of the Bible are the direct revelations from the triune God of the gospel. Everyone who observes the world in which we live and move is unavoidably confronted with the question as to how all creation received its order and origin. When observing a house, car, swimming pool, jet, or skyscraper, we intuitively know there was planning and engineering involved in making such things—in short, we know there is a builder, creator, and intelligent force behind its creation.

The same principles hold true for our universe and all created things. They point to a builder, creator, and an intelligent designer behind everything that exists. But what do we know about this uncreated creator behind all that exists?

As Christians, we have the incredible understanding that God in His infinite wisdom, mercy, and love has chosen to reveal Himself to us in a special and direct way. First, He has given us His written word which we call the Bible. Second, the Father has given us His Son, the eternal Word: the Lord Jesus Christ who came to "exegete" (explain) God to man (cf. John 1:1, 14, 18). In His life, death, resurrection, and ascension Jesus makes it possible for man to have a personal relationship with God. Christianity is not a religion of human speculation or philosophy; it is a revealed religion from God Himself.

Many believe the Bible is nothing more than a collection of books written by men. Thus they conclude the Bible, like any other book, is fallible. It is true that if the Bible was just a book written by only men it would be fallible and inadequate at best. That's because man's intelligence, in and of itself, falls woefully short of being able to fathom who God is. The intellectual faculties of man, even exercised in its greatest potential, are futile apart from supernatural intervention. If man is to know and explain anything about God truly, he must receive that knowledge from God Himself. God announced the limited nature of the human intellect and intuitive powers through the prophet Isaiah and Apostle Paul when He says:

> *Isaiah 55:8-9,* *"For my thoughts are not your thoughts, neither are your ways my ways," declares the Lord. "As the heavens are higher than the earth, so are my ways higher than your ways and my thoughts than your thoughts."*

> *1 Corinthians 2:16,* *Who has known the mind of the Lord so as to instruct him?*

Revelation, Inspiration, and Illumination

Revelation, inspiration, and illumination are essential doctrines to consider in order to better understand the nature of God speaking light into the darkness of man's fallen reasoning. *Revelation* is a direct act of God communicating divine truths to mankind; while *inspiration* is the act of God helping man in transferring this divine knowledge into language which others may understand; and *illumination* is the act of God in allowing biblical readers to understand God's written word properly.

One could ask why revelation is necessary at all? There are several answers to this question.

First, revelation is necessary because God is inaccessible and unknowable without revelation. Because of the finiteness of mankind, God's infinite knowledge and character could not be known without divine revelation. Read the words of Isaiah again:

> *Isaiah 55:8-9,* *"For my thoughts are not your thoughts, neither are your ways my ways," declares the Lord. "As the heavens are higher than the earth, so are my ways higher than your ways and my thoughts than your thoughts."*

Second, revelation is necessary because of the fall of mankind. Because of Adam's sin, mankind's relationship with God was broken. Right after Adam sinned, God spoke to Adam which is divine revelation.

Genesis 3:9-18, But the Lord God called to the man, "Where are you?" He answered, "I heard you in the garden, and I was afraid because I was naked; so I hid." And he said, "Who told you that you were naked? Have you eaten from the tree that I commanded you not to eat from?" The man said, "The woman you put here with me—she gave me some fruit from the tree, and I ate it." Then the Lord God said to the woman, "What is this you have done?" The woman said, "The serpent deceived me, and I ate." So the Lord God said to the serpent, "Because you have done this, cursed are you above all livestock and all wild animals! You will crawl on your belly and you will eat dust all the days of your life. And I will put enmity between you and the woman, and between your offspring and hers he will crush your head, and you will strike his heel." To the woman he said, "I will make your pains in childbearing very severe; with painful labor you will give birth to children. Your desire will be for your husband, and he will rule over you." To Adam he said, "Because you listened to your wife and ate fruit from the tree about which I commanded you, 'You must not eat from it,' cursed is the ground because of you; through painful toil you will eat food from it all the days of your life. It will produce thorns and thistles for you, and you will eat the plants of the field."

If Adam needed divine revelation immediately after his fall, how much more do we need divine revelation? Since the effect of Adam's sin was passed down to all mankind, our sin likewise brings spiritual separation which creates a need for divine revelation. Therefore, divine revelation is needed because of the chasm sin forms between God and man. God must cross the chasm since man is stained by sin.

Other questions should be addressed as well when speaking of revelation: Does God wish to reveal Himself to mankind? If so, *why?*

Scripture is clear that God desires to reveal Himself to mankind because of His great love for us. Therefore, divine revelation is an act of God that He chooses to do in His own good pleasure for the sake of His glory and man's joy in Him. Read Ephesians 1:3-5:

Ephesians 1:3-5, Praise be to the God and Father of our Lord Jesus Christ, who has blessed us in the heavenly realms with every spiritual blessing in Christ. For he chose us in him before the creation of the world to be holy and blameless in his sight. In love he predestined us for adoption to sonship through Jesus Christ, in accordance with his pleasure and will...

How God Chose to Reveal Himself

God has chosen to reveal Himself in various ways. First, in creation. The created world is the handiwork of God which reveals that God is infinitely powerful and wise. He has carefully designed the world through intelligence for a purpose. This is what theologians refer to as General or Natural Revelation. Scripture testifies to this facet of revelation when it says:

> *Psalm 19:1-2,* The heavens declare the glory of God; the skies proclaim the work of his hands. Day after day they pour forth speech; night after night they reveal knowledge.

God has also chosen to reveal Himself through man's conscience, or what many have described as God-consciousness, which is possessed by every person. This is evident in that man still has a sense or desire for moral and spiritual worth. Also, this can be easily observed through philanthropic enterprises and man's desire for law and justice. This God-consciousness fleshes itself out in mankind's historical and almost universal desire to worship something or someone. In every culture and in every age mankind has searched for a god to worship. This idea is found in both Romans and Genesis.

> *Romans 1:21-23,* For although they knew God, they did not honor him as God or give thanks to him, but they became futile in their thinking, and their foolish hearts were darkened. Claiming to be wise, they became fools, and exchanged the glory of the immortal God for images resembling mortal man and birds and animals and creeping things.

God also reveals Himself through what is called a *theophany*. A theophany is a physical manifestation of the divine presence of God. Examples of theophanies are seen in Scripture:

> *Genesis 17:1,* When Abram was ninety-nine years old, the Lord appeared to him and said, "I am God Almighty; walk before me faithfully and be blameless."

God has also chosen to reveal Himself through miracles and signs. The purpose of these miracles and signs was to gain man's attention and to demonstrate God's power. Examples of these miracles and signs can be found in the flood (Genesis 6-9); the burning bush, the plagues of Egypt, and the cloud and fire found in Exodus 3-15. Our Lord also used miracles and signs to testify to His identity as the Son of God (e.g., water to wine, raising Lazarus from the dead, feeding 5000, etc.). Many other examples can also be seen throughout Scripture.

God also revealed Himself to mankind through the Old Testament Prophets. These Prophets (men such as Samuel, Isaiah, and Jeremiah) were entrusted with God's direct speech to proclaim and herald to the nation of Israel or specific people within Israel. However, all of these Old Testament Prophets were only a shadow of someone greater, someone who would come as God's perfect Word to man—Jesus Christ. The Supreme revelation of God was provided in the person and work of Jesus Christ who was born at God's appointed time. The Bible declares very plainly that Jesus came to reveal God to us in a personal way, because Jesus was both sent by God the Father and is one substance with the Father. Jesus is God's mystery revealed to us and in whom are hidden all the treasures, wisdom, and knowledge of God.

> _Hebrews 1:1-2, Long ago, at many times and in many ways, God spoke to our fathers by the prophets, but in these last days he has spoken to us by his Son, whom he appointed the heir of all things, through whom also he created the world._

Finally, God reveals Himself to us through Scripture. All of the other forms of revelation that we have studied are confirmed, contained, and preserved in the Word of God. Scripture shows how God has revealed himself to mankind, and provides a picture of God in His glory and all of His attributes. We see mankind in his proper place in relation to an eternally triune God. Scripture reveals the love that God possess and demonstrates for mankind.

Additionally, theophanies give a clear view the salvation which God offers and the spiritual blessings He bestows upon all those who are in saving union with His Son, Jesus Christ. The Scriptures give a view of God's plan from eternity past, the present circumstances, and into eternity future. Scripture shows how God dealt with Israel, the Gentiles, the Church, and ultimately how God will deal with all mankind in the future. It is the Scriptures that reveal to us what God has done, is doing, and will do in Christ by the Spirit. God has chosen to reveal Himself to us and in doing that He has given us the greatest book in the world—the Bible.

Inspiration

Inspiration refers to the act of God enabling biblical authors to write divine truth down exactly the way God intends for it to be written such that it is simultaneously the words of the biblical writer and the true word of God. The Apostle Paul declared:

> _2 Timothy 3:16-17, All Scripture is God-breathed and is useful for teaching, rebuking, correcting and training in righteousness, so that the servant of God may be thoroughly equipped for every good work._

The word "God-breathed" is translated inspired in many translations. God-breathed comes from the combination of two Greek _"theo-pneustos."_ "Theos" means God and _"pneustos"_ means breath. Therefore, the best and most accurate translation of that word is "*God-breathed,*" and it refers to all Scripture.

It should be pointed out that there are various views of the inspiration of the Bible. First, there is what has been called *Natural Inspiration.* That who hold to natural inspiration believe the Bible is only a remarkable human book but is devoid of divine inspiration. The writers of the Bible are said to have literary genius just like many other gifted writers, poets, and musicians who have created masterpieces. For them, the Bible is classified as mere exceptional literature and placed on the same literary level as Homer's *Odyssey*, Dante's *Divine Comedy*, and the many writings of Shakespeare. Some will even go so far as to suggest that the Bible although not divinely inspired, is the greatest of all human writings as Christ was the greatest of all human teachers.

A second view of inspiration is that of *Partial Inspiration.* According to this view, inspiration applies to doctrinal teachings and precepts, but historical, geographical, or scientific statements in the Scriptures are not inspired and subject to error. This view also maintains that inspiration had only to do with the writer's thoughts, not with the actual words he wrote. *Partial Inspiration* holds to view that God suggested the ideas in the general trend of the revelation then left man free to express them in his own language as he desired. Along with this view is the idea that some portions of Scriptures are more inspired than others. This view clearly rejects the truth that *all* of Scripture is "God-breathed."

It must be noted at this point, that *Partial Inspiration* falls short of the clear teaching of Scripture and does extensive damage to the teaching of the Bible itself. If some of the words of the Bible are not inspired, then the study of some parts of Scripture would be meaningless because the words would be without divine authority. This is in direct contradiction to what Scripture itself teaches because the Bible itself insists on the authority of its very words.

> <u>Hebrews 4:12,</u> *For the word of God is alive and active. Sharper than any double-edged sword, it penetrates even to dividing soul and spirit, joints and marrow; it judges the thoughts and attitudes of the heart.*

Not only does *Partial Inspiration* fall short of the teaching of Scripture itself, there are two other problems that are created: 1) *Partial Inspiration* renders the reader helpless in determining what parts of Scripture are inspired and which parts are not and 2) *Partial Inspiration* actually sets the reader in authority over the words of Scripture in that each individual person is responsible to determine what parts of Scripture are divinely inspired and which parts they do not believe are inspired.

A third theory of inspiration is called *Degrees of Inspiration.* This theory is based on the assumption that some parts of the Bible are more inspired than others. This view gives latitude for the contention that the Bible contains errors. Many claim that the Bible is full of myths, legends, and folklore which have been carried down through the years. It is maintained that we may accept the humanistic side of the Bible, but when we come to the divine aspect, then it is attributed to hyper-spiritual exaggeration. As with *Partial Inspiration*, those who hold to the theory of *Degrees of Inspiration* set themselves up as the judge of what is inspired and what is not. The product of this teaching is an "anything goes" theology which becomes devoid of any divine light and legitimacy.

A fourth view of Inspiration is the *Mechanical* or *Dictation Theory* concerning the Bible. This theory of inspiration asserts that God dictated the Scriptures to men and controlled them in a mechanical way as they wrote. A biblical author then is wholly passive in the process transmitting of the revelation, similar to a court reporter. In this view, the human author's personality is completely set aside to the point where he is really no author at all. This view is certainly an attempt to defend and uplift Scripture's divine origin and authority. However, it is not consistent with the array of writing styles portrayed in Scripture. If the *Mechanical* or *Dictation Theory* is correct, and God did dictate the Scripture in the fashion suggested by the theory, then the Bible would be uniform in its structure and style. However, the reader of Scripture can easily see that the message of the Bible is wholly consistent, but Scripture is written in many different times, styles, and structures. Examples of these different styles can easily be seen in that Luke uses a very pure, sophisticated Greek; Paul uses choppy, more difficult Greek; and John employs a simple, easy-to-read Greek. The writings of John, Paul, and Luke are literarily distinct and represent their respective styles and perspectives.

The final view of Inspiration we shall consider is called *Verbal* or *Plenary Inspiration*. *Verbal Inspiration* means that in the original writings, the Spirit guided in the choice of words which were to be used. However, the unique perspectives and personalities of the writers were preserved. Their styles and vocabularies were used but without any blemish, error, or falsehood.

Plenary Inspiration means that the accuracy which *Verbal Inspiration* secures is extended to every part of the Bible. The word plenary means full, complete, and absolute. This means that all of Scripture, from beginning to end, is divinely inspired, error-free, and authoritative for faith and life. The view of Verbal or Plenary Inspiration is the only view that is consistent logically and the one that is supported throughout the Bible—specifically by the word *"theo-pneustos"* which means *"God-breathed"*:

> *2 Timothy 3:16-17, All Scripture is God-breathed and is useful for teaching, rebuking, correcting and training in righteousness, so that the servant of God may be thoroughly equipped for every good work.*

> *2 Peter 1:21, For no prophecy was ever produced by the will of man, but men spoke from God as they were carried along by the Holy Spirit.*

There is internal evidence of divine inspiration. Simply stated, that means the Bible itself claims divine inspiration. First, in considering the matter of the divine inspiration of the Bible, it is helpful and appropriate to first look at the words of Jesus. Jesus affirmed the divine inspiration of the Old Testament when He says,

> *Matthew 5:18, For truly I tell you, until heaven and earth disappear, not the smallest letter, not the least stroke of a pen, will by any means disappear from the Law until everything is accomplished.*

In this passage, Jesus was referring to the Old Testament and affirming its Divine Inspiration. On many other occasions, Jesus quoted from the Old Testament as authoritative, demonstrating that He considered it to be inspired by God as the true, infallible, and authoritative Word of God.

The continuity of the Bible's message is another internal effect of divine inspiration. This is actually one of the strongest evidences of the Bible's divine inspiration and authorship. Simply stated, the golden thread that runs through all the pages of the Bible is God reconciling the world to Himself in Christ (2 Cor 5:19). The Scriptures are a single volume composed of sixty-six smaller books written over the span of sixteen centuries by over forty different human authors who were inspired by the Holy Spirit. Even over the long time span, using numerous human authors, and diversity in literary form, Scripture's unity and clarity is astonishing. The unity of Scriptures can be seen through the steady unfolding of God's plan of salvation through His Son Jesus Christ, and God's plan of salvation and redemption of mankind unfolds from Genesis and Revelation.

In Genesis 1, the creation of the world occurs, and in Genesis 2 there is a poetic account of the creation of the first man and woman. In Genesis 3, the serpent (Satan) and temptation enter the world and mankind, in willful and sinful autonomous rebellion, disobeys God. In Genesis 4-11, sin becomes a universally destructive factor. In chapter 12, God promises a blessed redeemer who would come through the seed of Abraham and the nation of Israel (see Genesis 12:1-3 and Galatians 3:16).

After the promise of a redeemer, the Law was given for the purpose of reminding mankind of its sinfulness before God and its inability to live a life which is acceptable to God. God used the nation of Israel to entrust with His Holy Oracles.

Romans 3:1-2, What advantage, then, is there in being a Jew, or what value is there in circumcision? Much in every way! First of all, the Jews have been entrusted with the very oracles of God.

God used the nation of Israel for the purpose of producing the divine seed which was to bless all nations, namely, the person of the the Lord Jesus Christ:

Genesis 15:1-7, After this, the word of the Lord came to Abram in a vision: "Do not be afraid, Abram. I am your shield, your very great reward." But Abram said, "Sovereign Lord, what can you give me since I remain childless and the one who will inherit my estate is Eliezer of Damascus?" And Abram said, "You have given me no children; so a servant in my household will be my heir." Then the word of the Lord came to him: "This man will not be your heir, but a son who is your own flesh and blood will be your heir." He took him outside and said, "Look up at the sky and count the stars—if indeed you can count them." Then he said to him, "So shall your offspring be." Abram believed the Lord, and he credited it to him as righteousness. He also said to him, "I am the Lord, who brought you out of Ur of the Chaldeans to give you this land to take possession of it."

In the New Testament, the Savior comes in fulfillment of the Old Testament's promises. In His earthly Ministry, Jesus time and time again expresses His purposes of fulfilling the Old Testament promises and prophecies. The Gospels record His incarnation, perfect life, divine teaching, death, resurrection, and ascension—all according to God's redemptive plan which was beginning to unfold in the Old Testament. The prophecies and teachings of the Old Testament are fulfilled in the New Testament, and more specifically, in the person of Jesus Christ (see 2 Cor 1:20).

In Acts 2, we see further progressive continuity of the Bible with the outpouring of the Holy Spirit which resulted in the birth of the Church. Through the Holy Spirit's empowerment and guidance, the gospel expanded throughout the book of Acts. The church continued to grow and develop its system of doctrines and teaching throughout the New Testament epistles.

The book of Revelation foretells of that final combat between good and evil, God and Satan, and an eternal state is set. All of this is seen in a continuous line running from Genesis to Revelation, expressing incredible continuity. In this divine continuity, we see the divine authorship of the Bible from beginning to end.

The Bible declares itself to be the very word of God. The Old Testament states some

3,808 times that its words are of divine origin. Some may question whether the Bible can be considered a good witness of itself. There are some who argue that the Scriptures ought not to be appealed to for their own vindication. It is maintained that to quote Scripture in support of its own nature seems to be arguing in circles or logically inconclusive. However, it must be noted that every document has the right to speak for Himself, and the Scriptures are no exception (e.g., the U.S. Constitution). The Bible is a trustworthy witness for so many subjects, therefore, why should its testimony concerning itself not be considered? After all, in God's infinite wisdom, He chose to write Scripture through human authors, so it has a right to be its own witness just like someone does in a court of law. Thus, in some 3,808 instances, the human authors don't claim authority for their words in themselves but attest to God as the ultimate source of their words and wisdom as contained in the Bible.

The biblical writers themselves claim divine inspiration in several ways: 1) The various writers' claim divine authorship and authority for their words.

Psalm 19:7, The law of the Lord is perfect, refreshing the soul. The statutes of the Lord are trustworthy, making wise the simple.

Psalm 119:89, Your word, Lord, is eternal; it stands firm in the heavens.

Isaiah 8:20, Consult God's instruction and the testimony of warning. If anyone does not speak according to this word, they have no light of dawn.

In the Bible, we find one book recognizing another book as speaking with divine authority.

Joshua 8:31-32, as Moses the servant of the Lord had commanded the Israelites. He built it according to what is written in the Book of the Law of Moses—an altar of uncut stones, on which no iron tool had been used. On it they offered to the Lord burnt offerings and sacrificed fellowship offerings. There, in the presence of the Israelites, Joshua wrote on stones a copy of the law of Moses.

Nehemiah 8:1, all the people came together as one in the square before the Water Gate. They told Ezra the teacher of the Law to bring out the Book of the Law of Moses, which the Lord had commanded for Israel.

Daniel 9:1-2, In the first year of Darius son of Xerxes (a Mede by descent), who was made ruler over the Babylonian kingdom—in the first year of his reign, I, Daniel, understood from the Scriptures, according to the word of the Lord given to Jeremiah the prophet, that the desolation of Jerusalem would last seventy years.

1 Peter 1:10-11, Concerning this salvation, the prophets, who spoke of the grace that was to come to you, searched intently and with the greatest care, trying to find out the time and circumstances to which the Spirit of Christ in them was pointing when he predicted the sufferings of the Messiah and the glories that would follow.

2 Peter 3:15-16, Bear in mind that our Lord's patience means salvation, just as our dear brother Paul also wrote you with the wisdom that God gave him. He writes the same way in all his letters, speaking in them of these matters. His letters contain some things that are hard to understand, which ignorant and unstable people distort, as they do the other Scriptures, to their own destruction.

Jesus affirmed Scripture and said it could not be broken. Jesus also declared that the Law of Moses, the Prophets, and the Psalms speak about Him, and He affirms that He did not come to destroy the Law but to fulfill it:

Luke 24:44, He said to them, "This is what I told you while I was still with you: Everything must be fulfilled that is written about me in the Law of Moses, the Prophets and the Psalms."

Matthew 5:17-18, "Do not think that I have come to abolish the Law or the Prophets; I have not come to abolish them but to fulfill them. For truly I tell you, until heaven and earth disappear, not the smallest letter, not the least stroke of a pen, will by any means disappear from the Law until everything is accomplished.

Therefore, those who affirm the complete divine inspiration of the Bible are in good company as they stand with Moses, Isaiah, Jeremiah, David, the Prophets, Paul, Peter, the Apostles, Jesus, the Holy Spirit, and the early church.

Another strong argument in favor of the Bible being the Word of God is reflected in the fulfillment of prophecy. The Bible itself indicates that the litmus test of all prophecy is its complete accuracy and fulfillment.

Deuteronomy 18:21-22, You may say to yourselves, "How can we know when a message has not been spoken by the Lord?" If what a prophet proclaims in the name of the Lord does not take place or come true, that is a message the Lord has not spoken.

If there were only a few prophecies in Scripture, one might dismiss them as mere chance or luck. However, when these predictions run into hundreds, the evidence is incontestable as to the divine inspiration of Scriptures. There are too many fulfilled prophecies to list. However, I will present just a few prophecies that were fulfilled concerning the person of Jesus Christ:

Nature of Prophecy - The Prophecy - The Fulfillment of the Prophecy

- Seed of a woman - Genesis 3:15 - Galatians 4:4
- Human generation - Genesis 12:3; 18:18 & 49 - John 1:45, Acts 3:25; 13:23, Galatians 3:8
- Time of His coming - Daniel 9:24-25 - John 1:41; 4:25-26
- Born of a Virgin - Isaiah 7:14; Micah 5:3 - Matthew 1:23 Luke 1:26-35
- Descendant of Shem - Genesis 9:7 - Luke 3:36
- Descendant of Abraham - Genesis 12:3 - Matthew 1:1-2, Luke 3:34
- Descendant of Isaac - Genesis 17:19 - Matthew 1:2, Romans 9:7
- Descendant of Jacob - Genesis 28:14 - Luke 3:34
- Tribe of Judah - Genesis 49:10 - Matthew 1:2; 2:6
- House of David - Isaiah 9:7 - Matthew 1:1, 6 Jeremiah 23:5 Luke 3:31
- Birthplace - Micah 5:2 - Matthew 2:1-6
- Massacre of innocents accompany His birth - Jeremiah 31:15 - Matthew 2:17-18
- Flight into Egypt - Hosea 11:1 - Matthew 2:15
- Ministry in Galilee - Isaiah 9:1-2 - Matthew 4:15-16
- A prophet - Deuteronomy 18:15 - John 1:45; 6:14
- Priest like Melchizedek - Psalms 110:4 - Hebrews 5:6; 6:20
- Purification of temple - Psalms 69:9 - John 2:17
- Rejected by Jews - Psalms 2:1 - John 6:66
- Spiritual graces - Psalms 45:7 - Luke 4:18
- Triumphant entry into Jerusalem - Isaiah 62:11 - Matthew 21:1-10; John 12:14-16
- Betrayal by a friend for 30 pieces of silver - Zechariah 11:12-13 - Matthew 26:15
- Silence against accusations - Psalms 38:13 Isaiah 53:7 - Matthew 26:63; 27:12-14
- Vicarious sufferings - Isaiah 53:4-6 - Hebrews 9:28
- Death with malefactors - Isaiah 53:9-12 - Matthew 27:38
- Piercing of hands and feet - Psalms 22:16 - John 20:27
- Insult-mocking Psalms - 109:25; 22:6-7 - Mark 15:29
- Offered vinegar - Psalms 69:21 - Matthew 27:34, 48
- Cast lots for vesture - Psalms 22:18 - Mark 15:24

- Not a bone broken - Exodus 12:46 - John 19:36
- Burial with the rich - Isaiah 53:9 - Matthew 27:57-60
- Resurrection - Psalms 16:10 - Matthew 28:6
- Ascension - Psalms 68:18; 110:1 - Luke 24:51

Before leaving the discussion of the evidences for Divine Inspiration, it is important to consider the matter of preservation and indestructibility of the Bible. Certainly, this is one of the most unusual arguments in favor of the Bible's divine origin. Never has a book or system of writing undergone the attacks and abuses which the Bible has suffered. It has been burned, banned, and ridiculed throughout the centuries, but it still remains today the world's number one selling book. Even in the countries where it has been banned, the Bible is still present, believed, read, and taught. The reason for this seems obvious because the word of God exposes the sinfulness of man, and for this reason, carnal man resents and rejects the Bible. There have been many attempts throughout the centuries to suppress and even destroy the Word of God.

Not too long ago, Sir Julian Huxley, the grandson of Thomas Huxley, predicted that the Bible and Christianity are doomed to extinction. Liberals, modernist, and skeptics all over the land are attacking and making fun of the Bible and those who read it. Yet the Word of God still convicts of sin, comforts the soul, and always represents the power of God unto salvation because it is the very word of God.

The Canon of the Bible

How do we determine the sixty-six books in the Bible were the ones to be deemed the Word of God? What guidelines were used in recognizing their inspiration and author-ity? Why were these particular sixty-six books chosen? What is the *canon*?

In pondering those questions, it would first be valuable to consider the meaning of the word "canon." Our English word "canon" comes from the Greek word *kanon* and has several simple meanings. Basically, it means a straight rod or bar, like one used by car-penters. It refers to keeping something straight or testing something to see if it is straight. In the metaphorical sense, it refers to that which serves to measure (to rule) and is the norm of standard. In a passive sense, it refers to that which has been measured or put to the test and accepted.

From these definitions, we can determine several facts about the canon of the Bible: First, it refers to the fact that the writings which were to be considered for canonicity were put through a strict set of tests. Second, various methods were used as a guideline. Third, the sixty-six books which are contained in the Bible have been examined and judged to be the Word of God.

The Old Testament has some very unique characteristics about its particular collection of books. It is unique in its relationship to the New Testament. The Old Testament is the foundation for and preparatory to the New Testament. There could be no accurately informed understanding of the New Testament without the Old Testament. Murrill F. Unger said, "Since the New Testament is infolded in the Old, and the Old Testament in the New, to separate the two and to treat each as an isolated, unconnected unity has resulted in irreparable harm and confusion."

B.B. Warfield described the Old Testament as a room that is "fully furnished but dimly lit," awaiting the light of the world to enter and give illumination. In other words, the Old Testament has all the necessary components to convey the gospel, but the New Testament illuminates the Old Testament so our eyes can clearly see it.

How did we come to have the Old Testament canon which now exists? First, the writers of the Old Testament were conscious of the fact that they were inspired by God and their writings were accepted almost immediately by the people to be inspired by God. The closing and the ratification of the Hebrew canon (Old Testament) came about in the 5th century before Christ when some of the notables such as Ezra, Nehemiah, and others making up the great assembly placed the Old Testament in the present division and declared it to be the Word of God.

Because both the Old and New Testaments are divinely inspired by God, it's not necessary to go through the Bible and point out book by book its inspiration, credibility, and attestation. We shall simply cite here the method used to determine whether a book or set of writings was to become part of the New Testament canon.

New Testament writers came to realize that some of the writings which they had were a product of God, and for this reason, they sought to preserve them. It was also recognized that there were other writings which did not deserve the title of divine authorship and a separation of the two had to be made. Since the Bible is a divine product, it is important to recognize that the Holy Spirit led these men to set up the original canon and the necessary guidelines to discern between truth and error. The providential care of the Holy Spirit must not be overlooked.

What were the guidelines used to determine whether or not a New Testament book was inspired by God? The first guideline was that of *Apostleship*. For a book to be considered part of the New Testament canon, it had to be authored by an Apostle or if the writer was credited as divinely inspired by an apostle. A second guideline was that the book was examined as to its contents to determine if the contents of the book were true in all its teachings related to doctrine and morality. The third guideline was it university used and confirmed by the early church? Finally, was the book characteristic of divine inspiration?

To some, the development of the canon may seem indefinite. However, it is clear that the choosing of the books of the New Testament was done with great care which provides us great confidence that we have the 27 books in the New Testament that God wanted. Should we doubt what we have now? Is there a single book that we would be willing to lose or remove from the New Testament? Or on the other hand, read the extra-canonical books and see if there is one that you would be willing to put on par with the books of the New Testament? No, God does not always lead the Church infallibly, but we do believe that He did eventually lead it unerringly to the specific books that He wanted in the New Testament.

H.C. Thiessen wrote years ago, "In recent times there has been little discussion of the question of the canon of the New Testament. There are perhaps few that would favor the omission of any of the books that we have in our English New Testament today, although many would ascribe varying degrees of value to the several books. The tendency at present is to accept all because of their traditional recognition, but to lower their dignity and to bring up some of the extra-canonical writings to a canonical level. Scholars try to show that the New Testament and the extra-canonical writings have much in common. In other words, present-day interest in the New Testament is more intellectual than spiritual. This is the logical consequence of the abandonment of the doctrine of verbal inspiration. While this is a popular trend at the present time... Divine Providence has overruled in the selection of the books that should constitute the canon and who were convinced from their own study of the twenty-seven books in our New Testament that they are supernaturally inspired and stand on an entirely different plane from all the extra-canonical books."

In conclusion, the sixty-six books referred to as the Bible were written by men who were divinely inspired by God both in their thoughts and words. The books these divinely inspired authors wrote are true, credible, and without error in their original manuscripts; evidence that it is truly the Word of God. The 39 books of the Old Testament and the 27 books of the New Testament went through a rigorous testing process before they were accepted by the New Testament Church as the 66 books that make up our Bible. Throughout the process, the Holy Spirit has done a wonderful thing inspiring godly men to write the sixty-six book and bring to us the revelation of God in written form.

It is this truth that allows us to celebrate with the prophet Isaiah who said, "The grass withers and the flowers fall, but the word of our God endures forever." (Isaiah 40:8)

THE DOCTRINE OF GOD

Until we grasp the proper biblical portrayal of God, we will not be able to understand anything else about theology, the Bible, or even the real purpose of life. The Bible, unsurprisingly, does not argue for God's existence, but assumes and announces Him instead (e.g., "In the beginning God..." Gen. 1:1).

One reason the Bible doesn't argue for the existence of God is because God Himself is the ultimate Author of the Bible. To use a simple illustration, the fact that I am writing this book on doctrine is proof enough that I exist. I do not need to argue my own existence because this book sufficiently shows that I do exist.

As we begin to examine the biblical portrayal of God, we must remember that there is no richer endeavor than to trace the footprints of God both in His word and creation. Our concept of God will inevitably determine our view on things such as evil, work, relationships, and our lifestyle. A distorted view of God will consequently pervert and misshape our view of every other doctrine or subject found in the Bible (not to mention all of our life circumstances as well). Especially in our pluralistic and relativistic age, there is a pressing need for the Christian to study and proclaim who God is and what He has done in creating, acting in, and reconciling the world. Kevin Vanhoozer agrees when he writes, "Christian doctrine is a dose of reality, a slap in the face that wakes up the bleary-eyed and hungover, all those who cannot open their eyes (or prefer to keep them shut) to the new thing God is doing in Christ through the Spirit."

God alone possesses ultimate glory and is the source of all physical and spiritual life. God started it all! He is the One who spoke the universe into existence by His power, and it is God who reigns supremely on His throne in heaven. God will also renew and redeem all things in accordance with His eternal design. As the Apostle Paul says:

> *Ephesians 1:3-12,* *Praise be to the God and Father of our Lord Jesus Christ, who has blessed us in the heavenly realms with every spiritual blessing in Christ. For he chose us in him before the creation of the world to be holy and blameless in his sight. In love he predestined us for adoption to sonship through Jesus Christ, in accordance with his pleasure and will—to the praise of his glorious grace, which he has freely given us in the One he loves. In him we have redemption through his blood, the forgiveness of sins, in accordance with the riches of God's grace that he lavished on us. With all wisdom and understanding, he made known to us the mystery of his will according to his good pleasure, which he purposed in Christ, to be put into effect when the times reach their fulfillment—to bring unity to all things in heaven and on earth under Christ. In him we were also chosen, having been predestined according to the plan of him who works out everything in conformity with the purpose of his will, in order that we, who were the first to put our hope in Christ, might be for the praise of his glory.*

Who is God and What is He Like? The Nature and Character of God

Three names are used to speak of God in the Bible. These three names speak to God's position, person, and title. The first word used in the Bible to refer to God is *Elohim.* The word is translated "God" 2,300 times in the Old Testament. *Elohim* is not the personal name of God, but it refers to God's official title as the Creator of the universe. The name *Elohim* also gives us an early glimpse of the triune Godhead or Trinity, as we know it.

The English language carries the idea of two basic numbers. There is "one" or "singular." The other number in the English language is "plural" which means two or more of someone or something. However, the Hebrew language has three number possibilities and is not limited to singular or plural. The Hebrew language allows for singular (one), dual (two), and plural (which denotes 3 or more).

Elohim denotes God as plural (*three* or more) and is found in the first verse of the Bible. Genesis 1:1, states, "In the beginning God created the heavens and the earth." While the first verse in the Bible tells us that God (Elohim) is three or more, the rest of Scripture identifies God as three distinct persons: Father, Son, and Holy Spirit. Not only does Elohim express that triune nature of God, but it also expresses God as the one who is power.

Yahweh (Hebrew: YHWH) is the second word the Bible uses to name God. It should be noted that *Yahweh* is pronounced as 'Jehovah' by many biblical scholars. The difference between Yahweh or Jehovah has nothing to do with the Hebrew word YHWH. Ancient Hebrew did not use vowels in its written form. Vowels were added in the spoken form of the Hebrew language but not recorded in the written form.

The King James Version popularized the term Jehovah as the name for God. However, many Hebrew scholars believe that *Yahweh* is the better translation and pronunciation of YHWH. While many will argue for and against the use of Jehovah or *Yahweh*, we must always remember that the most important thing is to know the God who is spoken of by the term YHWH. *Yahweh* is the personal name of God that speaks of His redemption, deliverance, and eternality as God. It should also be noted that some Bible translations avoid the word choice of Jehovah or Yahweh altogether and simply translate YHWH as "LORD" or "LORD God."

Adonai is the third term which is used to express who God is. It is most often translated "Lord" or Lord God." Adonai expresses the idea of God's sovereignty, dominion, and authority over the earth and all who live in it. *Adonai* occurs approximately 300 times in the Old Testament. Like *Elohim, Adonai* is a plural noun that expresses the idea of the Trinity.

God is Spirit

The Bible informs us that God is spirit, or immaterial, but this must not be confused as unreal. Jesus said, "God is spirit, and his worshipers must worship in spirit and in truth" (John 4:24). God the Father is not flesh and bone as we are. God is, in fact, spiritual substance, not material substance. Many people today try and reduce God to the material world—the trees, animals, or natural substances. However, we must always remember that those material substances are creations of the ultimate spiritual substance—i.e., God!

Although God the Father does not possess a body as we think of a physical body, the Bible does use figurative language to refer to God that we can understand. The Bible speaks of God's hands, feet, eyes, and ears. This way of speaking of God is anthropological (attributing human characteristics to that which is non-human).

Genesis 3:8, Then the man and his wife heard the sound of the Lord God as he was walking in the garden in the cool of the day, and they hid from the Lord God among the trees of the garden.

Psalm 34:15, The eyes of the Lord are on the righteous, and his ears are attentive to their cry.

Isaiah 65:2, All day long I have held out my hands to an obstinate people, who walk in ways not good, pursuing their own imaginations.

This anthropological language is used to help our finite minds understand the reality of an infinite God. However, we should never reduce God to the material because ultimately God is spirit.

God is Personal

There are many today who consider God to be only a force or influence in the universe and not personal. Accordingly, they believe it is impossible to have any kind of personal relationship with God. While it is true, from our previous point that God is spirit and is not confined to the limitations of matter, it is not true that God is an impersonal force.

The Bible makes abundantly clear that God is extremely personal. The Bible describes God as being volitional, wrathful, compassionate, loving, patient, etc.

Psalm 104:27-30, All creatures look to you to give them their food at the proper time. When you give it to them, they gather it up; when you open your hand, they are satisfied with good things. When you hide your face, they are terrified; when you take away their breath, they die and return to the dust. When you send your Spirit, they are created, and you renew the face of the ground.

God is very personal and intimately involved in His created order. He has a personality and desires to have an individual relationship with His image-bearers. It is wonderful to think that the same God who is powerful enough to speak the world into existence also desires to have an active personal relationship to those He has created.

The fact that God is personal is one of the greatest truths in the Bible. God's personal nature means that He is caring, comforting, loving, and understanding toward us. The Bible also affirms that God's personal connection with us is so deep that he even knows the number of hairs on our heads:

Matthew 6:25-30, Therefore I tell you, do not worry about your life, what you will eat or drink; or about your body, what you will wear. Is not life more than food, and the body more than clothes? Look at the birds of the air; they do not sow or reap or store away in barns, and yet your heavenly Father feeds them. Are you not much more valuable than they? Can any one of you by worrying add a single hour to your life? And why do you worry about clothes? See how the flowers of the field grow. They do not labor or spin. Yet I tell you that not even Solomon in all his splendor was dressed like one of these. If that is how God clothes the grass of the field, which is here today and tomorrow is thrown into the fire, will he not much more clothe you—you of little faith?

Matthew 10:29, Are not two sparrows sold for a penny? Yet not one of them will fall to the ground outside your Father's care. And even the very hairs of your head are all numbered.

God is both spirit and personal. However, don't ever forget the transcendence of God. God is bigger and greater than anything we imagine. God cannot be and is not limited by anything. God is even far greater than our wildest imaginations can manufacture. The writer of the book of Hebrews puts it well:

Hebrews 1:10, He also says, "In the beginning, Lord, you laid the foundations of the earth, and the heavens are the work of your hands. They will perish, but you remain; they will all wear out like a garment. You will roll them up like a robe; like a garment they will be changed. But you remain the same, and your years will never end."

God is Trinity

The doctrine of the Trinity is perhaps the most intricate and mysterious doctrine presented in all of God's Word. For this reason, one cannot presume to understand it or give an exhaustive explanation. This is not surprising because God is infinitely greater than us and it should not discourage us that we cannot fully understand Him. We must remember that even though we are *creature* and He is *Creator*, we can truly and accurately know God!

Fred Sanders makes an astute observation on the Trinity when he writes, "The doctrine of the Trinity has a peculiar place in the minds and hearts of evangelical Christians. We tend to acknowledge the doctrine with a polite hospitality but not welcome it with any special warmth."

While the Trinity is a mystery, this does not give us warrant to treat this doctrine coldly as a misplaced, contradictory concept that only confuses God's people. Rather, the doctrine of the Trinity should be cherished, preserved, and proclaimed by the church for what it truly is: the beautiful reality that the God of the gospel has been, is, and always will be a loving tri-personal community of Father, Son, and Holy Spirit.

This section sets forth the fundamental truths of the Trinity. These truths will be important to grasp because, in the words of John Webster, "the doctrine of the Trinity is *the Christian understanding of God*; and so the doctrine of the Trinity shapes and determines the entirety of how we think of God's nature." Not only is the doctrine of the Trinity vital to our conception of God, but it is also essential to our understanding of the gospel—the good news of God saving sinners.

Kevin Vanhoozer makes this clear when he says, "The doctrine of the Trinity is the beginning and end, the source and substance, of the Christian message of salvation." In other words, the Trinity gives us the proper and necessary framework to understand the truth of the Father reconciling the world to Himself in Christ through the Spirit. Before digging deeper into the idea of the Trinity, it might help to note a few definitions of the Trinity given by others.

> "God eternally exists as three persons, Father, Son, and Spirit, and each person is fully God, and there is one God." (Wayne Grudem, Systematic Theology)

> "The Trinity is composed of three united persons without separate existence so completely united as to form one God. The divine natures subsists in three distinctions Father, Son, and Holy Spirit." (Lewis Sperry Chafer)

> "The Doctrine of the Trinity may be expressed in the six following statements: (1) In Scripture, there are three who are recognized as God. 2) These three are so described in Scripture that we are compelled to conceive of them as distinct persons. 3) The tri-personality of the divine nature is not merely economic and temporal, but is eminent and eternal. 4) This tri-personality is not tritheism; for while there are three persons, there is but one essence. 5) The three persons, Father, Son, and Holy Spirit are equal. 6) Inscrutable yet not self-contradictory, this doctrine furnishes the key to all other doctrines." (A.H. Strong, Systematic Theology)

"Trinity" is the best word to explain God in human terms. The word "Trinity" is the combination of two Latin words "Tri-Unity." So, when we say Trinity, we are saying that God is a "Tri-Unity." The Trinity is the One True God existing in three persons. However, these three distinct persons are not three different gods.

It should be noted that the word "Trinity" is not found in Scripture, but that should not discourage us or cause us to shrink from using it. The concepts represented in the word "Trinity" do exist within Scripture. Trinity is simply the term used to describe the triune God—three coexistent, coeternal Persons who make up the Godhead.

There is One God

Deuteronomy 6:4, Hear, O Israel: The Lord our God, the Lord is one.

Galatians 3:20, A mediator, however, implies more than one party; but God is one.

1 Timothy 2:5, For there is one God and one mediator between God and mankind, the man Christ Jesus,

It should be noted that not everyone believes there is one God. The biblical idea of one true God is rejected by polytheists like Hindus, Animists, New Age teachers, and Mormons.

The One God Exist in Three Persons

As discussed earlier, the Hebrew name for God *"Elohim"* is in the plural form referring to two or more. Scripture delineated that the number is three to be exact: the Father, the Son, and the Holy Spirit. Several passages that help us understand this threeness of the One True God are:

Genesis 1:26, Then God said, "Let us make mankind in our image, in our likeness, so that they may rule over the fish in the sea and the birds in the sky, over the livestock and all the wild animals, and over all the creatures that move along the ground."

Isaiah 6:8, Then I heard the voice of the Lord saying, "Whom shall I send? And who will go for us?"

Matthew 3:16-17, As soon as Jesus was baptized, he went up out of the water. At that moment heaven was opened, and he saw the Spirit of God descending like a dove and alighting on him. And a voice from heaven said, "This is my Son, whom I love; with him I am well pleased."

Matthew 28:19, Therefore go and make disciples of all nations, baptizing them in the name of the Father and of the Son and of the Holy Spirit,

2 Corinthians 13:14, May the grace of the Lord Jesus Christ, and the love of God, and the fellowship of the Holy Spirit be with you all.

The Father is God

John 6:27, Do not work for food that spoils, but for food that endures to eternal life, which the Son of Man will give you. For on him God the Father has placed his seal of approval."

Romans 1:7, To all in Rome who are loved by God and called to be his holy people: Grace and peace to you from God our Father and from the Lord Jesus Christ.

1 Peter 1:2, who have been chosen according to the foreknowledge of God the Father, through the sanctifying work of the Spirit, to be obedient to Jesus Christ and sprinkled with his blood: Grace and peace be yours in abundance.

The Son is God

John 1:1, In the beginning was the Word, and the Word was with God, and the Word was God.

John 1:14, The Word became flesh and made his dwelling among us. We have seen his glory, the glory of the one and only Son, who came from the Father, full of grace and truth.

Colossians 2:9, For in Christ all the fullness of the Deity lives in bodily form.

The Holy Spirit is God

Acts 5:3-4, Then Peter said, "Ananias, how is it that Satan has so filled your heart that you have lied to the Holy Spirit and have kept for yourself some of the money you received for the land? Didn't it belong to you before it was sold? And after it was sold, wasn't the money at your disposal? What made you think of doing such a thing? You have not lied just to human beings but to God."

Matthew 28:19, Therefore go and make disciples of all nations, baptizing them in the name of the Father and of the Son and of the Holy Spirit,

2 Corinthians 13:14, May the grace of the Lord Jesus Christ, and the love of God, and the fellowship of the Holy Spirit be with you all.

The Bible is clear in its teaching related to the Trinity that the Father, the Son, and the Holy Spirit are one God while remaining distinct persons. Certainly, this is a difficult concept to understand with our limited and finite reasoning powers. However, the fact that the three persons of the Trinity are distinct is taught through the pages of Holy Scripture.

- The Father is not the Son

John 3:16, *For God so loved the world that he gave his one and only Son, that whoever believes in him shall not perish but have eternal life.*

Luke 22:42, *"Father, if you are willing, take this cup from me; yet not my will, but yours be done."*

- The Son is Not the Holy Spirit

John 14:16, *And I will ask the Father, and he will give you another advocate to help you and be with you forever.*

John 16:7, *But very truly I tell you, it is for your good that I am going away. Unless I go away, the Advocate will not come to you; but if I go, I will send him to you.*

- The Holy Spirit is Not the Father

John 14:26, *But the Advocate, the Holy Spirit, whom the Father will send in my name, will teach you all things and will remind you of everything I have said to you.*

John 15:26, *When the Advocate comes, whom I will send to you from the Father—the Spirit of truth who goes out from the Father—he will testify about me.*

The above outline of the Trinity gives direct biblical support for the three distinct persons of the one triune God of the gospel—God the Father, God the Son, and God the Holy Spirit. Thus, affirming what the Bible teaches: there is One God with three distinct persons composing the Godhead. Each of these persons is entirely equal with the other in substance, essence, and glory.

This core outline of the Trinity is clearly set forth in the Bible. The Father is God, the Son is God, and the Holy Spirit is God while at the same time, the Father, the Son, and the Holy Spirit are one God. This is the doctrine of the Trinity presented in God's Word. The fact that finite minds find it hard to understand and reconcile the idea of three-ness in oneness is not surprising nor cause for concern. For the God of the Bible is infinitely greater and higher than we are. Remember the words God spoke through the prophet Isaiah:

> *Isaiah 55:8-9, "For my thoughts are not your thoughts, neither are your ways my ways," declares the Lord. "As the heavens are higher than the earth, so are my ways higher than your ways and my thoughts than your thoughts."*

Also, remember the words of the Apostle Paul:

> *Romans 11:33-34, Oh, the depth of the riches of the wisdom and knowledge of God! How unsearchable his judgments, and his paths beyond tracing out! "Who has known the mind of the Lord? Or who has been his counselor?"*

In conclusion, regarding the doctrine of the Trinity, it is found throughout the pages of Scripture and the truth that God is an eternally tri-personal fellowship of life and love should be cherished.

The Attributes of God

An attribute is a quality, trait, or characteristic of a person place or thing. The "attributes of God" refers to the quality, trait, or characteristic of the triune God of the gospel which separates and distinguishes Him from all other beings. God's attributes are not acquired, but natural qualities that are essential to His Being. Mankind possesses certain qualities that distinguish it from all animal and plant life. Thus, man is distinctly and uniquely man. In a similar manner, God is far above mankind as mankind is above the lowest form of life. God is God, and there is no other that can compare to Him.

> *1 Chronicles 17:20, There is no one like you, Lord, and there is no God but you...*

> *Isaiah 45:5, I am the Lord, and there is no other; apart from me there is no God.*

God possesses certain attributes that only He can possess (these are called "incommunicable" or "natural" attributes). For example, man is intelligent, but only God is all-knowing. Man can demonstrate a substantial amount of power, but only God is all-powerful. Man demonstrates great wisdom, but only God is all-wise. History and man are constantly changing, but only God is unchanging in His Being and purposes.

God's attributes are commonly divided into two classes: incommunicable and communicable.

God's incommunicable attributes are those traits of God that are not true, and cannot be true, of man. For example, God is present everywhere, and that will never be true of man.

God's communicable attributes are those attributes that man can imitate, and Christians are called to do. For example, God is love, and we are called to be and can be loving.

Incommunicable Attributes of God

- Omniscience - God has always known, knows, and will always know all that is possible to know in every physical and spiritual realm of creation.
- Omnipotence - God is able to do everything and anything that is consistent with His nature and fitting for His purposes.
- Omnipresence - God, who is not limited or confined to space, is present in every point of the universe.
- Eternality - God is neither limited nor confined to time such that He is able to know all of time with the same intimacy. In the words of Wayne Grudem, "God sees and knows all events—past, present, and future—with equal vividness" (Grudem, *Christian Beliefs*, 25).
- Immutability - God is unchangeable in His Being, character, and purposes.

Communicable Attributes of God

- Holiness - God's holiness refers to His existence as being the unutterable summation and perfection of all that is incorruptibly good and pure.
- Faithfulness - God's firm commitment, in all circumstances, to stay true to His word of covenantal promise.
- Mercy - God's kind favor toward those who deserve His just wrath.
- Love - God's love is His proactive favor to act for the good of others such that they get more knowledge, experience, and intimacy with Him.
- Truth - Grudem helpfully notes, "All his knowledge and all his words are both true and the final standard of truth" (Grudem, *Christian Beliefs*, 28)
- Justice - God's justice is His unwavering acting in accordance with what is most morally excellent and forensically righteous (i.e., He is always true to His nature as God).

In this study, there will be no attempt to present an exhaustive study of each of God's attributes. If this were to be done, "the world itself could not contain the books that would be written" (John 21:25).

Natural Attributes

God's Self-Existence: The Bible declares that God is self-existent and eternal. The Bible does not refer to a beginning of God. Unlike mankind and creation, God has always existed, and He owes His existence only to Himself. Everything we know had a beginning, except God Himself. The Bible declares, *"In the beginning God..."*(Genesis 1:1).

There was a time when God was all there was—God in His triune fellowship of love and life. There was no universe, no heaven, no earth, no angels, just the triune God—Father, Son, and Spirit—existing in the perfect unity of love. This is referred to as eternity past. In eternity past, God was alone, self-loving, self-sufficient, and in need of nothing. The Father, Son, and Spirit were completely satisfied in their fellowship of love (the Father and Son eternally loving each other in the power and bond of the Holy Spirit). This truth makes God's gracious and merciful dealings with mankind all the more amazing. He is eternal as it relates to the past, but God is also eternal as it relates to the future in that God will never cease to exist.

> *Exodus 3:14, "God said to Moses, 'I AM WHO I AM.' And he said, 'Say this to the people of Israel: I AM has sent me to you.'"*

> *Isaiah 44:6, "This is what the Lord says— Israel's King and Redeemer, the Lord Almighty: I am the first and I am the last; apart from me there is no God."*

Omnipotence: In addition to the attribute of self-existence or eternality, God also possesses the quality of omnipotence. "Omnipotent" means all-powerful or almighty and reveals that God is able to do whatever He wills. God's omnipotence means that God has the power to save, keep those whom He has saved, and has control over the future. J.I. Packer defines God's omnipotence as His "power to do everything that in his rational and moral perfection God wills to do" (J.I. Packer *Concise Theology*, 36).

God's omnipotence also means that nothing is too hard for Him because He possesses unlimited power to do anything *according to His nature*. This is a comforting thought: God's omnipotence assures us that He has the power over our daily life as well as the power over death.

A final point to remember concerning the omnipotence of God is that if there are any limitations placed on God's power, they are self-imposed. It is true that man can reject God's moral will in a matter such as shunning the salvation in Jesus Christ (God is "not wishing that any should perish, but that all should reach repentance" 2 Peter 3:9). But, that rejection is only because God has allowed man to reach his desired end: life apart from God. Thus, God limits Himself to some degree by His choice to work through man.

> *1 Peter 1:5*, *who through faith are shielded by God's power until the coming of the salvation that is ready to be revealed in the last time.*

> *Matthew 10:28*, *Do not be afraid of those who kill the body but cannot kill the soul. Rather, be afraid of the One who can destroy both soul and body in hell.*

> *Matthew 19:26*, *Jesus looked at them and said, "With man this is impossible, but with God all things are possible."*

> *Genesis 18:14*, *Is anything too hard for the Lord? I will return to you at the appointed time next year, and Sarah will have a son.*

Omniscient: In addition to God's omnipotence, we see in Scripture that God is also omniscient. The word "omniscient" means God is all-knowing and has perfect knowledge. God knows all things past, present, and future. The Bible declares that God's knowledge is perfect and that it is beyond comparison to man's knowledge. God knows everything. He knows our secrets, our ways, our days, and our thoughts. The Psalmist was so overwhelmed by the knowledge of God that he declared God's knowledge to be infinite. A.W. Tozer defines God's omniscience well when he writes, "To say that God is omniscient is to say that He possesses perfect knowledge and therefore has no need to learn. But it is more: it is to say that God has never learned and cannot learn." (Tozer, *Knowledge of the Holy*)

Paul declared that the foolishness of God is wiser than the greatest wisdom of man (1 Corinthians 1:25). There is nothing that God does not know. What a blessing it is to have a personal relationship with this One True omniscient God!

> *Job 36:4-5*, *Be assured that my words are not false; one who has perfect knowledge is with you. God is mighty, but despises no one; he is mighty, and firm in his purpose.*

> *Matthew 10:29-30*, *Are not two sparrows sold for a penny? Yet not one of them will fall to the ground outside your Father's care. And even the very hairs of your head are all numbered.*

> *Psalm 44:21*, *would not God have discovered it, since he knows the secrets of the heart?*

> *Psalm 94:9-11*, *Does he who fashioned the ear not hear? Does he who formed the eye not see? Does he who disciplines nations not punish? Does he who teaches*

mankind lack knowledge? The Lord knows all human plans; he knows that they are futile.

Omnipresence: The next attribute of God to consider is His Omnipresence. Because God is infinite, He has no boundaries with reference to space. The fact that God is everywhere present at the same time is beyond human comprehension, but it is nevertheless true. Timothy George helpfully notes, "Just as God's omnipresence refers to his sovereignty over time, so the attribute of omnipresence denotes that, as the eternal Creator of all that is, God is not bounded by space" (George, *A Theology for the Church*, 198). Scripture makes it clear that God is omnipresent in both heaven and earth.

> *Jeremiah 23:24*, "Who can hide in secret places so that I cannot see them?" declares the Lord. "Do not I fill heaven and earth?" declares the Lord.

> *Joshua 2:11*, When we heard of it, our hearts melted in fear and everyone's courage failed because of you, for the Lord your God is God in heaven above and on the earth below.

> *Psalm 139:3-5*, You discern my going out and my lying down; you are familiar with all my ways. Before a word is on my tongue you, Lord, know it completely. You hem me in behind and before, and you lay your hand upon me.

Immutability: The next attribute of God that demands consideration is His immutability. The doctrine of immutability teaches that God never changes. Immutability is not that God does not change; it is that God cannot change. God is already perfect in all ways, and thus there is no need for God to change. God is unchangeable in His attributes, His being, His nature, and His eternal plan. God is absolute and perfect. He does not grow nor does He need to. His love, word, and promises always remain the same. But, His unchangeable nature still allows Him to "act or feel differently in response to different situations" (Grudem, *Christian Beliefs*, 24).

The Bible informs us that God is not changeable like man. God's counsel is forever, and His Word is settled in heaven (Psalm 119:89). God does not faint or grow weary. God's word is unchangeable, His love is unchangeable, His being is unchangeable, His power is unchangeable, and His loving commitment to His children is unchangeable. God is unchangeable or immutable in every area.

> *Hebrews 13:8*, Jesus Christ is the same yesterday and today and forever.

> *Malachi 3:6*, I the LORD do not change.

James 1:17, Every good and perfect gift is from above, coming down from the Father of the heavenly lights, who does not change like shifting shadows.

Numbers 23:19, God is not human, that he should lie, not a human being, that he should change his mind. Does he speak and then not act? Does he promise and not fulfill?

Psalm 33:11, But the plans of the Lord stand firm forever, the purposes of his heart through all generations.

Infinite: The next attribute of God which must be acknowledged is that God is infinite. This means God has no natural limitations. It has already been stated, but it is worth restating that the only limitations that God experiences are those He imposes upon Himself. God's understanding is infinite, and He fills the heaven and the earth with His being and presence. God is so infinite and glorious that the heavens cannot even contain Him.

Psalm 147:5, Great is our Lord and mighty in power; his understanding has no limit.

Jeremiah 23:24, "Who can hide in secret places so that I cannot see them?" declares the Lord. "Do not I fill heaven and earth?" declares the Lord.

1 Kings 8:27, But will God really dwell on earth? The heavens, even the highest heaven, cannot contain you. How much less this temple I have built!

Holiness: Holiness is the next attribute of God we will consider. God is totally and completely free from and unblemished by all evil—He is holy! Without a doubt, one of the greatest truths that man could ever learn concerning God is that He is holy. The Bible teaches that God is absolutely unstained by sin and God cannot even be tempted to sin. Thomas Oden notes that "holiness implies that every excellence fitting to the Supreme Being is found in God without blemish or limit" (Thomas Oden, *The Living God*, 95). Because of the holiness of God, sin separates sinners from God. Not only is God holy, but He also expects holiness from His children.

The holiness of God reveals several important truths concerning our relationship with God. First, God's holiness brings to light the utter perversity of man's sin. The holiness of God amplifies the true condition of man. Remember, the Bible does not look at man through human eyes but through the eyes of God. Since God is perfectly holy, only He has the authority to determine that which is holy and that which is unholy. God's absolute holiness also magnifies and reveals the unsearchable riches of God's love and mercy for fallen humanity.

God's holiness also causes us to marvel at the sacrifice of Jesus Christ on man's behalf (Romans 5:6). We must see that man is not saved because of what he is, but man is saved from what he is in order to become like God. The holiness of God causes us to boast in God's grace because through grace we have been reconciled to God (Romans 5:10-11), justified before Him (Romans 3:21-31), made partakers of the divine nature (2 Peter 1:4), and become new creatures in Christ (2 Corinthians 5:17).

1 John 1:5, This is the message we have heard from him and declare to you: God is light; in him there is no darkness at all.

Luke 1:49, for the Mighty One has done great things for me— holy is his name.

James 1:13, When tempted, no one should say, "God is tempting me." For God cannot be tempted by evil, nor does he tempt anyone;

Leviticus 19:2, Speak to the entire assembly of Israel and say to them: "Be holy because I, the Lord your God, am holy."

Romans 8:32, He who did not spare his own Son, but gave him up for us all—how will he not also, along with him, graciously give us all things?

Ephesians 1:3, Praise be to the God and Father of our Lord Jesus Christ, who has blessed us in the heavenly realms with every spiritual blessing in Christ.

The Sovereignty of God

The sovereignty of God means that as Creator of all things, God is the owner of all things, and He has absolute rule over all creation. God's sovereignty means that He exercises His authority in the universe based on His wisdom, holiness, and love. Several Scriptures speak to God's sovereign control of the universe Psalm 115:3, Daniel 4:35, and Isaiah 45:9.

God's sovereignty, or control, of the universe, does not only speak to God's attitude as a controller, but to His nature as the One who is in ultimate control of all things. God's sovereignty does not simply speak to the fact that God takes charge of all things, but instead, God's sovereignty means that God is always in charge.

God's sovereignty can be broken down into two fundamental subjects: The doctrine of Preservation and the doctrine of Providence.

The Doctrine of Preservation

The doctrine of Preservation means that God did not leave His creation to chance, but continuously maintains the existence of all things He created. There are some who teach that after creating the world and mankind, God has now assumed the passive position of simply being an observer who intervenes in the affairs of man only on rare occasions. However, contrary to this view, the Bible teaches that God is very interested and involved in His creation.

The Bible teaches clearly that God is interested, oversees, guides, and holds all things together that He has created.

> *Nehemiah 9:6, You alone are the Lord. You made the heavens, even the highest heavens, and all their starry host, the earth and all that is on it, the seas and all that is in them. You give life to everything, and the multitudes of heaven worship you.*

> *Colossians 1:17, He is before all things, and in him all things hold together.*

> *Psalm 36:6, Your righteousness is like the highest mountains, your justice like the great deep. You, Lord, preserve both people and animals.*

> *Proverbs 2:8, for he guards the course of the just and protects the way of his faithful ones.*

The Doctrine of Providence or God's Directing Care

The doctrine of providence means that God not only created heaven and earth through His power, but he also actively preserves and controls His creation. The sovereign control of God of His creation is called providence. The doctrine of providence maintains that God allows all of the events of the world—physical, mental, and moral phenomena—to work according to His purposes. Though sin has entered into the universe, sin in no way has power to halt or frustrate God's benevolent, wise, and holy purposes.

God's providential control of heaven and earth is seen clearly in Scripture. Scripture also affirms that God provides for the needs of His people. What a true blessing it is to know that God is sovereign—not lacking power, strength, or wisdom. It is actually refreshing to be conscious of the truth that God preserves and watches over His creation. God cares about everything that occurs in the life of His children. Similarly, there is no situation that God could not cure, provide for, or sustain us. When one looks at the world today, it appears as though things are chaotic, but let's remember that God sits on His throne in all His glory, power, and wisdom—forever and always sovereign!

Job 12:10, *In his hand is the life of every creature and the breath of all mankind.*

Psalm 4:8, *In peace I will lie down and sleep, for you alone, Lord, make me dwell in safety.*

Psalm 103:19, *The Lord has established his throne in heaven, and his kingdom rules over all.*

Psalm 121:3, *He will not let your foot slip— he who watches over you will not slumber;*

Luke 1:52, *He has brought down rulers from their thrones but has lifted up the humble.*

Romans 8:28, *And we know that in all things God works for the good of those who love him, who have been called according to his purpose.*

THE DOCTRINE OF JESUS CHRIST

No greater subject can occupy the mind of a believer than that of Jesus Christ. To even undertake a thorough discussion of Jesus Christ is a profound blessing. This study will present a concise and understandable portrayal of the person and work of Jesus Christ as it is presented in the word of God.

Today, as it has been since the beginning of the Church age, many would pervert the biblical teachings concerning the Son of God. Therefore, it is the purpose of this study to affirm Jesus Christ to be the very Son of God—the Creator and Sustainer of the universe who died on the cross for the sins of humanity and was resurrected in power.

> _Colossians 1:16-18, For in him all things were created: things in heaven and on earth, visible and invisible, whether thrones or powers or rulers or authorities; all things have been created through him and for him. He is before all things, and in him all things hold together. And he is the head of the body, the church; he is the beginning and the firstborn from among the dead, so that in everything he might have the supremacy._

> _Acts 4:12, Salvation is found in no one else, for there is no other name under heaven given to mankind by which we must be saved._

The Deity of Jesus Christ

Many of the written words about Jesus today focus on His humanity, work, teaching, and death. Many would prefer us to believe that Jesus was simply a mere man or noble martyr. Some claim that Jesus was only a very committed man carrying out a worthy mission and that His life ended in tragedy. Yet, the death of Jesus is more than another tragic martyrdom—it is a divine sacrifice. It is a divine sacrifice in that the Bible makes exceedingly clear that Jesus Christ, the Son of God made flesh, offered himself in glad obedience to the Father, even to the point of death on a cross. Jesus Christ is indeed divine, in every aspect being eternal God, possessing all divine attributes as the second person of the Trinity.

> *Romans 4:25, He was delivered over to death for our sins and was raised to life for our justification.*

Fulfilled prophecy is the first evidence of the deity of Jesus Christ. Jesus Himself referenced fulfilled prophecy as proof of His divine nature.

> *Luke 24:27, And beginning with Moses and all the Prophets, he explained to them what was said in all the Scriptures concerning himself.*

Over the years, some skeptics have objected to the notion of fulfilled prophecy by saying that Scripture was written after Jesus' birth and thus was not fulfilled prophecy at all. However, this idea simply does not stand up to the facts that the Old Testament was written, recorded, and copied well before the time of Jesus. Thus the charges of collaboration hold no credibility.

The 39 books of the Old Testament are dated long before the time of Jesus for a number of reasons: a) Jesus and many New Testament writers frequently quote from the Old Testament; b) Even Jewish theologians who reject Jesus as their Messiah agree that the Old Testament predates the life of Jesus by over 300 Years; c) The Septuagint (abbreviated as LXX) is the Greek translation of the Old Testament that was completed 2-3 centuries before the life and ministry of Jesus; d) The recent discovery of the Dead Sea Scrolls only further confirm the fact that the Old Testament was completed well before Jesus' earthly ministry. Therefore, the array of evidence thoroughly disapproves the objection to the fulfilled prophecy that the Old Testament was written after the time of Jesus.

Another objection to the idea of fulfilled prophecy in Jesus affirming His deity is that some say the fulfilled prophecies were nothing more than a coincidence. Sure, it is true that you could find an individual here or there who might fulfill a couple of the prophecies. However, the Bible doesn't simply have a few prophecies that were fulfilled in Jesus. Careful study of the Old Testament shows about 60 prophecies concerning the Messiah that have over 270 specific details or ramifications for the Messiah.

Peter W. Stoner looked at the probabilities of a person fulfilling just eight of the 60 major prophecies and determined that probability to be 10 to the 17th power. That's a 1 in 100,000,000,000,000,000 chance. Stoner went on to illustrate this probability with the analogy of taking 10 to the 17th silver dollars and lay them on the state of Texas. That many silver dollars would cover the state of Texas two feet deep. Then mark one of those silver dollars mix them all up, blindfold a person and give them one shot to pick the right silver dollar. That's inconceivable, to say the least, but those are the odds of an individual fulfilling just *eight* of the Messianic prophecies.

In his book, *More Than a Carpenter*, Josh McDowell wrote, "Now these prophecies were either given by inspiration of God or the prophets just wrote them as they thought they should be. In such a case the prophets had just one chance in 10^{17} of having them come true in any man, but they all came true in Christ. This means that the fulfillment of these eight prophecies alone proves that God inspired the writing of those prophecies to a definiteness which lacks only one chance in 10^{17} of being absolute." Therefore, the coincidence objection just simply holds no legitimate validity.

Another objection to the fulfillment of Messianic prophecies in the life of Jesus was that He tried to fulfill these prophecies. In response to this objection, Louis Lapides wrote:

> "For a few of the prophecies, yes, that's certainly conceivable that Jesus could have intentionally fulfilled them, as some claim. But there are many others for which this just wouldn't have been possible. For instance, how would he control the fact that the Sanhedrin offered Judas thirty pieces of silver to betray him? How could he arrange for his ancestry, or to be born when and where he was, or his methods of execution, or that soldiers gambled for his clothing, or that his legs remained unbroken on the cross? How would he arrange perfect miracles in front of skeptics? How would he arrange for his resurrection? When you interpret Daniel 9:24-26, it foretells that the Messiah would appear a certain length of time after King Artaxerxes issued a decree for the Jewish people to go from Persia to rebuild the walls in Jerusalem. That puts the anticipated appearance of the Messiah at the exact moment in history when Jesus showed up. Certainly that's nothing he could have prearranged."

Years ago, the Christian Victory Publishing Company offered a reward if someone could find a person other than Jesus, either living or dead, who could fulfill half of the predications concerning the Messiah. To date, they have never had to pay up. A silly example such as this reminds us that the fulfillment of prophecy in the life of Jesus is a true affirmation of His deity.

Since the Bible is the final authority, it is important to see what it has to say about the deity of Jesus Christ. When the Scriptures are carefully examined, it is difficult to miss both the direct and indirect teachings concerning the deity of Jesus Christ.

The Bible declares Jesus Christ to be the Creator of all things. Scripture is clear that the power to create is a quality which can only be attributed to God. Therefore, if Jesus is the Creator of all things, then it can be naturally assumed that He is fully and truly God.

John 1:1-3, In the beginning was the Word, and the Word was with God, and the Word was God. He was with God in the beginning. Through him all things were made; without him nothing was made that has been made.

Colossians 1:15-18, The Son is the image of the invisible God, the firstborn over all creation. For in him all things were created: things in heaven and on earth, visible and invisible, whether thrones or powers or rulers or authorities; all things have been created through him and for him. He is before all things, and in him all things hold together. And he is the head of the body, the church; he is the beginning and the firstborn from among the dead, so that in everything he might have the supremacy.

Jesus is often referred to as "Immanuel, which literally means "God with us."

Isaiah 7:14, Therefore the Lord himself will give you a sign: The virgin will conceive and give birth to a son, and will call him Immanuel.

Matthew 1:21-23, "She will give birth to a son, and you are to give him the name Jesus, because he will save his people from their sins." All this took place to fulfill what the Lord had said through the prophet: "The virgin will conceive and give birth to a son, and they will call him Immanuel" (which means "God with us").

Scripture expounds that Jesus is equal with the Father (see John 5:23) and He is even called God (see Titus 2:13). It is also apparent that He is God because He has the power to forgive sins (see Colossians 3:13). The Pharisees correctly stated that only God can forgive sins. Jesus, knowing that to be their attitude, expressed the fact that He has the power to forgive sins declaring that He is equal with God, being God Himself.

Mark 2:7-10, "Why does this fellow talk like that? He's blaspheming! Who can forgive sins but God alone?" Immediately Jesus knew in his spirit that this was what they were thinking in their hearts, and he said to them, "Why are you thinking these things? Which is easier: to say to this paralyzed man, 'Your sins are forgiven,' or to say, 'Get up, take your mat and walk'? But I want you to know that the Son of Man has authority on earth to forgive sins."

In Acts 3:14 Jesus is declared to be the Holy and Righteous One. In Hebrews 1:8-12 Jesus is described as Eternal God and Creator. Another title used to equate Jesus with

God is "King of Glory" (see Psalm 24:7-10). The prophet Isaiah described Jesus as the Mighty God (see Isaiah 9:6).

Throughout Scripture, God is the only one who is to be worshiped (see Hebrews 1:6). Jesus is said to be the object of all true worship, thus He must be considered truly God.

Jesus is said to be the object of our faith, and throughout Scripture, we are told to have faith in God. Therefore Jesus must be God.

John 14:1, Do not let your hearts be troubled. You believe in God; believe also in me.

Jesus declared Himself to be one with the Father. The religious leaders of the day complained about this because they rightly understood that in saying this, Jesus was declaring Himself to be God and co-equal with God in all things.

John 14:7-10, "If you really know me, you will know my Father as well. From now on, you do know him and have seen him." Philip said, "Lord, show us the Father and that will be enough for us." Jesus answered: "Don't you know me, Philip, even after I have been among you such a long time? Anyone who has seen me has seen the Father. How can you say, 'Show us the Father'? Don't you believe that I am in the Father, and that the Father is in me? The words I say to you I do not speak on my own authority. Rather, it is the Father, living in me, who is doing his work."

Jesus is the eternal Son of God in human flesh, the only begotten of God, which means He possesses true and full deity. Being eternally begotten of the Father, He possesses the nature of the Father just like one who is fathered by a human has the nature of a human being. The fact that Jesus was the only begotten of the Father is attested to throughout the Bible.

John 1:14 The Word became flesh and made his dwelling among us. We have seen his glory, the glory of the one and only Son, who came from the Father, full of grace and truth.

John 3:16, For God so loved the world that he gave his one and only Son, that whoever believes in him shall not perish but have eternal life.

Jesus is declared to be the fullness of deity in bodily form in Colossians 2:9, "For in Christ all the fullness of the Deity lives in bodily form..." In Revelation, Jesus is identified as the King of Kings and the Lord of Lords (see Revelation 17:14).

Thus, from Genesis to Revelation the deity of Jesus is confirmed time and time again. His deity is never questioned by biblical writers. The biblical writers use names and words to describe Jesus that are reserved solely for the One true eternal God who made

41

heaven and earth. Additionally, actions are performed by Jesus that are understood to be actions only God Himself performs. Jesus' chief adversaries understood clearly that others perceived Jesus to be God. We cannot conclude any less of Jesus than the biblical writers themselves do—Jesus is God!

Jesus Has Divine Attributes

There were certain characteristics which can only be attributed to God. In other words, certain qualities exist in His nature, which distinguishes Him from all others, making Himself alone God. In looking at the Scriptures concerning the person of Jesus Christ, the Bible makes it clear that Jesus Christ eternally possesses all of the divine attributes. For example, the Bible declares Jesus Christ to be eternal and pre-existent, a quality which can only be attributed to God.

Eternality: Jesus Christ is not just pre-existent, but He is also eternal. He is not, as some teach, a being created by God the Father. There was never a time when He did not exist, for He is in fact eternal. In considering the eternity of Jesus Christ, we are to understand that He is also declared to be self-existent. That is, He is not dependent upon anything outside Himself.

John 8:58, "Very truly I tell you," Jesus answered, "before Abraham was born, I am."

Colossians 1:16-17, For in him all things were created: things in heaven and on earth, visible and invisible, whether thrones or powers or rulers or authorities; all things have been created through him and for him. He is before all things, and in him all things hold together.

If Jesus is eternal, then it is wise to consider at this point the relationship between the eternality of Jesus Christ and the incarnation of Jesus Christ. In other words, as God, the Son of God has always existed—He is eternal. However, as a man, Jesus was born, assuming a true human nature, which is the incarnation. The Apostle Paul tells us very clearly in Philippians 2 that when Jesus Christ was born, He "made Himself nothing" by taking the nature of servant.

Philippians 2:5-11, In your relationships with one another, have the same mindset as Christ Jesus: Who, being in very nature God, did not consider equality with God something to be used to his own advantage; rather, he made himself nothing by taking the very nature of a servant, being made in human likeness. And being found in appearance as a man, he humbled himself by becoming obedient to death—even death on a cross! Therefore God exalted him to the highest place and gave him the name that is above every name, that at the name of Jesus every knee should bow, in heaven and on earth and under the earth, and every tongue acknowledge that Jesus Christ is Lord, to the glory of God the Father.

In the Son of God leaving heaven and coming to earth, C.S. Lewis used the analogy of a man diving for pearls by saying:

"One may think of a diver, first reducing himself to nakedness, then glancing in mid-air, then gone with a splash, vanishing rushing down through the green and warm water into the black and cold water, down through the increasing pressure into the deathlike region of ooze and slime and old decay; then up again, back to the colour and light, has lungs almost bursting, till suddenly he breaks the surface again, holding in his hand the dripping, precious thing he went down to recover. He and it are both coloured now that they have come up into the light: down below it was colorless in the dark, he lost his color too." (Miracles, chapter 14).

Perhaps the simplest way to understand Jesus' incarnation is with the phrase "Jesus limited himself by becoming fully man, but Jesus did not lessen Himself since he remained fully God."

Jesus was still fully God when he walked this earth. Although Jesus' divine attributes were veiled by Him taking the form of a servant during His earthly ministry, we still see glimpses of His divine nature throughout His life. Here are few examples:

He had the power to forgive sins.

Matthew 9:6, "But I want you to know that the Son of Man has authority on earth to forgive sins." So he said to the paralyzed man, "Get up, take your mat and go home."

He had the power over His own life.

John 10:18, No one takes it from me, but I lay it down of my own accord. I have authority to lay it down and authority to take it up again. This command I received from my Father.

He had the power to give eternal life.

John 17:2, For you granted him authority over all people that he might give eternal life to all those you have given him.

He had the power to heal and cast out demons.

Mark 1:23-27, Just then a man in their synagogue who was possessed by an impure spirit cried out, "What do you want with us, Jesus of Nazareth? Have you come to destroy us? I know who you are—the Holy One of God!" "Be quiet!" said Jesus sternly. "Come out of him!" The impure spirit shook the man violently and came out of him with a shriek. The people were all so amazed that they asked each other,

"What is this? A new teaching—and with authority! He even gives orders to impure spirits and they obey him."

Currently, at the right hand of the Father, the man Jesus Christ still exercises authority as fully and truly God:

He has the power to transform our bodies to be like His resurrected, glorified body.

Philippians 3:21, who, by the power that enables him to bring everything under his control, will transform our lowly bodies so that they will be like his glorious body.

He has the power to save forever.

Hebrews 7:25, Therefore he is able to save completely those who come to God through him, because he always lives to intercede for them.

He has the power to guard us.

2 Timothy 1:12, That is why I am suffering as I am. Yet this is no cause for shame, because I know whom I have believed, and am convinced that he is able to guard what I have entrusted to him until that day.

Immutability: Another quality of deity, which is attributed to Jesus is immutability (i.e., He is "unchangeable") (see Hebrews 13:8).

All of these Scriptures lead to one conclusion: Jesus Christ is truly and fully God, possessing and demonstrating all attributes of God, being very God of very God. In other words, while on this earth, Jesus may have limited Himself by becoming a servant man, but Jesus never lessened Himself because He remained fully God.

The Work of Christ in Creation

The Church has affirmed throughout her existence the biblical teaching that creation took place by a free act of God., In spite of the various attempts to explain the source of life, fallen man has come up short at every turn with every feeble attempt. These attempts continue to demonstrate the fact that man, left to himself, cannot discover, understand, or even explain one of the most fundamental truths of life—creation. Creation is a doctrine which can be understood only by revelation from the Creator Himself. It is true that creation is generally attributed to the work of the Father; however, Scriptural evidence reveals that creation is the work of the triune God of the gospel.

Scripture is clear that each person of the Trinity—Father, Son, and Holy Spirit— were all active agents in the creation of heaven and earth.

Genesis 1:1, In the beginning God created the heavens and the earth.

Psalm 104:30, When you send your Spirit, they are created, and you renew the face of the ground.

1 Corinthians 8:6, yet for us there is but one God, the Father, from whom all things came and for whom we live; and there is but one Lord, Jesus Christ, through whom all things came and through whom we live.

Therefore, creation was not a solitary act of any one person of the Trinity. For it is inconceivable that any member of the Godhead would or could work independently of the other two. The emphasis in both John's gospel and Colossians is on the creative powers of the Jesus the Son. Yet, at no point does this minimize the role of the Father or the Holy Spirit in creation. It is important to examine the powers of Jesus Christ, the second person of the Trinity in human flesh, as they relates to the creation story.

Jesus is Creator

In Colossians 1:16, we see the extent of the creative powers of the Lord Jesus Christ by the words "thrones...powers....rulers...authorities." This verse is directed toward the angel worship of the Colossian people. The Colossians had developed a system of grades for angels as mediums for communication with God. Paul pointed out that this was an insult and a degradation to Christ who created them all. The Word of God very clearly and plainly states that Jesus Christ is the Creator of all things:

Colossians 1:16, For in him all things were created: things in heaven and on earth, visible and invisible, whether thrones or powers or rulers or authorities; all things have been created through him and for him.

Remember, Jesus, as God, had a significant part in setting up God's plan for creation. Christ was directly involved in the plan and activity of the triune God to create heaven and earth.

Jesus is the Preserver of All Things

Scripture also says He "is before all things" and "holds all things together" (see Colossians 1:17). Jesus is in the distinct place of preservation and providential care of His creation. The phrase "before all things" expresses the 'priority' of Jesus in position, not in time. He is "before" all things not in the sense that He was created first (time), but He is "before all things" in the sense that He is above, transcended in terms of priority to all created things since the Son, as truly God, was not created. So, Jesus is stated to be both pre-existent and eternal as Creator God. Therefore, Jesus is "before all things" since He is eternally God. That short phrase speaks to Christ's deity, eternality, and priority.

The next phrase "holds all things together" points to the fact that Jesus is the sustainer of the universe and the unifying principle of life—qualities reserved for God alone. Jesus holds the universe together because of His divine power. Apart from Jesus Christ the universe would be in chaos. It is through Christ that life makes sense, for apart from Him all things are chaos and without meaning.

Jesus in the Old Testament

Jesus, as the eternal Son, is also evident throughout the Old Testament. The word "theophany" comes from the Greek word for God, "*theos*" and the Greek word *phaino*, which means to appear. Thus, a theophany is a brief physical appearance of God on earth. For the purposes of this section, theophanies here will more specifically refer to the physical manifestations of God in the Old Testament. It should also be noted that some commentators refer to a *Christophany*, which is a word designated as the appearance of Christ in the Old Testament. Another term used for an appearance in the Old Testament is an *Angelophany* which is the appearance of an angel.

Throughout the Old Testament, the major theophanies occur with the "Angel of the Lord." It is the well-studied opinion of most biblical scholars that the manifestations of the Angel of the Lord are understood to be appearances of the eternal Son of God.

It must be conceded at this point that we are not explicitly told that every appearance of the Angel of the Lord is in fact, Jesus. We do know that every theophany is a foreshadowing of the incarnation of Christ that is found in the New Testament. Some will use the term Christophany to designate an Old Testament theophany as an appearance of the pre-incarnate Christ.

The Angel of the Lord demonstrates the active presence of the Son of God in the Old Testament to deal with sin, provide for those in need, guide in the way of the will of God, protect His people from their enemies, and execute the will of God. As this study of the work of the angel of the Lord will reveal, the term designates the pre-incarnate Word and His work during the Old Testament. Thus, the Angel of the Lord in the Old Testament is none other than the Son of God Himself before His incarnation in the New Testament.

Here is a list of the appearances of the Angel of the Lord and His ministry through the Old Testament:

- He appeared to Hagar and told her to return and submit to Saria. In addition, He prophesied that He would greatly multiply her (Genesis 16:7-14).
- He appeared to Abraham and stopped him from slaying Isaac (Genesis 22:11-18).
- He told Jacob that He would prosper him in the face of Laban's unfair dealings (Genesis 31:11-13).
- He appeared to Moses in a flame of fire out of the bush and asked him not to draw near, for the ground was holy (Exodus 3:2-5 in verse 4, He is called "God.").
- He went before Israel when they left Egypt (Exodus 19; 23:20; 33:34).
- Paul says that the Rock that followed Israel was Christ (1 Corinthians 10:4).
- When Balaam came to curse Israel, He was intercepted by the Angel of the Lord and instructed as to what to say (Numbers 22:22-35).
- He came to Gideon when he was threshing wheat and told him to go and deliver Israel (Judges 6:11-23).
- He appeared to Manoah and promised a son, whom his wife called Samson (Judges 13:2-25).
- When David sinned in numbering the people, God sent the angel of the Lord with pestilence (1 Chronicles 21:1-27).
- When Elijah fled before Jezebel, He came and refreshed him under the juniper tree (1 Kings 19:5-7).
- When Sennacherib invaded Judah, the angel came to the rescue of the Jews and killed 185,000 Assyrians in one night (2 Kings 19:35).
- He is seen standing among the myrtle trees and receiving the reports of various messengers (Zechariah 1:11).
- Joshua, the high priest, is said to be standing for Him. (Zechariah 3:1).

Therefore, it can be concluded that Christ had a distinct personal existence in the Old Testament period as the Angel of the Lord.

Other instances of the Angel of the Lord, can be seen in the form of a man accompanied by two angels. During His conversation with Abraham about the birth of a son and the destruction of Sodom, the Angel is referred to as the Lord. There is little doubt that this is an Old Testament appearance of Jesus Christ. Also, Jacob wrestled with an angel, and some have concluded that Jacob was, in fact, wrestling with the pre-incarnate Jesus.

People are often confused about salvation in the Old Testament. The doctrine of Old Testament soteriology (God's plan for salvation) is founded upon particular truths. First, is the universal fall of humanity into sin. Genesis 3 explains that through Satan's subtlety, man was drawn away from God into an act of rebellion which resulted in sin and the fall of man. The term "fall" means that man fell from the elevated position which he occupied with God prior to the sin. In Genesis 3:15, we have God's promise concerning a coming Savior to undo the tragedy of Eden.

> *Genesis 3:15, And I will put enmity between you and the woman, and between your offspring and hers; he will crush your head, and you will strike his heel.*

This verse is the first Messianic prophecy in the Bible. Scholars refer to this as the "Protoevangelium" (i.e., the first gospel). The Bible makes it plain that this was not an afterthought by God but according to His eternal plan. As the Old Testament unfolds, we begin to get a glimpse of God's revelation in regard to the way of salvation in the Old Testament.

What conditions for salvation are expressed in the Old Testament? First, there was the necessity of faith.

> *Romans 4:1-8, What then shall we say that Abraham, our forefather according to the flesh, discovered in this matter? If, in fact, Abraham was justified by works, he had something to boast about—but not before God. What does Scripture say? "Abraham believed God, and it was credited to him as righteousness." Now to the one who works, wages are not credited as a gift but as an obligation. However, to the one who does not work but trusts God who justifies the ungodly, their faith is credited as righteousness. David says the same thing when he speaks of the blessedness of the one to whom God credits righteousness apart from works: "Blessed are those whose transgressions are forgiven, whose sins are covered. Blessed is the one whose sin the Lord will never count against them."*

After faith, the second condition of salvation was the promised death of Jesus Christ on the cross for the sins of man.

> *Romans 3:21-26, But now apart from the law the righteousness of God has been made known, to which the Law and the Prophets testify. This righteousness is given through faith in Jesus Christ to all who believe. There is no difference between Jew and Gentile, for all have sinned and fall short of the glory of God, and all are*

justified freely by his grace through the redemption that came by Christ Jesus. God presented Christ as a sacrifice of atonement, through the shedding of his blood—to be received by faith. He did this to demonstrate his righteousness, because in his forbearance he had left the sins committed beforehand unpunished—he did it to demonstrate his righteousness at the present time, so as to be just and the one who justifies those who have faith in Jesus.

It is important to consider the matter of faith in the Old Testament, and ask the simple question, "In what did Old Testament believers have faith?" Obviously, God could not hold the Old Testament believer responsible for truths which were not revealed until New Testament times. Thus, the faith required was faith in the promise of God insofar as they were revealed.

It must be noted that the saving work of God was gradually unfolded throughout the Old Testament. For Adam and Eve, this was faith in the promised seed of the woman which was to bruise the serpent's head. For Abraham, it was faith in God's ability to uphold His promises for offspring and land. Thus, faith in the Old Testament took the form of trust in God to provide a sufficient means of salvation. Those who believe in Him and trusted in Him for deliverance and forgiveness were, therefore, saved (see Hebrews 11:6-10).

We should not forget that salvation in the Old Testament from the divine side was based on the reality of the cross. Although Old Testament believers did not possess adequate knowledge of the coming Christ, it was according to God's economy that all forgiveness is on the basis of Christ's atoning death on the cross. Therefore, from God's viewpoint, all salvation in the Old Testament was based upon Jesus Christ.

Romans 3:24-25, and all are justified freely by his grace through the redemption that came by Christ Jesus. God presented Christ as a sacrifice of atonement, through the shedding of his blood—to be received by faith. He did this to demonstrate his righteousness, because in his forbearance he had left the sins committed beforehand unpunished...

Therefore, God provides salvation in the Old Testament through His grace and restraint to actually leave man's sins unpunished before they receive adequate and just punishment on the cross of Christ. God then "passed over" the sins that had been committed in Old Testament times before Christ. In this sense, God was able to pass over sin for the time being and save the Old Testament saint. God knew, in His eternal plan to unite all things in Christ (Ephesians 1:10), that payment for sin was coming in Jesus Christ.

When Christ died, sins were judged and passed away, thus leaving God's just wrath satisfied. Therefore, all of the Old Testament ordinances, laws, and sacrifices were all anticipatory of the coming of Christ. All of the sins which God forgave in the Old Testament were forgiven (passed over) with the cross in mind. However, after the cross and to this day, God calls all people to repent with an offer of immediate forgiveness in Christ.

> *Acts 17:30, In the past God overlooked such ignorance, but now he commands all people everywhere to repent.*

What about the Old Testament sacrifices? The sacrifices that God commanded in the Old Testament were the means by which believers could manifest their inward faith in God for a coming acceptable sacrifice. We must carefully note that the sacrifices in and of themselves could not save anyone.

> *Hebrews 10:1-4, The law is only a shadow of the good things that are coming— not the realities themselves. For this reason it can never, by the same sacrifices repeated endlessly year after year, make perfect those who draw near to worship. Otherwise, would they not have stopped being offered? For the worshipers would have been cleansed once for all, and would no longer have felt guilty for their sins. But those sacrifices are an annual reminder of sins. It is impossible for the blood of bulls and goats to take away sins.*

If an unbeliever offered a sacrifice, his or her sacrifice would be entirely unacceptable to God. The mere offering of a bull or goat can by no means save anyone. Therefore, the sacrifices were both types and symbols of the Lamb of God who was slain from the foundation of the world (Revelation 13:8). Old Testament sacrifices were simply the means by which individuals could demonstrate their faith in God and His promise of salvation.

> *1 Peter 1:18-21, For you know that it was not with perishable things such as silver or gold that you were redeemed from the empty way of life handed down to you from your ancestors, but with the precious blood of Christ, a lamb without blemish or defect. He was chosen before the creation of the world, but was revealed in these last times for your sake. Through him you believe in God, who raised him from the dead and glorified him, and so your faith and hope are in God.*

Hence, we are to understand that Jesus is the Savior in the Old Testament just as He is in the New Testament. Man was not saved in the Old Testament by keeping the Law, but by expressing faith in God, His word, and His promises. The ultimate promise, of course, being that God would provide a perfect sacrifice as a complete payment for sins. This plan of God would provide the way for humanity to be brought back into fellowship with God by having his or her sins cleansed by the blood of Jesus Christ.

Hebrews 9:11-15, But when Christ came as high priest of the good things that are now already here, he went through the greater and more perfect tabernacle that is not made with human hands, that is to say, is not a part of this creation. He did not enter by means of the blood of goats and calves; but he entered the Most Holy Place once for all by his own blood, thus obtaining eternal redemption. The blood of goats and bulls and the ashes of a heifer sprinkled on those who are ceremonially unclean sanctify them so that they are outwardly clean. How much more, then, will the blood of Christ, who through the eternal Spirit offered himself unblemished to God, cleanse our consciences from acts that lead to death, so that we may serve the living God! For this reason Christ is the mediator of a new covenant, that those who are called may receive the promised eternal inheritance—now that he has died as a ransom to set them free from the sins committed under the first covenant.

The Person and Work of Jesus Christ

John 21:25, Jesus did many other things as well. If every one of them were written down, I suppose that even the whole world would not have room for the books that would be written.

In this verse, the Apostle John declares that if all the works of Jesus were written down in detail, even the world itself would not be able to contain the books. We have somewhat of an understanding as to how impossible it would be to write an exhaustive study on the person of Jesus Christ. Isaiah the prophet prophesied this about Jesus,

Isaiah 9:6, For to us a child is born, to us a son is given, and the government will be on his shoulders. And he will be called Wonderful Counselor, Mighty God, Everlasting Father, Prince of Peace.

To even attempt to consider this verse, would lead one to a study beyond the limits of mere expression of who Jesus is. Jesus is the Lord of Glory, Wonderful Counselor, and the Prince of Peace. With this in mind, when approaching any study of the person of Jesus Christ, we must certainly be reminded of the words which God spoke to Moses from the burning bush. We are standing on Holy Ground.

The person of Jesus Christ is not a casual subject matter. We are to understand that we are speaking and thinking about the incarnation of God! Whenever we attempt to prepare or to teach a study on Jesus, we must do so with the greatest reverence. Total dependence upon the Holy Spirit is required. So, let us approach with great reverence. Let us, with our finite minds, search to understand some of the One who is infinite. Let us be glad that God, in His eternal wisdom, chose to give us His Word so that we may at least touch the hem of His garment.

The Incarnation and Character of Jesus Christ

Throughout all time, there has existed without beginning or end the triune God of the gospel: God the Father, God the Son, and God the Holy Spirit. Therefore, we have seen that there is an eternally divine person who is the Son of God; the Lord Jesus Christ. It is critical to investigate the incarnation of the second person of the Trinity, the eternal Son in human flesh: Jesus Christ.

The word "incarnation" comes from a Latin word meaning "becoming flesh." Although the word "incarnation" is not a biblical term, it does reflect the biblical truth "the word became flesh" found in John 1:14. Indeed, as one theologian helpfully explains, the mystery of the incarnation is that "God, without ceasing to be God, actually became what he created in order to reconcile us to himself" (*The Incarnation of God*, 47). The incarnation is the advent of Jesus into the human family. This participation in the human family was for the purpose of redemption.

The means which God used to enter the human family was the virgin birth. When considering the virgin birth of Christ, the following truths must be taken into account. First, the acceptance and understanding of the virgin birth of Jesus Christ is based on a proper understanding of His eternal divinity as the second person of the Trinity. Although the virgin birth is difficult to grasp—it certainly is miraculous—it is also natural considering the fact that Jesus' birth was accompanied by a star, heralded by the angels, and testified to shepherds.

Furthermore, the virgin birth seems fitting considering that miracles were a constant part of Jesus' public ministry and that after dying for the sins of the world, Jesus Christ was resurrected in power. When considering the star, angel, shepherds, wise men, miracles, and the resurrection, then the virgin birth seems both suitable and fitting for such a magnificent Savior. When one comes to believe in the deity of Jesus Christ, questions concerning the Virgin birth seem to fade. The glorious person and miraculous life of Jesus Christ both requires and affirms the fact of the virgin birth.

The second truth which we are to understand is that the acceptance of the virgin birth of Christ is based on the validity and integrity of Scripture. When the Bible is accepted as the Holy Spirit authored Word of God, there should be no problem concerning the Virgin Birth because the Bible plainly declares that Jesus was born of a virgin.

Isaiah 7:14, Therefore the Lord himself will give you a sign: The virgin will conceive and give birth to a son, and will call him Immanuel.

> *Matthew 1:22-23,* All this took place to fulfill what the Lord had said through the prophet: "The virgin will conceive and give birth to a son, and they will call him Immanuel" (which means "God with us").

The word "virgin" comes from the Greek word *parathenos* and means maiden or unmarried daughter. It is used of Mary (Matthew 1:23), the ten virgins (Matthew 25:1-11), and the daughters of Philip in Acts 21:9. So, Scripture affirms that Jesus' birth was brought about through an earthly mother who was a virgin.

The virgin conception of Jesus is an entirely divine act. It was divine in several ways: First, the person who was born is divine (Luke 1:31-35); Second, the manner in which the Virgin Birth was announced was divine (Luke 1:26-32); Third, the conception of the eternal Son in the womb of a virgin was brought about by overshadowing of the Holy Spirit (Matthew 1:18; Luke 1:35).

> *Luke 1:35,* The angel answered, "The Holy Spirit will come on you, and the power of the Most High will overshadow you. So the holy one to be born will be called the Son of God."

While the idea of the Virgin Birth might be difficult for our finite minds to understand, we must remember that if God can create man, form him out of the dust of the ground, breathe into him and make him a living being, then He certainly has the capacity to bring about a virgin birth. All of these events and circumstances attest to the fact that the birth of Jesus Christ was no ordinary incident.

Furthermore, The involvement of the angels (Luke 2:9-14); the experience of Mary and Elizabeth (Luke 1:41-45); the shepherds (Luke 2:8-20); the star (Matthew 2:2); and the wise men (Matthew 2:1-2) all cooperate in the advent of the Son of God becoming eternally man.

To deny the virgin birth of Christ is to go against the testimony of both the Old and New Testament revelation. If one denies the authoritative biblical revelation concerning the birth of Christ, then why would one believe anything else written about Christ? If Christ has not been born of a virgin then He would have the same sin nature as an earthly father and, therefore, would not be capable of saving the world from sin and death. In sum, the clear teaching of Scripture is that the birth of Jesus was accomplished by God through the miracle of the immaculate conception.

The Son of God assumed a full, true human nature in the incarnation. Thus, making Him the most unique person ever to live by possessing two natures: divine and human. Scripture plainly asserts the deity of Christ even after His incarnation. It has already been discussed that Jesus is truly and fully God. However, one of the most difficult doctrines to consider and understand is the truth of Christ's two natures in one person. This truth is difficult for our finite minds to understand, to say the least. Jesus Christ is truly and fully God and at the same time truly and fully man.

In 451 A.D., the Council of Chalcedon was held to come to a decisive, Orthodox statement on the two natures of Jesus Christ. The product of the council's work led to what is referred to as the Chalcedonian definition about Jesus Christ:

> "Jesus exists in two natures which exist without confusion, without change, without division, without separation the difference of the the natures having been in no wise taken away by reason of the union, but rather properties of each other being preserved, and both concurring into one person."

What does that mean? It has been said:

- Jesus was 100 percent God and 100 percent man 100 percent of the time.
- Jesus was not God indwelling a man. He was not a man who became God. He was not God appearing to be a man. He had two natures combined into one personality: He was fully God and fully man and eternally exists as *one* person.
- Without ceasing to be who He was as the eternal Son of God, Jesus Christ became what he created: a true man with a full human nature.

Let's attempt to clarify this subject by stating that Jesus did not possess one nature divided into two parts consisting of God and man—half God and half man. The Bible makes it clear that Christ possesses, in His incarnate state, two full and complete natures. Namely, full and perfect God (deity), and full and perfect humanity (true humanity without a sinful nature). This combination of human and divine natures is what makes Jesus Christ unique as both the Son of God and the Son of Man.

> *1 John 5:10,* Whoever believes in the Son of God accepts this testimony. Whoever does not believe God has made him out to be a liar, because they have not believed the testimony God has given about his Son.

He possesses a perfect divine nature and an unfallen human nature. This union of two complete natures is described by the term "Hypostatic Union." This Hypostatic Union of the human and divine natures of Jesus is clearly attested to in the Bible:

- Jesus has always been fully God: John 1:1-3, "In the beginning was the Word, and the Word was with God, and the Word was God. He was with God in the beginning. Through him all things were made; without him nothing was made that has been made."

- Jesus became fully man without ceasing to be what He was—fully God: Colossians 2:9, "For in Christ all the fullness of the deity lives in bodily form."
- Jesus continues to exist as both God and man. Acts 1:11, "This same Jesus, who has been taken from you into heaven, will come back in the same way you have seen him go into heaven."

So, Jesus is fully man and fully God at the same time. But, what is the result of this combination of His two natures? Jesus' divine nature could not experience physical and mental suffering; however, His human nature could. Thus, through the suffering of His human nature, Christ became our compassionate High Priest.

> Hebrews 4:15, For we do not have a high priest who is unable to empathize with our weaknesses, but we have one who has been tempted in every way, just as we are—yet he did not sin.

It should be pointed out that understanding the unity of Jesus' two natures can be difficult because, at times, Jesus could be weak and all-powerful. He could increase His knowledge and be all-knowing at the same time. He could be finite and infinite at the same time. Without an understanding of the Hypostatic Union of the two natures of Jesus Christ, these ideas could be exceedingly confusing.

However, it was just this combination of the divine and human natures which made the death of Christ sufficient for salvation. As man, Jesus could die for our sins, but only as God could, His death has sufficient value to provide for salvation. We must remember that in His incarnation, the Son of God assumed unfallen humanity in order to redeem fallen humanity. At the same time, Jesus Christ could not have saved the world unless He was both fully God and fully man.

> 1 John 2:1-2, My dear children, I write this to you so that you will not sin. But if anybody does sin, we have an advocate with the Father—Jesus Christ, the Righteous One. He is the atoning sacrifice for our sins, and not only for ours but also for the sins of the whole world.

One cannot thoroughly appreciate the incarnation of Jesus Christ without an understanding of the term kenosis. If Jesus is the eternal Son of God, then it is wise to discuss at this point the relationship between the eternality of Jesus Christ and the incarnation of Jesus Christ. In other words, as God, the Son has always existed—He is eternal.

However, as a man, Jesus was born, assuming a true human nature, which is the incarnation. The Apostle Paul tells us very clearly in Philippians 2 that when Jesus Christ was born He "made Himself nothing" (*kenosis*) by taking the form of a servant. The *kenosis* of Jesus Christ reveals to us the love of God and the high price which Christ paid for our salvation. It should also be noted at the beginning of the discussion on the idea of *kenosis,* that any attempt to fully explain or understand this will always fall short because Jesus was God and any attempt to explain God fully always falls short. The *kenosis* of Jesus is portrayed in Philippians 2:5-11.

> *Philippians 2:5-11, In your relationships with one another, have the same mindset as Christ Jesus: Who, being in very nature God, did not consider equality with God something to be used to his own advantage; rather, he made himself nothing by taking the very nature of a servant, being made in human likeness. And being found in appearance as a man, he humbled himself by becoming obedient to death—even death on a cross! Therefore God exalted him to the highest place and gave him the name that is above every name, that at the name of Jesus every knee should bow, in heaven and on earth and under the earth, and every tongue acknowledge that Jesus Christ is Lord, to the glory of God the Father.*

In this passage, we find several things: First, we see the eternal position of Jesus Christ. Verse 6 states that Jesus truly exists "being in very nature God" which means Jesus continues to be what He had always been: God.

Next, verse 6 says, "Who, being in very nature God, did not consider equality with God something to be used to his own advantage." This means that Jesus chose not to assert His equality with God the Father. This doesn't mean that He didn't value His equality with God; rather, it reveals that there was something of greater significance which required this surrender and could not be accomplished apart from it: the redemption of mankind. Therefore, in light of His desire to obey the Father by saving men from their sins, Christ did not consider the expression of His divine essence a treasure that should be trumpeted in the public square.

Verse 7 says that Jesus "...made himself nothing by taking the very nature of a servant, being made in human likeness." Those words "made himself nothing" come from the Greek word *kenosis.* The *Amplified Bible* tries to capture the essence of *kenosis* with this translation:

> *Philippians 2:7, but emptied Himself [without renouncing or diminishing His deity, but only temporarily giving up the outward expression of divine equality and His rightful dignity] by assuming the form of a bond-servant, and being made in the*

likeness of men [He became completely human but was without sin, being fully God and fully man].

So what does it mean "made himself nothing"? As the Amplified Translation clearly states, Jesus was not renouncing or diminishing His deity. Although Jesus did take on the form of a servant man, He was still God. God cannot change; therefore "making himself nothing" did not refer to any change in His divine nature.

Thus, "made himself nothing" is best understood in two statements: 1) Jesus limited Himself while He was on earth, but 2) Jesus did not *lessen* Himself while he was on this earth.

The question is, what does it mean that Jesus "made himself nothing"? To be sure, Jesus did not cease to be God, nor did He become less God. Theologians from the past often used the phraseology that Jesus divinity was "veiled" by His form of a servant. Perhaps the simplest way to understand Jesus' incarnation is with the phrase "Jesus limited himself by becoming fully man, but Jesus did not lessen Himself since he remained fully God."

The truth of Scriptures is that in His incarnation Jesus limited Himself: by taking the form of a servant (Phil 2:6-8), by limiting His presence to one place at a time, by taking a position in which the Father was greater (John 14:28), and by limiting His knowledge (Matthew 24:36).

> *John 14:28, You heard me say, "I am going away and I am coming back to you." If you loved me, you would be glad that I am going to the Father, for the Father is greater than I.*

> *Matthew 24:36, But about that day or hour no one knows, not even the angels in heaven, nor the Son, but only the Father.*

> *John 5:19, Jesus gave them this answer: "Very truly I tell you, the Son can do nothing by himself; he can do only what he sees his Father doing, because whatever the Father does the Son also does."*

> *John 5:30, By myself I can do nothing; I judge only as I hear, and my judgment is just, for I seek not to please myself but him who sent me.*

Perhaps these ideas from John MacArthur will explain this idea a little better. He said, "Jesus remained God, but renounced His privileges." MacArthur believes:

- He renounced His privileges to "heavenly glory." Christ gave up the glory of face-to-face relations with God for the muck of this earth. He gave up the ador-ing presence of the angels for the spittle of men. He gave up the shining bril-liance of heaven's glories

John 17:5, And now, Father, glorify me in your presence with the glory I had with you before the world began.

- Christ renounced His independent authority. He completely submitted Himself to the will of the Father and learned to be a servant;

Matthew 26:39, Going a little farther, he fell with his face to the ground and prayed, "My Father, if it is possible, may this cup be taken from me. Yet not as I will, but as you will."

- Christ renounced the voluntary use of His divine attributes. He did not give up any of His deity, but He did give up the free exercise of His attributes;

John 5:30, By myself I can do nothing; I judge only as I hear, and my judgment is just, for I seek not to please myself but him who sent me.

- Christ renounced His personal riches;

2 Corinthians 8:9, For you know the grace of our Lord Jesus Christ, that though he was rich, yet for your sake he became poor, so that you through his poverty might become rich.

- Christ renounced His favorable relationship with the Father and being sepa-rate from sin, to become sin on our behalf.

2 Corinthians 5:21, God made him who had no sin to be sin for us, so that in him we might become the righteousness of God.

Jesus was still fully God when he walked this earth. Although Jesus' divine attri-butes were veiled during His time on this earth, glimpses of His divine nature are evident throughout His earthly ministry.

John 5:18, For this reason they tried all the more to kill him; not only was he break-ing the Sabbath, but he was even calling God his own Father, making himself equal with God.

John 14:9, Jesus answered: "Don't you know me, Philip, even after I have been among you such a long time? Anyone who has seen me has seen the Father."

John 8:58, Very truly I tell you," Jesus answered, "before Abraham was born, I am!"

Colossians 2:9, For in Christ all the fullness of the Deity lives in bodily form

All of these Scriptures lead to one conclusion: Jesus Christ is the eternal Son of God, possessing and demonstrating all of the divine attributes of God. In other words, we must always remember that while on this earth, "Jesus may have limited Himself by becoming a man, but Jesus never lessened Himself because He remained fully God.

The Death of Jesus Christ

Just outside the city of Jerusalem, there was a place reserved for public executions called Golgotha, the place of the skull (named for the shape of the hill). It was a place of horror, sheer agony, intense suffering, and excruciating pain. Golgotha was a malignant place reserved for the sadistic, where the perverted would find joy in watching human suffering.

Lingering death, moans, and cries beyond description and an indescribable death made it an infamous place. Yet, this little hill which had become famous for its agony was about to take its place in the salvation of the world. This day was to be the greatest day in history. Upon Golgotha, instead of an execution, there was a divine sacrifice. This place of ignominy was about to become a place of glory. This place of suffering was about to become a place of healing. This place of death was about to become a place of life. This place of fear was about to become a place of peace. This place of disgrace was about to become a place of comfort. This place of physical death was about to become a place of spiritual victory. On that day, that little hill, Golgotha, the place of the skull, was Calvary.

The hands of the Lord Jesus Christ were nailed to the cross so that our hands could be freed from sin and the captivity of sin. His feet were nailed to the cruel cross, so that those who would believe in Him might walk in fellowship with God. His heart was ruptured, so that our hearts might be repaired and might be made right with him. His side was pierced and wounded, so that our bodies might be restored to fellowship with God. His blood was shed for our cleansing. He died so we might live!

There are two major factors concerning God's plan of salvation which must not be overlooked. First, there must be a proper understanding of the finished work of the Savior on Calvary. Secondly, there must be the personal application of that work to those who believe. One must remember that the death of Christ will be of no value to anyone unless His work on Calvary is claimed by faith and personally applied to the individual by the power of the Spirit.

The death of the Lord Jesus Christ is to be considered one of His works, for it did not happen to Him, and was not forced upon Him, but resulted from a definite choice on His part. In other words, Cavalry was part of the eternal plan and design of God the Father for the purpose of providing redemption for lost humanity.

It will be of great value for us to consider some significant facts concerning the death of Christ. One of which is that the death of Christ was predicted in the Old Testament. There are those today who would tell us that the death of Jesus came as an interruption to the healing ministry of Christ. However, a careful study of the Bible will show us that the death of Christ, was not an accident, but was, in fact, part of God's eternal plan and design.

As we search the pages of Scripture, we will readily find that the Old Testament is laden with types, symbols, and prophecies concerning the death of Christ. One of which is the prophecy regarding the fact that the Messiah was to be betrayed:

> *Psalm, 41:9-11, Even my close friend, someone I trusted, one who shared my bread, has turned against me. But may you have mercy on me, Lord; raise me up, that I may repay them. I know that you are pleased with me, for my enemy does not triumph over me.*

The Old Testament prophecies also describe in vivid detail some of the trials of the Lord, like Jesus being falsely accused, spat upon, and sold for money:

> *Zechariah 11:12-13, I told them, "If you think it best, give me my pay; but if not, keep it." So they paid me thirty pieces of silver. And the Lord said to me, "Throw it to the potter"—the handsome price at which they valued me! So I took the thirty pieces of silver and threw them to the potter at the house of the Lord.*

The crucifixion of Jesus is described in detail in both Isaiah 53:1-6 and Psalm 22:1-8:

> *Isaiah 53:1-6, Who has believed our message and to whom has the arm of the Lord been revealed? He grew up before him like a tender shoot, and like a root out of dry ground. He had no beauty or majesty to attract us to him, nothing in his appearance that we should desire him. He was despised and rejected by mankind, a man of suffering, and familiar with pain. Like one from whom people hide their faces he was despised, and we held him in low esteem. Surely he took up our pain and bore our suffering, yet we considered him punished by God, stricken by him, and afflicted. But he was pierced for our transgressions, he was crushed for our iniquities; the punishment that brought us peace was on him, and by his wounds we are healed. We all, like sheep, have gone astray, each of us has turned to our own way; and the Lord has laid on him the iniquity of us all.*

Psalm 22:1-8, My God, my God, why have you forsaken me? Why are you so far from saving me, so far from my cries of anguish? My God, I cry out by day, but you do not answer, by night, but I find no rest. Yet you are enthroned as the Holy One; you are the one Israel praises. In you our ancestors put their trust; they trusted and you delivered them. To you they cried out and were saved; in you they trusted and were not put to shame. But I am a worm and not a man, scorned by everyone, despised by the people. All who see me mock me; they hurl insults, shaking their heads. "He trusts in the Lord," they say, "let the Lord rescue him. Let him deliver him, since he delights in him."

The Old Testament does not simply speak in general terms but offers specificity concerning the death of Christ. For example, there are predictions such as the fact that He would be struck and the sheep scatter, He would be put to death and have nothing, and He would be brutally beaten and disfigured:

Zechariah 13:7, "Awake, sword, against my shepherd, against the man who is close to me!" declares the Lord Almighty. "Strike the shepherd, and the sheep will be scattered, and I will turn my hand against the little ones."

Daniel 9:26, After the sixty-two 'sevens,' the Anointed One will be put to death and will have nothing. The people of the ruler who will come will destroy the city and the sanctuary. The end will come like a flood: War will continue until the end, and desolations have been decreed.

Isaiah 52:14, Just as there were many who were appalled at him—his appearance was so disfigured beyond that of any human being and his form marred beyond human likeness—

The Old Testament prophecies also offer specific details about the trials and crucifixion of Jesus Christ in such explicit terms that it even predicted that not one bone of His body would be broken.

Psalm 34:20, he protects all his bones, not one of them will be broken.

And finally, His resurrection from the dead was predicted.

Psalm 16:8-10, I keep my eyes always on the Lord. With him at my right hand, I will not be shaken. Therefore my heart is glad and my tongue rejoices; my body also will rest secure, because you will not abandon me to the realm of the dead, nor will you let your faithful one see decay.

One of the significant facts concerning the death of Jesus Christ is that it was predicted in the Old Testament and therefore part of the triune God's plan throughout the ages. Another important fact is the prominence and importance of the death of Christ in the New Testament.

The last three days of the life of Christ occupy about 1/5th of the four Gospels. It has been suggested that if all of the three and a half years of His public ministry had been written out fully as the last three days of the life of the Lord, we would have a volume of some 84,000 pages of the life of Christ. It has been estimated that the death of Christ is mentioned over 175 times in the New Testament. It is plain to see the whole life of Christ was directed toward one place: Calvary!

The death of Jesus Christ was also the climax of the eternal Son taking the form of a servant. Indeed, obedience to the point of death, even death on a cross is the true testimony of the Son's total obedience to the Father. It is a simple fact that Christ came into the world for one purpose, and that is to die on the cross for the sins of humanity.

While it is not the purpose of this section, it is good to note that there are several false beliefs concerning the crucifixion of Jesus. Some believe that Jesus was a martyr who teaches us about total commitment to a cause. Others believe that the primary purpose of Jesus' life and death was so the He could be an example how we should live. Still, others believe that Jesus' death was a great moral lesson as to how much God loves us.

Yes, it is true that Jesus was a martyr in that he died for His cause, but His death on the cross was much more than that. Yes, Jesus was the best example ever as to how we should live, but His death on the cross was much more than that. Yes, Jesus' death on the cross was, in fact, a great demonstration of God's love for us, but His death on the cross was much more than that.

To state that Jesus was merely a martyr, an example, or a moral teacher, would fall woefully short of the real purpose of His death. The chief reason for the incarnation of Jesus Christ was so that He would reconcile fallen humanity to God.

> *Hebrews 2:9, But we do see Jesus, who was made lower than the angels for a little while, now crowned with glory and honor because he suffered death, so that by the grace of God he might taste death for everyone.*

The death of Christ is the heart of the gospel. Without the death of Christ on Calvary, there would be no gospel; there would be no good news, there would be no salvation. Christianity is distinguished from all other religions in that its Founder took upon Himself the sins of the man and died for our redemption. Doing away with the vicarious atonement of Jesus Christ would reduce Christianity to another system of teaching or religious practice.

Thus, the death of the Lord Jesus Christ is central to the heart Christianity. Not only that, but the Bible makes it plain because mankind's sinful condition deserved the wrath of God which made the death of Christ essential to salvation. Therefore, God sent His Son into the world to die for our sins that we might be saved.

> *John 3:14-16,* *Just as Moses lifted up the snake in the wilderness, so the Son of Man must be lifted up, that everyone who believes may have eternal life in him....For God so loved the world that he gave his one and only Son, that whoever believes in him shall not perish but have eternal life.*

It is important to understand a few theological words and their meanings as they relate to the death of Jesus. If one reads much of the death of Christ, the word *vicarious* is sure to come up. The death of Jesus is said to be a vicarious death. The Bible tells us that Jesus did not die for His own sins since He is entirely without sin. Vicariousness speaks of someone doing something on behalf of another person. A vicar is a substitute individual who takes the place of another and acts on his or her behalf. Thus, the suffering of Jesus was vicarious in that He was suffering for someone else and that someone else was sinful humanity. Jesus took sin upon Himself and suffered the just, divine punishment that mankind might be brought into a right standing with God. The truth of Christ's vicarious suffering is found through Scripture:

> *Isaiah 53:5-6,* *But he was pierced for our transgressions, he was crushed for our iniquities; the punishment that brought us peace was on him, and by his wounds we are healed. We all, like sheep, have gone astray, each of us has turned to our own way; and the Lord has laid on him the iniquity of us all.*

Another theological term which is used in reference to the death of Christ is that of *satisfaction*. When man sinned, God's holiness was offended. In addition, God's holiness demands that sin be punished. When Christ died on the cross for our sins, the holiness of God was satisfied with the work done. It is finished! The death of Christ satisfied the justice of God, and the death of Christ satisfied the demands of God's Law.

The death of Christ also involved a term known as *redemption*. Basically, the term redemption has in view the payment of the price demanded by a Holy God for the deliverance of the believer from the bondage and the burden of sin.

Propitiation is another word which is used in reference to the sacrificial death of Christ on the cross. The term propitiation embodies the concept that the death of Christ fully satisfied the demands of a righteous God in respect to His judgment upon the sinner. Thus, by His death on the cross, Christ appeased God's holy wrath against sin and turned His wrath to favor for those who would believe.

1 John 2:2, My dear children, I write this to you so that you will not sin. But if any-body does sin, we have an advocate with the Father—Jesus Christ, the Righteous One. He is the atoning sacrifice for our sins, and not only for ours but also for the sins of the whole world.

Some people prefer to shy away from any mention of the blood of Jesus Christ because they consider it unacceptable, outdated, too graphic or even not socially ac-ceptable. One cannot rightly understand the sacrificial offering of Jesus Christ without understanding the significance and meaning of the blood. God did not provide a Savior who would be acceptable to man; rather the Father provided a Savior who would be an acceptable sacrifice to Himself. The Bible places great emphasis on the blood of Jesus Christ, and so should we.

First, Scripture is clear that God's eternal plan of salvation was brought about through the blood of Christ.

1 Peter 1:18-20, For you know that it was not with perishable things such as silver or gold that you were redeemed from the empty way of life handed down to you from your ancestors, but with the precious blood of Christ, a lamb without blemish or defect. He was chosen before the creation of the world, but was revealed in these last times for your sake.

Second, it was the blood of Jesus Christ that brought about the *propitiation* for sins of the world. Propitiation is not a word we use very often, but it has great significance. Propitiation carries two basic ideas: a) the idea of appeasement or satisfaction of the wrath God against sin; b) because of that appeasement of wrath, there is now a possible reconciliation to God.

Many like the second idea of reconciliation but reject the first idea of appeasing God's wrath. However, Scripture clearly teaches both aspects of proportion that was brought about by the blood of Christ.

Romans 5:9, Since we have now been justified by his blood, how much more shall we be saved from God's wrath through him!

Romans 3:25, God presented Christ as a sacrifice of atonement, through the shed-ding of his blood—to be received by faith. He did this to demonstrate his righteous-ness, because in his forbearance he had left the sins committed beforehand unpun-ished

In addition to the propitiation for our sins, the blood of Jesus also brought about our redemption, forgiveness, justification, and spiritual adoption into the family of God.

Ephesians 1:7, In him we have redemption through his blood, the forgiveness of sins, in accordance with the riches of God's grace

The blood of Jesus Christ also provided the purchase price for the believer to become God's own possession.

1 Corinthians 6:19-20, Do you not know that your bodies are temples of the Holy Spirit, who is in you, whom you have received from God? You are not your own; you were bought at a price. Therefore honor God with your bodies.

Through the blood of Jesus Christ, we are redeemed: a) We are redeemed from every lawless deed; b) We are redeemed from the curse of the law; c) We are redeemed from the bondange of the law; d) We are redeemed from the power of sin; e) We are redeemed from a futile way of life.

Titus 2:14, who gave himself for us to redeem us from all wickedness and to purify for himself a people that are his very own, eager to do what is good.

Galatians 3:13, Christ redeemed us from the curse of the law by becoming a curse for us, for it is written: "Cursed is everyone who is hung on a pole."

1 Peter 1:18, For you know that it was not with perishable things such as silver or gold that you were redeemed from the empty way of life handed down to you from your ancestors,

The blood of Jesus Christ allows us to be reconciled to God.

Colossians 1:19-20, For God was pleased to have all his fullness dwell in him, and through him to reconcile to himself all things, whether things on earth or things in heaven, by making peace through his blood, shed on the cross.

Finally, the blood of the Lamb enables people from every tribe, language, and nation to sing a new song.

Revelation 5:9, And they sang a new song, saying: "You are worthy to take the scroll and to open its seals, because you were slain, and with your blood you purchased for God persons from every tribe and language and people and nation."

The Resurrection of Jesus Christ

The resurrection of Christ is vital to the gospel message and Christian hope. It is the center of gravity for the Christian faith. Men and women of the early church entrenched themselves in the truth and hope of the resurrection. Christianity stands or falls on the historical fact of the resurrection of Jesus Christ. Therefore, Christianity stands alone as the one and only supernatural religion. While humanism is struggling desperately to teach men how to die well, Christ offers life and life to the full! While the world promotes the weak and lifeless philosophies of dead and dying men, the Apostle Paul points us to the truth of the resurrection of Jesus Christ.

The historical fact of the resurrection of Jesus Christ rightly occupies a prominent place in the Christian confession. It was the resurrection of Jesus Christ that was preached by the Apostles, attested to by the angels, and hatefully acknowledged by His enemies as a game changer for everyone involved.

Acts 25:19, Instead, they had some points of dispute with him about their own religion and about a dead man named Jesus who Paul claimed was alive.

Luke 24:4-7, While they were wondering about this, suddenly two men in clothes that gleamed like lightning stood beside them. In their fright the women bowed down with their faces to the ground, but the men said to them, "Why do you look for the living among the dead? He is not here; he has risen! Remember how he told you, while he was still with you in Galilee: 'The Son of Man must be delivered over to the hands of sinners, be crucified and on the third day be raised again.' "

Matthew 28:11-15, While the women were on their way, some of the guards went into the city and reported to the chief priests everything that had happened. When the chief priests had met with the elders and devised a plan, they gave the soldiers a large sum of money, telling them, "You are to say, 'His disciples came during the night and stole him away while we were asleep.' If this report gets to the governor, we will satisfy him and keep you out of trouble." So the soldiers took the money and did as they were instructed. And this story has been widely circulated among the Jews to this very day.

It is important to understand that the resurrection of Jesus Christ was brought about by both His own power and the power of God the Father.

John 10:18, No one takes it from me, but I lay it down of my own accord. I have authority to lay it down and authority to take it up again. This command I received from my Father."

Acts 2:24, But God raised him from the dead, freeing him from the agony of death, because it was impossible for death to keep its hold on him.

The Bible makes it abundantly clear that the significance of the resurrection of Jesus Christ is seen in that it is absolutely necessary for effective faith, forgiveness of sin, the fulfillment of Scripture, eternal hope, and justification of the believer.

> *1 Corinthians 15:14-17*, *And if Christ has not been raised, our preaching is useless and so is your faith. More than that, we are then found to be false witnesses about God, for we have testified about God that he raised Christ from the dead. But he did not raise him if in fact the dead are not raised. For if the dead are not raised, then Christ has not been raised either. And if Christ has not been raised, your faith is futile; you are still in your sins.*

Furthermore, the fact of the resurrection of Jesus in an infallible proof that Jesus Christ was indeed the Son of God.

> *Romans 1:4*, *and who through the Spirit of holiness was appointed the Son of God in power by his resurrection from the dead: Jesus Christ our Lord.*

We must understand that the resurrection of Jesus Christ was an actual physical, bodily resurrection. There are some who believe the Jesus did not actually die but fainted because of the ordeal of the cross, and later because of the cool air and spices in the tomb, He was revived. However, we know from historical evidence that this "Swoon Theory" holds no weight.

Still, others acknowledge that Jesus did die on the cross but suggest His body was stolen by His disciples, so they could perpetuate the story of Christ's resurrection. Indeed this "Stolen Body Theory" could have happened, but it does not explain how the disciples who had been so fearful at his betrayal became so brave as to steal the body after Jesus death while it was being guarded by Roman Soldiers. This objection also fails to account for all the appearance Jesus made to over 500 people.

Some have affirmed that Jesus' resurrection did happen, but suggest His resurrection was spiritual and not physical. They would say His death and resurrection are merely two sides of the same experience. In His death, Jesus passed out of this physical life, and in His resurrection, He passed into the spiritual life. Thus His appearances to people was simply spiritual. However, this does not take into account that Jesus ate and had physical contact with those he came into contact with after His resurrection. Surely, had Jesus' resurrected body been purely spiritual this would have been noted by the biblical writers.

Some have suggested that the resurrection of Jesus was simply a case of "Mass Hallucinations" by his followers. This "Hallucination Theory" seems plausible to some but does not deal with that fact that Jesus didn't just appear to His followers, but His tomb was in fact empty.

As a response to some of these objections to the resurrection, Gary R. Habermas and Michael Licona, authors of *The Case for the Resurrection of Jesus*, write:

> *One might speculate that the disciples experienced grief hallucinations. But grief hallucinations cannot account for the empty tomb or the conversion of the church persecutor Paul, who had viewed Jesus as a false prophet and would not have grieved over his death. One cannot argue that the disciples were lying about appearances and stole Jesus' body from the tomb, since we can establish that they truly believed that the risen Jesus had appeared to them. This would not have been the case if they had been lying. We can also rule out the theory that the Resurrection story was a legend that developed over time and was not actually taught by the original disciples, since we can establish that those original disciples sincerely believed that the risen Jesus had appeared to them and taught it within a very short period of time after his crucifixion.*

While these theories and others deny the literal, bodily resurrection of Jesus Christ, they actually acknowledge several clear facts. Those facts are: the tomb was empty, the physical body of Jesus was gone, those who crucified Jesus were distressed that the tomb was empty, and had the body of Jesus simply been produced, Christianity would have been proved false within hours of the message of the resurrection being first preached. Therefore, these objections to the physical resurrection of Jesus just simply don't hold under the weight of scrutiny.

The Bible makes it clear that the resurrection of Jesus Christ was a genuine bodily resurrection! Let us note some Scriptural facts that make it plain that Christ had a real, glorified body after His resurrection. Luke's gospel declares that the resurrected Jesus had a real body. The women who met Christ on the resurrection morning are said to have held Him by the feet.

> *Luke 24:39-40, Look at my hands and my feet. It is I myself! Touch me and see; a ghost does not have flesh and bones, as you see I have." When he had said this, he showed them his hands and feet.*

The Old Testament prophecy of David declared that the physical body of Christ would see no corruption.

> *Psalm 16:10, because you will not abandon me to the realm of the dead, nor will you let your faithful one see decay.*

> *Acts 2:31, Seeing what was to come, he spoke of the resurrection of the Messiah, that he was not abandoned to the realm of the dead, nor did his body see decay.*

Luke's gospel also records that Jesus ate actual food after His resurrection.

Luke 24:41-45, And while they still did not believe it because of joy and amazement, he asked them, "Do you have anything here to eat?" They gave him a piece of broiled fish, and he took it and ate it in their presence. He said to them, "This is what I told you while I was still with you: Everything must be fulfilled that is written about me in the Law of Moses, the Prophets and the Psalms." Then he opened their minds so they could understand the Scriptures.

The fact that Jesus had an actual body is seen after His resurrection. He was recognized by those who knew Him even down to the nail wounds.

John 20:25-28, So the other disciples told him, "We have seen the Lord!" But he said to them, "Unless I see the nail marks in his hands and put my finger where the nails were, and put my hand into his side, I will not believe." A week later his disciples were in the house again, and Thomas was with them. Though the doors were locked, Jesus came and stood among them and said, "Peace be with you!" Then he said to Thomas, "Put your finger here; see my hands. Reach out your hand and put it into my side. Stop doubting and believe." Thomas said to him, "My Lord and my God!"

The resurrection of Jesus clearly attests to and affirms the deity of Christ. Matthew, John, and the Apostle Paul said that the resurrection of Jesus Christ declared Him to be the Son of God.

Romans 1:4, and who through the Spirit of holiness was appointed the Son of God in power by his resurrection from the dead: Jesus Christ our Lord.

The resurrection of Jesus Christ also assures us that He has in fact purchased salvation for all who receive Him as Savior and Lord. If Christ had not risen from the grave physically, we could not be sure if God would save us or not. It has been said that the resurrection of Jesus Christ was God's "amen" to all that Jesus said and taught about salvation.

Through the resurrection of Jesus Christ, He has become the one Mediator between God and man.

1 Timothy 2:5-6, For there is one God and one mediator between God and mankind, the man Christ Jesus, who gave himself as a ransom for all people. This has now been witnessed to at the proper time.

The Bible also lists many other blessings which the resurrection of Christ purchase and assure for His followers—such as a personal realization of salvation which He provided, the assurance of salvation, and the power to live for Him.

Ephesians 1:18-20, I pray that the eyes of your heart may be enlightened in order that you may know the hope to which he has called you, the riches of his glorious in-

heritance in his holy people, and his incomparably great power for us who believe. That power is the same as the mighty strength he exerted when he raised Christ from the dead and seated him at his right hand in the heavenly realms...

The resurrection of Jesus is also God's guarantee that our bodies will also be resurrected from the dead.

1 Corinthians 15:20-23, But in fact Christ has been raised from the dead, the firstfruits of those who have fallen asleep. For as by a man came death, by a man has come also the resurrection of the dead. For as in Adam all die, so also in Christ shall all be made alive. But each in his own order: Christ the firstfruits, then at his coming those who belong to Christ.

The resurrection of Christ testifies to the truth that He will bring about the end time judgment of both the just and the unjust alike.

Acts 10:42, He commanded us to preach to the people and to testify that he is the one whom God appointed as judge of the living and the dead.

Finally, the resurrection of Jesus is our assurance that we have eternal life in Christ even if we die.

John 11:25-26, Jesus said to her, "I am the resurrection and the life. The one who believes in me will live, even though they die; and whoever lives by believing in me will never die. Do you believe this?"

The Ascension and Exaltation of Jesus Christ

After Christ finished His redemptive ministry and work on earth, it was time for Him to return to His home in glory. Following the final instructions to His disciples, Jesus ascended into heaven in front of them. He ascended with, and still possess an actual, glorified human body. Earthly or human flesh is perishable, but heavenly bodies are imperishable because they are created to indwell the New Earth, and Jesus' resurrected body is also referred to as a "glorious body."

Philippians 3:20-21, But our citizenship is in heaven. And we eagerly await a Savior from there, the Lord Jesus Christ, who, by the power that enables him to bring everything under his control, will transform our lowly bodies so that they will be like his glorious body.

What is the Son of God doing in glory now? The ascension of Christ marked the end of His "making Himself Nothing" (*Kenosis*) throughout His earthly ministry. Christ, when

He returned to glory, ended His time of intentionally giving up of divine prerogatives, and He is now reigning in all His glory. When Christ came to earth, He temporarily laid aside His pre-incarnate glory, but now He has received eternal glory from the Father. Scripture testifies that He is now highly exalted. As such, Christ is said to be the firstfruits of the resurrection being the forerunner for all the saints who shall someday follow Him into that same state of eternally glorified bodies.

> *Hebrews 2:8,* "*...and put everything under their feet.*" *In putting everything under them, God left nothing that is not subject to them. Yet at present we do not see everything subject to them.*

In addition to this, according to the promise of the Lord Jesus, He has entered into heaven to prepare a place for His children. We are not told how or what He is actually doing in this preparation, but we are confident some day He shall receive to Himself in that gloriously prepared place.

> *John 14:1-6,* "*Do not let your hearts be troubled. You believe in God; believe also in me. My Father's house has many rooms; if that were not so, would I have told you that I am going there to prepare a place for you? And if I go and prepare a place for you, I will come back and take you to be with me that you also may be where I am. You know the way to the place where I am going.*" *Thomas said to him,* "*Lord, we don't know where you are going, so how can we know the way?*" *Jesus answered,* "*I am the way and the truth and the life. No one comes to the Father except through me.*"

Finally, Christ has entered into a state of glory in order to begin His present ministry on behalf of the saints. Christ has come into glory to prepare for His coming again which is referred to as the return of Christ in all His Glory.

Summary of Belief

The following is a statement of belief concerning the person and work of the Lord Jesus Christ. First, we believe that Jesus Christ is the eternal Son of God, being very God Himself. It is to be understood that Jesus Christ did not become God's Son at His birth, but has been God's Son throughout all eternity (John 1:1-3). For the pre-incarnate ministry of the Lord Jesus Christ see Colossians 1:16-17 and 1 Corinthians 8:6.

Secondly, we believe that Jesus Christ was born of a virgin and lived an impeccable life on earth. The Bible teaches that the birth of Jesus Christ was a miraculous act of God (Matthew 1:18-25). All true born-again believers will readily and without hesitation accept the reality of the virgin birth of Christ. While here on earth, Christ was both perfect God and perfect man (Romans 1:3-4).

The theological term that is used to describe the coming of God in the flesh is *incarnation*. The incarnation of Jesus Christ is described as the "mystery of godliness" (1 Timothy 3:16). There are seven basic reasons for the incarnation given to us in the Bible. In Isaiah 53:1-6, Christ came to confirm God's promises. In John 1:18, we are told that Jesus Christ came in order to reveal the Father. In Hebrews 4:14-16, we are told that Jesus Christ came to be a faithful high priest. In Hebrews 9:26-28, we are told that the purpose of Jesus Christ coming into the world was to put away sin and destroy the works of the devil. (1 John 3:8). Jesus Christ came to give us an example of the holy life (1 John 1:5-7), and to prepare for the second advent (Hebrews 9:28).

Thirdly, we believe that Jesus Christ died an efficacious death for the sins of the world. The Bible makes it plain that Jesus Christ was not a martyr, but His death was one of eternal and efficacious value (1 Timothy 2:5-6; Titus 2:14).

As we have stated, His death was not an accident, nor was it an act of martyrdom, but was in accordance to the perfect will of God (Genesis 3:15; Isaiah 53:1-5; Acts 2:23). It is declared in the Scriptures that Jesus Christ was and is the only one who could have died for the sins of man (Acts 4:10-12). The death of Jesus Christ has made it possible for all who believe in Him and receive Him as Lord and Savior to have forgiveness of sin (1 Timothy 2:1-6).

Fourthly, we believe in the literal, physical resurrection of Jesus Christ. There are many theories concerning the resurrection of Jesus Christ, none of which are worthy of the occupation of any space in this study. The Bible makes it clear that Jesus Christ was literally and physically resurrected by the power of God (1 Timothy 3:16). Biblical revelation declares that He was resurrected on the third day as He promised. There is no small amount of evidence in the Bible concerning the resurrection of Jesus Christ. His order of appearance after His resurrection is as follows: He appeared to Mary Magdalene (Mark 16:9-11); to the women returning from the tomb (Matthew 28:8-10); to Peter (Luke 24:34); to the disciples on the road to Emmaus (Mark 16:12); to the disciples with Thomas not present (Mark 16:14); a second time to the disciples with Thomas present (John 20:26-31); to the seven beside the Sea of Galilee (John 21); to the apostles and over five hundred people (Matthew 28:16-20; 1 Corinthians 15:6); to James, the Lord's half-brother (1 Corinthians 15:7); and at His ascension (Acts 1:3-12).

The Scriptures attest to the importance of the resurrection of Christ in relation to

God's plan of salvation (1 Corinthians 15:12-20).

Fifthly, we believe that Jesus Christ lives today at the right hand of the Father. The scope of His present-day ministry is as follows. He is declared to be Savior (Romans 10:13; 1 Timothy 2:3-4; Hebrews 7:25). In fact, the Bible identifies Jesus Christ as being the Mediator between God and man (1 Timothy 2:5). Hebrews 7:23-28 and Hebrews 4:15-16 states that Jesus Christ is now the believer's High Priest. How good it is to know that every born-again believer in Jesus Christ by virtue of his relationship with God through Christ now has the right and privilege to go directly to the Father through our High Priest, the Lord Jesus Christ. In Hebrews 7:25, He is identified as our Intercessor. In 1 John 2:1, He is seen as our Advocate, the One who stands before the Father and pleads our case before Him when we fall in sin. The Bible says that it is through Him and by Him that the world is held together (Colossians 1:16-17). The present day ministry of Jesus Christ is that of holding His creation together. He is today seen to be the Head of the Church (Colossians 1:18).

Sixthly, we believe in the personal, literal, and visible return of Jesus Christ. He will come first for His church (1 Thessalonians 4:13-18). This is to be understood as the Rapture of the Church; and secondly, Christ will come to the earth with His Church to defeat the armies of the Antichrist, and to set up His earthly kingdom. Revelation 19 explains this to be the Revelation of Jesus Christ.

This study must not be concluded without a personal appeal. You may have a perfect theology concerning the person of the Lord Jesus Christ. You may believe all the right things about the Lord and understand what the Bible says about Him. However, the real issue is, whether or not there has ever been a time in your life when you have personally received Jesus Christ as your Lord and Savior?

C. S. Lewis wrote these words about Jesus that are still a great challenge for us today:

> *"I am trying here to prevent anyone saying the really foolish thing that people often say about Him, 'I am ready to accept Jesus as a great moral teacher, but I don't accept His claim to be God.' That is one thing we must not say. A man who was merely a man and said the things Jesus said would not be a great moral teacher. He would either be a lunatic—on the level with the man who says he is a poached egg--or else he would be the Devil of Hell. You must make your choice. Either this man was, and is, the Son of God; or else a madman or something worse...You can try to shut Him up for a fool, you can spit at Him and call Him a demon, or you fall at His feet and call Him Lord and God. But let us not come up with any patronizing nonsense about His being a great human teacher. He has not left that open to us; He did not intend to."*

The Bible says in Romans 10:9-10 that, "If you confess with your mouth Jesus as Lord, and believe in your heart that God raised Him from the dead, you shall be saved, for with the heart man believes, resulting in righteousness, and with the mouth he confesses, resulting in salvation." Then in verse 13, we are told, "...for whoever will call upon the name of the Lord will be saved."

The promise is simple: if you will personally invite Jesus Christ to come into your heart and ask Him to save you and forgive you of all sins, He will do so and make you His child. If there has never been a time when you know that you received Christ as your Lord and Savior, don't miss this opportunity to invite Christ to come into your heart and to forgive you of all your sins and make you His child.

THE DOCTRINE OF THE HOLY SPIRIT

There are few biblical subjects more fundamental to the Christian faith than that of the Holy Spirit. A study of the Holy Spirit is critical because the Spirit is the source of all spiritual knowledge and power. Apart from the ministry of the Holy Spirit, there can be no maturity in the Christian journey. One cannot be saved except through the mystery of the Holy Spirit, nor can one live the Christian life. The Holy Spirit is the One who guides us into all truth, empowers us for service, intercedes on our behalf to the Father, unifies the body of Christ, imparts unto each believer spiritual gifts, seals the believer until the day of redemption, and genuinely provides the presence of God in each believer. For this reason, it is important that every believer understands the ministry of the third person of the Trinity: the Holy Spirit.

The Deity of the Holy Spirit

In too many circles of Christianity, the Holy Spirit is treated more as a thing or an impersonal *it*. In the last several years, there has been considerable misunderstanding in the Christian community concerning the person and work of the Holy Spirit. Therefore, it's important to study the Holy Spirit by pointing out the divine truth that the Holy Spirit is truly and fully God and is to be treated with all adoration and reverence due God. The Holy Spirit is the third person of the Trinity, and the believer should understand and embrace the fact that He is a divine person. The Holy Spirit is indeed God!

We should note that the writers of Scripture have chosen to refer to the Holy Spirit as God. In Acts 5, the Apostle Peter rebuked Ananias and Sapphira for their sin, and declared that Satan had filled their hearts for the purpose of lying to the Holy Spirit. As such, Peter says they lied to God and not man, thus affirming the Holy Spirit is in fact, God.

> *Acts 5:3-4, Then Peter said, "Ananias, how is it that Satan has so filled your heart that you have lied to the Holy Spirit and have kept for yourself some of the money you received for the land? Didn't it belong to you before it was sold? And after it was sold, wasn't the money at your disposal? What made you think of doing such a thing? You have not lied just to human beings but to God."*

Elsewhere, the Apostle Paul described the children of God as the "Temple of God." The reality of the indwelling of the Holy Spirit makes believers the temple of God because the Holy Spirit is truly and fully God.

> *1 Corinthians 3:16, Don't you know that you yourselves are God's temple and that God's Spirit dwells in your midst?*

The evidence for the deity of the Holy Spirit is abundant elsewhere in Scripture. The Holy Spirit is described as the Spirit of God, the Spirit of the Lord, or the Spirit of the Living God:

> *Genesis 1:2, Now the earth was formless and empty, darkness was over the surface of the deep, and the Spirit of God was hovering over the waters.*

> *Luke 4:18, The Spirit of the Lord is on me, because he has anointed me to proclaim good news to the poor. He has sent me to proclaim freedom for the prisoners and recovery of sight for the blind, to set the oppressed free...*

> *1 Corinthians 6:11, And that is what some of you were. But you were washed, you were sanctified, you were justified in the name of the Lord Jesus Christ and by the Spirit of our God.*

> *2 Corinthians 3:3, You show that you are a letter from Christ, the result of our ministry, written not with ink but with the Spirit of the living God, not on tablets of stone but on tablets of human hearts.*

Also, God refers to the Holy Spirit as "My Spirit."

> *Genesis 6:3, Then the LORD said, "My Spirit will not contend with humans forever, for they are mortal; their days will be a hundred and twenty years."*

In the word of God, there are several titles which show the relation of the Holy

Spirit to the Son of God. The Holy Spirit is called the Spirit of Christ or the Spirit of Jesus:

> *Romans 8:9, You, however, are not in the realm of the flesh but are in the realm of the Spirit, if indeed the Spirit of God lives in you. And if anyone does not have the Spirit of Christ, they do not belong to Christ. (see also 1 Peter 1:11; Philippians 1:19; Acts 16:7)*

Thus, we see from biblical revelation that the deity of the Holy Spirit is considered a cardinal doctrine of the Christian faith. In our study on the doctrine of the God, it was noted that God possesses certain attributes which make Him uniquely Divine. We discover that the word of God ascribes these divine attributes to the Holy Spirit.

The Holy Spirit coming to Mary is seen to be a demonstration of the Power of the Most High.

> *Luke 1:35, The angel answered, "The Holy Spirit will come on you, and the power of the Most High will overshadow you. So the holy one to be born will be called the Son of God."*

The Holy Spirit is also said to be omniscient when Paul declared that it is the Holy Spirit who has the capacity to search all things, even the depths of God. Only God can possess and understand the depths of His own knowledge.

> *1 Corinthians 2:10, these are the things God has revealed to us by his Spirit. The Spirit searches all things, even the deep things of God.*

The Holy Spirit is also seen to be omnipresent. The Psalmist expresses this idea in the form of several questions. The clear answers to these rhetorical questions express the idea that there is no place one can go to escape the presence of the Holy Spirit. Thus, declaring the Holy Spirit possesses the divine quality of omnipresence.

> *Psalm 139:7-10, Where can I go from your Spirit? Where can I flee from your presence? If I go up to the heavens, you are there; if I make my bed in the depths, you are there. If I rise on the wings of the dawn, if I settle on the far side of the sea, even there your hand will guide me, your right hand will hold me fast.*

Eternality is a clear attribute or characteristic of God, and it is also stated in Scripture about the Holy Spirit.

> *Hebrews 9:14, How much more, then, will the blood of Christ, who through the eternal Spirit offered himself unblemished to God, cleanse our consciences from acts that lead to death, so that we may serve the living God!*

The Holy Spirit also possesses the divine attribute of love.

Romans 15:30, I urge you, brothers and sisters, by our Lord Jesus Christ and by the love of the Spirit, to join me in my struggle by praying to God for me.

The Holy Spirit has the divine attribute of holiness. The very name "Holy Spirit" indicates the holiness of the person and character of the Holy Spirit.

Ephesians 4:30, And do not grieve the Holy Spirit of God, with whom you were sealed for the day of redemption.

In regard to the deity of the Holy Spirit, the Bible teaches that the Holy Spirit is capable of performing divine acts. The Holy Spirit was involved in creation, regeneration, and the resurrection of Jesus Christ.

Genesis 1:1-2, In the beginning God created the heavens and the earth. Now the earth was formless and empty, darkness was over the surface of the deep, and the Spirit of God was hovering over the waters.

John 3:3-8, Jesus replied, "Very truly I tell you, no one can see the kingdom of God unless they are born again." "How can someone be born when they are old?" Nicodemus asked. "Surely they cannot enter a second time into their mother's womb to be born!" Jesus answered, "Very truly I tell you, no one can enter the kingdom of God unless they are born of water and the Spirit. Flesh gives birth to flesh, but the Spirit gives birth to spirit. You should not be surprised at my saying, 'You must be born again.' The wind blows wherever it pleases. You hear its sound, but you cannot tell where it comes from or where it is going. So it is with everyone born of the Spirit."

Romans 8:11, And if the Spirit of him who raised Jesus from the dead is living in you, he who raised Christ from the dead will also give life to your mortal bodies because of his Spirit who lives in you.

The Scriptures make it clear that the Holy Spirit is very much involved in the divine act of salvation.

1 Corinthians 6:11, And that is what some of you were. But you were washed, you were sanctified, you were justified in the name of the Lord Jesus Christ and by the Spirit of our God.

The above examples show that the Holy Spirit is to be recognized as God. For example, in the Great Commission, Jesus places the Holy Spirit alongside the Father and the Son indicating His equality with them and His place in the Trinity.

Matthew 28:18-20, Then Jesus came to them and said, "All authority in heaven and on earth has been given to me. Therefore go and make disciples of all nations, baptizing them in the name of the Father and of the Son and of the Holy Spirit, and teaching them to obey everything I have commanded you. And surely I am with you always, to the very end of the age."

Paul places the Holy Spirit alongside the Lord Jesus Christ and God the Father.

2 Corinthians 13:14, May the grace of the Lord Jesus Christ, and the love of God, and the fellowship of the Holy Spirit be with you all.

John records that the believer is commanded to heed and obey what the Holy Spirit has to say.

Revelation 3:22, Whoever has ears, let them hear what the Spirit says to the churches.

The Apostle Paul also states that the Holy Spirit is the administrator of spiritual gifts.

1 Corinthians 12:4-6, There are different kinds of gifts, but the same Spirit distributes them. There are different kinds of service, but the same Lord. There are different kinds of working, but in all of them and in everyone it is the same God at work.

Believers are commanded to depend upon the Holy Spirit in the time of need.

Mark 13:11, Whenever you are arrested and brought to trial, do not worry beforehand about what to say. Just say whatever is given you at the time, for it is not you speaking, but the Holy Spirit.

Finally, the Holy Spirit can be sinned against just like God.

Matthew 12:31-32, Therefore I tell you, every sin and blasphemy will be forgiven people, but the blasphemy against the Spirit will not be forgiven. And whoever speaks a word against the Son of Man will be forgiven, but whoever speaks against the Holy Spirit will not be forgiven, either in this age or in the age to come.

The Holy Spirit is fully and truly God. For this reason, we are to treat Him with the reverence and awe that He rightfully deserves. He sould be worshipped and obeyed as our divine Teacher and Sanctifier. The Holy Spirit is not some impersonal *it* to the believer. Rather, He is truly and fully God!

The Holy Spirit and Jesus Christ

The Holy Spirit was very involved in the earthly ministry of the Lord Jesus Christ. In fact, Jesus in His physical state was entirely dependant upon the Father and the ministry of the Holy Spirit.

Jesus Christ was conceived by the power of the Holy Spirit. The virgin conception of Mary is the Holy Spirit of God actually doing the work of impregnating the virgin Mary so that she might be able to produce the Holy Child. (Refer to the Doctrine of Jesus for a more thorough discussion of the Virgin Birth.)

> *Luke 1:35, The angel answered, "The Holy Spirit will come on you, and the power of the Most High will overshadow you. So the holy one to be born will be called the Son of God."*

Throughout the earthly ministry of the Lord Jesus Christ, the ministry of the Holy Spirit is evident. The Holy Spirit was present at the Baptism of Jesus as John tell us that the Holy Spirit descended upon Jesus like dove.

> *John 1:32, Then John gave this testimony: "I saw the Spirit come down from heaven as a dove and remain on him."*

Jesus was anointed by the Holy Spirit for the purpose of introducing His earthly ministry in Luke 4, which was the fulfillment of a prophecy from Isaiah 61.

> *Luke 4:18-19, The Spirit of the Lord is on me, because he has anointed me to proclaim good news to the poor. He has sent me to proclaim freedom for the prisoners and recovery of sight for the blind, to set the oppressed free, to proclaim the year of the Lord's favor.*

Peter spoke of this anointing by the Spirit of Jesus in Acts 10.

> *Acts 10:38, how God anointed Jesus of Nazareth with the Holy Spirit and power, and how he went around doing good and healing all who were under the power of the devil, because God was with him.*

The Old Testament clearly announced that the Messiah would be clothed with the Holy Spirit.

> *Isaiah 11:1-2, A shoot will come up from the stump of Jesse; from his roots a Branch will bear fruit. The Spirit of the LORD will rest on him—the Spirit of wisdom and of understanding, the Spirit of counsel and of might, the Spirit of the knowledge and fear of the LORD—*

In the Old Testament, the priests and Kings received an unction oil which was a foreshadowing that Jesus Christ, our King and High Priest, would also be anointed with the Holy Spirit.

> *1 Samuel 16:12-13, So he sent for him and had him brought in. He was glowing with health and had a fine appearance and handsome features. Then the LORD said,*

"Rise and anoint him; this is the one." So Samuel took the horn of oil and anointed him in the presence of his brothers, and from that day on the Spirit of the LORD came powerfully upon David. Samuel then went to Ramah.

Not only was Jesus Christ anointed by the Holy Spirit, but we find that He was also sealed by the Holy Spirit. This seal was proof of His heavenly origin and His divine Sonship. It was also proof of His authenticity as the true Messiah.

Matthew 3:16-17, As soon as Jesus was baptized, he went up out of the water. At that moment heaven was opened, and he saw the Spirit of God descending like a dove and alighting on him. And a voice from heaven said, "This is my Son, whom I love; with him I am well pleased."

The Holy Spirit is said to live in the person of the Lord Jesus Christ, and He was clothed with the power of the Holy Spirit.

John 1:33, And I myself did not know him, but the one who sent me to baptize with water told me, 'The man on whom you see the Spirit come down and remain is the one who will baptize with the Holy Spirit.'

Jesus Christ was filled with the Holy Spirit and clothed with His power.

John 3:34, For the one whom God has sent speaks the words of God, for God gives the Spirit without limit.

Luke 4:14, Jesus returned to Galilee in the power of the Spirit, and news about him spread through the whole countryside.

Jesus cast out demons by the power of the Holy Spirit.

Matthew 12:28, But if it is by the Spirit of God that I drive out demons, then the kingdom of God has come upon you.

Jesus gave instructions to His disciples and continually demonstrated the fruit of the Holy Spirit.

Acts 1:2, until the day he was taken up to heaven, after giving instructions through the Holy Spirit to the apostles he had chosen.

Galatians 5:22-23, But the fruit of the Spirit is love, joy, peace, forbearance, kindness, goodness, faithfulness, gentleness and self-control. Against such things there is no law.

Jesus is said to have offered Himself as a divine sacrifice through the Holy Spirit.

Hebrews 9:14, How much more, then, will the blood of Christ, who through the eternal Spirit offered himself unblemished to God, cleanse our consciences from acts that lead to death, so that we may serve the living God!

Finally, Jesus Christ was raised from the dead through the power of the Holy Spirit.

Romans 8:11, And if the Spirit of him who raised Jesus from the dead is living in you, he who raised Christ from the dead will also give life to your mortal bodies because of his Spirit who lives in you.

The Holy Spirit and the Church

When studying the person and ministry of the Holy Spirit, one must not overlook the important relationship the Holy Spirit has with the Church—the Body of Christ. The New Testament reveals various aspects of the Church's life which are associated with the Holy Spirit. In relation to the Church, the work of the Holy Spirit is twofold: a) The work of the Holy Spirit in the individual believers' life; and b) the work of the Holy Spirit in the Church. Whatever the Holy Spirit does is for the benefit of the Church, the Body of Christ, and for the ultimate purpose of glorifying the Lord Jesus Christ.

1 Corinthians 12:7, Now to each one the manifestation of the Spirit is given for the common good.

Why did the Holy Spirit come on the day of Pentecost?

Acts 2:1-12, When the day of Pentecost came, they were all together in one place. Suddenly a sound like the blowing of a violent wind came from heaven and filled the whole house where they were sitting. They saw what seemed to be tongues of fire that separated and came to rest on each of them. All of them were filled with the Holy Spirit and began to speak in other tongues as the Spirit enabled them. Now there were staying in Jerusalem God-fearing Jews from every nation under heaven. When they heard this sound, a crowd came together in bewilderment, because each one heard their own language being spoken. Utterly amazed, they asked: "Aren't all these who are speaking Galileans? Then how is it that each of us hears them in our native language? Parthians, Medes and Elamites; residents of Mesopotamia, Judea and Cappadocia, Pontus and Asia, Phrygia and Pamphylia, Egypt and the parts of Libya near Cyrene; visitors from Rome (both Jews and converts to Judaism); Cretans and Arabs—we hear them declaring the wonders of God in our own tongues!" Amazed and perplexed, they asked one another, "What does this mean?"

The answer to the question, "what does this mean?" can be seen in the reality and the fact that the Holy Spirit came on the day of Pentecost for the purpose of forming the Church, which is the Body of Christ. The unique thing about Christianity is that God actually indwells every believer permanently and this is what the Holy Spirit began doing at Pentecost.

> *1 Corinthians 6:19-20, Do you not know that your bodies are temples of the Holy Spirit, who is in you, whom you have received from God? You are not your own; you were bought at a price. Therefore honor God with your bodies.*

Therefore, whenever an individual receives the Lord Jesus Christ as His personal Savior, that person becomes a part of the temple of God by virtue of the fact that the Holy Spirit indwells him or her. This is not the complete extent of the ministry of the Holy Spirit, for it is the ministry of the Holy Spirit to make up and to establish the Church. It is the Holy Spirit, for example who unites each believer to Christ and makes each believer a member of the body of Christ.

> *1 Corinthians 12:13, For we were all baptized by one Spirit so as to form one body— whether Jews or Gentiles, slave or free—and we were all given the one Spirit to drink.*

The Holy Spirit convinces the sinner of their need for Christ, and brings them carefully to and ultimately through this door to salvation. Thus, it is the Holy Spirit who actually places the believer into the Body of Christ.

> *John 16:8-11, When he comes, he will prove the world to be in the wrong about sin and righteousness and judgment: about sin, because people do not believe in me; about righteousness, because I am going to the Father, where you can see me no longer; and about judgment, because the prince of this world now stands condemned.*

Just as the Holy Spirit physically formed the earthly body of Christ in the incarnation, so the Holy Spirit also forms the spiritual body of Christ, the Church.

The Bible makes it clear that that Holy Spirit brings together and unifies the church.

> *Ephesians 2:21-22, In him the whole building is joined together and rises to become a holy temple in the Lord. And in him you too are being built together to become a dwelling in which God lives by his Spirit.*

> *Ephesians 4:3, Make every effort to keep the unity of the Spirit through the bond of peace.*

The believer is encouraged to maintain the unity of the Spirit in the bond of peace. It is one of the ministries of the Holy Spirit to bring about unity in the body of Christ among believers. Unity is never created in the church by anyone other than the Holy Spirit. Members and believers can either help or hinder the unity of the church. We should remember that the Holy Spirit, as the Spirit of Truth, will unify us by correcting our doctrine and continually testifying to the saving person and work of Jesus Christ that saves and unites us.

> *Ephesians 4:11-13,* So Christ himself gave the apostles, the prophets, the evangelists, the pastors and teachers, to equip his people for works of service, so that the body of Christ may be built up until we all reach unity in the faith and in the knowledge of the Son of God and become mature, attaining to the whole measure of the fullness of Christ.

The Holy Spirit brings about unity through divine union. This divine union is the beautiful reality that the Holy Spirit actually and truly abides in every believer. Thus, every believer is "in Christ" by virtue of the work and presence of the Holy Spirit. The Holy Spirit allows us to abide in Christ (i.e., be united to Christ).

> *1 Corinthians 3:16,* Don't you know that you yourselves are God's temple and that God's Spirit dwells in your midst?

Through the Holy Spirit, we not only receive a true, living union with Jesus Christ but we also become members of one another as the body of Christ:

> *John 17:11,* I will remain in the world no longer, but they are still in the world, and I am coming to you. Holy Father, protect them by the power of your name, the name you gave me, so that they may be one as we are one.

When the Holy Spirit carries out His ministry unhindered, then we shall truly experience the beautiful reality of the Church being united in Jesus Christ. One writer put it this way in a equation speaking to the Church's unity: Union + Communion = Unity.

Over the years, some have pointed out that the Holy Spirit is the executive member of the Godhead. It is the Holy Spirit's business to execute in the world the plans and purposes of God the Father and God the Son. The ministry of the Holy Spirit is absolutely necessary for the operation of the Church. Without the ministry of the Holy Spirit, the Church would be reduced to an ineffective force. Without the ministry of the Holy Spirit, the Church would be totally inadequate to fulfill her divine purposes on earth and to war against the power of darkness present in this world.

Worship: The clear teaching of Scripture is that that true worship must be done through the ministry of the Holy Spirit.

John 4:23, Jesus said, "Yet a time is coming and has now come when the true worshipers will worship the Father in the Spirit and in truth, for they are the kind of worshipers the Father seeks."

Witness: Scripture also teaches that effective witness for Christ is empowered by the Holy Spirit.

Acts 1:8, But you will receive power when the Holy Spirit comes on you; and you will be my witnesses in Jerusalem, and in all Judea and Samaria, and to the ends of the earth."

Prayer: True, effective prayer is brought about through the ministry of the Holy Spirit.

Ephesians 6:18, And pray in the Spirit on all occasions with all kinds of prayers and requests. With this in mind, be alert and always keep on praying for all the Lord's people.

Romans 8:26, In the same way, the Spirit helps us in our weakness. We do not know what we ought to pray for, but the Spirit himself intercedes for us through wordless groans.

Mission: The Holy Spirit empowers our mission work.

Acts 13:2, While they were worshiping the Lord and fasting, the Holy Spirit said, "Set apart for me Barnabas and Saul for the work to which I have called them."

Fellowship: The Holy Spirit brings about true fellowship.

Philippians 2:1, Therefore if you have any encouragement from being united with Christ, if any comfort from his love, if any common sharing in the Spirit, if any tenderness and compassion,

Guidance: Guidance for ministries in the church comes from the the Holy Spirit.

Romans 8:14, For those who are led by the Spirit of God are the children of God.

Acts 16:6-7, Paul and his companions traveled throughout the region of Phrygia and Galatia, having been kept by the Holy Spirit from preaching the word in the province of Asia. When they came to the border of Mysia, they tried to enter Bithynia, but the Spirit of Jesus would not allow them to.

Thus, the Holy Spirit is the true Administrator of the work of the Church. Or to put it another way, God the Father is the owner of the Church, God the Son is the Head of the Church, God the Holy Spirit is the administrator or executive overseeing the work of the church. In Revelation 2-3, you see this phrase repeated over and over to the seven churches "let them hear what the Spirit says to the church." (Revelation 2:7, 2:11, 2:17, 2:29, 3:6, 3:13, 3:22). This is because it is the Holy Spirit who speaks to the Church in the every area including worship, witness, prayer, missions, fellowship, and guidance for ministry.

The Holy Spirit equips and guides the church. In 1 Corinthians 12 and Romans 12, the ministry of the Holy Spirit endows believers with spiritual gifts.

> *Romans 12:6-8, We have different gifts, according to the grace given to each of us. If your gift is prophesying, then prophesy in accordance with your faith; if it is serving, then serve; if it is teaching, then teach; if it is to encourage, then give encouragement; if it is giving, then give generously; if it is to lead, do it diligently; if it is to show mercy, do it cheerfully.*

> *1 Corinthians 12:4-11, There are different kinds of gifts, but the same Spirit distributes them. There are different kinds of service, but the same Lord. There are different kinds of working, but in all of them and in everyone it is the same God at work. Now to each one the manifestation of the Spirit is given for the common good. To one there is given through the Spirit a message of wisdom, to another a message of knowledge by means of the same Spirit, to another faith by the same Spirit, to another gifts of healing by that one Spirit, to another miraculous powers, to another prophecy, to another distinguishing between spirits, to another speaking in different kinds of tongues, and to still another the interpretation of tongues. All these are the work of one and the same Spirit, and he distributes them to each one, just as he determines.*

Spiritual gifts are Spirit-given capacities to perform useful functions for God, especially in the area of service in the church. Just as the human body has members with different capacities and responsibilities, so it is with individual Christians in the church having different capacities, skills, abilities, and spiritual gifts.

These particular spiritual gifts help individuals contribute to the welfare of the Church, as well as bear a dynamic and effective witness to the world. The Church simply cannot function properly apart from the gifts of the Holy Spirit. Spiritual gifts are bestowed by God's sovereign choice and need to be exercised in the power and under the direction of the Holy Spirit.

There is a great deal of talk today among certain groups concerning the gifts of the Holy Spirit. Actually, when it boils down to their particular theology, they are not talking about the gifts of the Holy Spirit but the gift of the Holy Spirit (namely, speaking in tongues). However, the Bible is clear in teaching several things: a) there are diversities of gifts; b) all do not have the same gift; c) no one has all the gifts; d) all gifts are given for the common good of the Church; and e) gifts are given according to the Holy Spirit's distribution.

> *1 Corinthians 12:4, There are different kinds of gifts, but the same Spirit distributes them.*

> *1 Corinthians 12:7, Now to each one the manifestation of the Spirit is given for the common good.*

The church is like an orchestra which is composed of many different instruments. All have different instruments (gifts), but they are all working together on the same song (the Great Commission). Thus, there is a diversity of gifts but the same Spirit just as there are many different members in the church but one body.

Not only does the Holy Spirit give gifts to the Church, but also, as Ephesians 4 makes clear, He bestows gifts for the leadership in the Church.

> *Ephesians 4:11-16, So Christ himself gave the apostles, the prophets, the evangelists, the pastors and teachers, to equip his people for works of service, so that the body of Christ may be built up until we all reach unity in the faith and in the knowledge of the Son of God and become mature, attaining to the whole measure of the fullness of Christ. Then we will no longer be infants, tossed back and forth by the waves, and blown here and there by every wind of teaching and by the cunning and craftiness of people in their deceitful scheming. Instead, speaking the truth in love, we will grow to become in every respect the mature body of him who is the head, that is, Christ. From him the whole body, joined and held together by every supporting ligament, grows and builds itself up in love, as each part does its work.*

Apostles and Prophets: From Ephesians 4, we see that the Holy Spirit gave the Church apostles who were special messengers and were part of the authoritative structure of the early Church. It must be noted that the office of Apostle no longer exists today. The Holy Spirit also gave prophets. A New Testament prophet was a man under the direct influence of God who was actually receiving and declaring the Word of God. Since we now have God's complete revelation, the Bible we have no need for prophets today. Thus, the office of prophet no longer exists.

There should be a differentiation between the office of a prophet in Ephesians 4, and the gift of prophecy found in Romans 12. The office of prophet speaks of those mean receiving direct revelation from God, while the gift of prophecy refers to those who are endowed with the ability to proclaim God's Word or the Scriptures.

Ephesians 4:11, So Christ himself gave the apostles, the prophets, the evangelists, the pastors and teachers...

Romans 12:6-8, We have different gifts, according to the grace given to each of us. If your gift is prophesying, then prophesy in accordance with your faith; if it is serving, then serve; if it is teaching, then teach; if it is to encourage, then give encouragement; if it is giving, then give generously; if it is to lead, do it diligently; if it is to show mercy, do it cheerfully.

Next, the Holy Spirit mentions the office of evangelist. New Testament evangelists were traveling missionaries sent out from the local church. Their ministry was to preach the gospel and plant churches. True New Testament evangelists were sent out under the authority of the local church for the purpose of beginning other churches.

Finally, we see the office or class of ministers spoken of as pastor-teachers. It should be noted carefully that the pastor-teacher is not to be understood as two different offices, but as one office: pastor-teacher. The purpose of these gifted leaders was to build up the body through the teaching of the Word of God. (More will be said about these various offices in our study of the Church)

The ministry of the Holy Spirit is also to guide the Church. It is the Holy Spirit who guides the Church into all truth and into ministry as John 16 clearly states:

John 16:13, But when he, the Spirit of truth, comes, he will guide you into all the truth. He will not speak on his own; he will speak only what he hears, and he will tell you what is yet to come.

Today, many churches have avoided teaching about the person of the work of the Holy Spirit out of fear for misunderstanding the gifts of the Spirit. This is indeed a grave tragedy because the word of God asserts that the Holy Spirit and His ministry are essential to the operation of the local church and the effective ministry of each individual believer. While we must be careful in studying the Holy Spirit, we must not be lacking in our teaching about the Holy Spirit.

Spirit Baptism

One of the fundamental doctrines of the Christian faith is the baptism of the Holy Spirit. However, it is also one of the most misunderstood doctrines. The baptism of the Holy Spirit is the sovereign act of God the Holy Spirit where He incorporates the believer into the body of Christ—the universal Church comprised of all believers—at the moment of salvation. Wayne Grudem notes in his *Systematic Theology* that to be baptized in the Spirit is for one to come "into the new covenant power of the Holy Spirit" which includes "the impartation of new spiritual life, cleansing from sin, a break with the power of sin, and empowering for ministry." Thus, it is through Spirit-baptism all believers are initiated as members of the body of Christ.

While this doctrine is important, there is much misunderstanding and confusion concerning the subject of baptism of the Holy Spirit. Division in the church has occurred in the recent years because of differing views of baptism of the Holy Spirit. Few doctrines have caused more confusion, division, false teaching, or, at times, hatred than this doctrine. This is a great paradox: the doctrine we are fighting over is about the Spirit who unites us in Christ. This very thought has caused many to throw the doctrine to the wind and proclaim that we should all just love one another. Certainly, every Christian would acknowledge that we should love one another. Yet, wouldn't it be just as beneficial to find out what the Bible really says concerning the baptism of the Holy Spirit so that we could truly love one another while being strengthened by truth?

Jesus Christ our Lord warned that the world could not receive the Holy Spirit.

John 14:17, the Spirit of truth. The world cannot accept him, because it neither sees him nor knows him. But you know him, for he lives with you and will be in you.

However, the great damage that has been done to the doctrine of the Spirit of God has come from the Christian community. Large groups of well-meaning, misinformed believers in their zeal to proclaim the neglected doctrine of the Holy Spirit have been led more by excitement than they have been by Scripture.

One of the major causes of confusion is an improper understanding of the distinctive character of the baptism of the Holy Spirit.

1 Corinthians 12:13, For we were all baptized by one Spirit so as to form one body— whether Jews or Gentiles, slave or free—and we were all given the one Spirit to drink.

Another source of confusion about the baptism of the Holy Spirit is improperly identifying the baptism of the Spirit with the filling of the Spirit. Some writers and teachers use the terms "baptism" as a synonym for "filling." This improper parallel to the baptism of the Holy Spirit has led to much confusion on the subject.

Still another reason for the misunderstanding concerning the baptism of the Spirit is the attempt on the part of some to link the baptism of the Spirit with certain gifts of the

Spirit and their use. Some falsely maintain that speaking in tongues is sole evidence of Spirit-baptism, and that the baptism by the Spirit does not come at the time of salvation. Those who believe this would assert that that the baptism of the Holy Spirit is a post-salvation experience, or a so-called "second blessing." In order to justify Spirit-baptism with tongues, some have attempted to make a distinction between the baptism by the Holy Spirit found in 1 Corinthians and the baptism with the Holy Spirit found in Acts.

According to this view, the baptism by the Holy Spirit places the believer into the body of Christ, while the baptism with the Holy Spirit produces tongues. However, in, both of the above verses mentioned, the Greek term *en pneumati* is used to express the baptism. Thus, it is dangerous to build two totally different doctrines with the exact same phrase. The results of the confusion over the doctrine of Spirit-baptism have been substantial, to say the least. Without question, the misunderstanding concerning the Spirit-baptism has had a profound effect on the Christian community. Through this misunderstanding, there have been great divisions among believers and harm brought to the real ministry of the Church; namely the preaching of the Gospel throughout all the world and the fulfillment of the Great Commission.

> *Matthew 28:18-20, Then Jesus came to them and said, "All authority in heaven and on earth has been given to me. Therefore go and make disciples of all nations, baptizing them in the name of the Father and of the Son and of the Holy Spirit, and teaching them to obey everything I have commanded you. And surely I am with you always, to the very end of the age."*

A lack of understanding of the baptism of the Holy Spirit has obscured the truth of the union every believer has with the living Christ. It has caused believers to seek that which they already possess, and to long for things which God has already given them, or does not desire to give them. Every believer, by virtue of his or her union with Christ, has everything that God has to offer ("every spiritual blessing" in Ephesians 1:3). Paul even told the carnal Corinthians that they lacked no spiritual gifts:

> *1 Corinthians 1:4-7, I always thank my God for you because of his grace given you in Christ Jesus. For in him you have been enriched in every way—with all kinds of speech and with all knowledge— God thus confirming our testimony about Christ among you. Therefore you do not lack any spiritual gift as you eagerly wait for our Lord Jesus Christ to be revealed.*

This misunderstanding has created much insecurity in the lives of the believers and caused many to doubt their salvation. As a result, many Christians have gone to great length to have some emotional experience in order to prove to other Christians, or themselves, that they are saved. In some circles, charismatic experiences, as it has been termed, becomes a status symbol of faith as a basis for acceptance and fellowship. This misunderstanding has created multiple levels of so-called spiritual superiority with those claiming to have had this "second blessing" to be a step above the lesser saints who have not had the second blessing.

What are the basic truths of Spirit-baptism? First, the baptism of the Holy Spirit is common to all believers:

> *1 Corinthians 12:13, For we were all baptized by one Spirit so as to form one body—whether Jews or Gentiles, slave or free—and we were all given the one Spirit to drink.*

Secondly, there is one, not two, baptisms of the Spirit. Paul says there is "one Lord, one faith, one baptism." The "one baptism" is Spirit-baptism and belongs to the same group with one Lord and one faith. Therefore, we can easily see that since there is only one Lord and one faith, there must also be only one spirit-baptism.

> *Ephesians 4:5, ...one Lord, one faith, one baptism.*

Third, there is no command to be baptized by the Holy Spirit. The fact that Spirit-baptism is universal among all believers is seen in the lack of Scriptural exhortations or commands to be baptized by the Holy Spirit. Nowhere in the Bible are believers ever commanded to be baptized by the Spirit or to seek such baptism. The Bible does command believers to be filled with the Spirit in Ephesians, but believers are never commanded to be baptized by the Spirit.

> *Ephesians 5:18, Do not get drunk on wine, which leads to debauchery. Instead, be filled with the Spirit...*

Scripture would command believers everywhere to be baptized by the Holy Spirit if this did not take place in all believers at the moment of salvation. The fact that such exhortations are missing is proof that Spirit-baptism is universal among all believers.

Conclusion: The baptism of the Holy Spirit occurs at the moment of salvation for all believers and is experienced only once by the believer. There are many fillings, but only one spirit-baptism.

One of the major results of the Spirit-baptism is that the Holy Spirit of God personally indwells him or her. At the moment of salvation, every believer without exception has by virtue of grace all the Holy Spirit he or she will ever have or need. There is no way a believer may receive more of the Holy Spirit or lose any of the Him. One of the greatest truths that we can try and comprehend is that the Holy Spirit of God actually lives within each child of God. Look at these words of Jesus:

> *John 14:16-17, And I will ask the Father, and he will give you another advocate to help you and be with you forever— the Spirit of truth. The world cannot accept him, because it neither sees him nor knows him. But you know him, for he lives with you and will be in you.*

Over the years, these verses have been commonly misunderstood or misapplied. Some have believed and taught that when a person believes, the Holy Spirit is only "with" the person until they actually "receive" the Holy Spirit at a later time, which is accompanied by the speaking in tongues. This teaching is related to the idea of the Holy Spirit being with Old Testament saints for temporary aid, but not permanently indwelling them.

However, Jesus said the Holy Spirit "lives with you and will be in you." This idea refers to the New Testament ministry of the Holy Spirit, which began at Pentecost. Today, the Holy Spirit dwells in all who receive Jesus Christ as Lord and Savior. The Apostle Paul made this teaching clear in Romans by saying:

> *Romans 8:9, You, however, are not in the realm of the flesh but are in the realm of the Spirit, if indeed the Spirit of God lives in you. And if anyone does not have the Spirit of Christ, they do not belong to Christ.*

It must be noted at this point that the absence of the Holy Spirit living "in" a person is evidence of an unsaved condition. Since we have seen that the Holy Spirit of God literally dwells within us, let us rejoice in this truth. Let us also note that the Holy Spirit does not indwell us in order to merely have some dwelling place, nor does He indwell us for our personal gratification. Rather, the Holy Spirit lives within every believer for the purpose of producing works which are pleasing to God. The Apostle Paul makes it clear that if we are to live a life which is acceptable to God, then we must have divine help. It is the Holy Spirit that provides the help needed for the believer to live a life that is pleasing and acceptable to God.

> *Galatians 5:16, 22-23, So I say, walk by the Spirit, and you will not gratify the desires of the flesh... But the fruit of the Spirit is love, joy, peace, forbearance, kindness, goodness, faithfulness, gentleness and self-control. Against such things is no law.*

Filled with the Holy Spirit

In Ephesians, the Apostle Paul commands us to "be filled with the Spirit."

Ephesians 5:17-18, Therefore do not be foolish, but understand what the Lord's will is. Do not get drunk on wine,which leads to debauchery. Instead, be filled with the Spirit...

A careful study of this verse helps one better understand what it means to be filled with the Holy Spirit. The word "filled" literally means "controlled," but both words can be used appropriately. If a particular thought controls our mind it is said to "fill" our minds. In the same way, if someone has full possession of our bodies it is said to "control" us. Similarly, being "filled" with the Holy Spirit is when the Holy Spirit has full possession or control of the believer's thoughts, words and actions.

Paul uses that example of being "drunk with wine" to convey the message of being filled or controlled. When one is drunk with wine, the alcohol controls his or her thoughts, words, and actions. Thus, the Apostle Paul says we should not be filled or controlled by wine, but we are to be filled and controlled by the Holy Spirit. This filling necessarily controls our thoughts, words, and actions.

In the Greek, to "be filled with the Spirit" is a command. Being filled with the Spirit is not an option or alternative, but a biblical command. In addition, it is in the plural, which indicates that all believers are to be filled or controlled by the Spirit. The filling is not for a select few who have experienced a second blessing, but for all believers.

Next, "be filled with the Spirit" is in the present tense, which speaks of a continual action. This is a process that must be continually experienced. Thus, the believer is commanded to be constantly filled with the Holy Spirit.

Finally, it is in the passive voice which means that the believer is to be acted upon rather than doing the acting. That is, the believer cannot fill oneself, but the Holy Spirit is the one who fills or controls the believer when the believer submits to the Spirit.

Experiencing the sweet and profound presence of the Holy Spirit should be a normal experience of the Christian life. The believer should be daily guided and empowered by the Holy Spirit. This is God's desire for every Christian. Being filled with the Holy Spirit occurs when the believer allows the Spirit to take over, direct, and lead him or her.

Wayne Grudem defines being filled with the Spirit as:

an event subsequent to conversion in which a believer experiences a fresh infilling with the Holy Spirit that may result in a variety of consequences, including greater love for God, greater victory over sin, greater power for ministry, and sometimes the receiving of new spiritual gifts (1242, Systematic Theology).

Being filled with the Holy Spirit is not receiving more of the Spirit of God, nor is it, as some falsely maintain, speaking in tongues. It is not having some emotional or sensational experiences, and it not a superior form of the Christian life. God is not in the habit of giving believers experiences that they can brag about. Rather, God desires for believers to be more sensitive to the Spirit's God-glorifying promptings to obedience to the word of God.

There is no specific place in the Bible that we are instructed on how one is to be filled with the Holy Spirit. However, one can note guidelines that are consistent throughout the New Testament as to how to be controlled or filled with the Holy Spirit.

Being filled with the Holy Spirit requires the absolute, unqualified surrender of our thoughts, words, and actions to God's will instead of our own. As noted earlier, when the believer is saved, the Holy Spirit abides within the believer. The result of that according to the Apostle Paul is that we should "honor God with your bodies."

1 Corinthians 6:19-20, Do you not know that your bodies are temples of the Holy Spirit, who is in you, whom you have received from God? You are not your own; you were bought at a price. Therefore honor God with your bodies.

At the same time, no believer is perfect in thought, word, or action because in one's sinful flesh we are imperfect and fall short of God's will for our lives. A believer who is filled with the Spirit will be marked by a quickness to confess and repent of sins

1 John 1:9, If we confess our sins, he is faithful and just and will forgive us our sins and purify us from all unrighteousness.

Believers must accept forgiveness and surrender again to the Holy Spirit for His control in our lives. The Bible does not encourage us to ask for the Spirit to fill us, although we certainly cannot state that it would be wrong to ask the Spirit to control us.

First, being filled with the Spirit affects the speech of the believer. The Spirit-filled or Spirit-controlled believer will change what he or she says and how he or she says it. It also means that the believer's speech will flow from a heart filled with godly joy.

Colossians 3:16, Let the message of Christ dwell among you richly as you teach and admonish one another with all wisdom through psalms, hymns, and songs from the Spirit, singing to God with gratitude in your hearts.

Ephesians 4:29-30, Do not let any unwholesome talk come out of your mouths, but only what is helpful for building others up according to their needs, that it may benefit those who listen. And do not grieve the Holy Spirit of God, with whom you were sealed for the day of redemption.

Second, the Spirit-controlled believers speech will be bold in witness for the Lord Jesus Christ. This does not mean that the believer only talks about spiritual matters, but it does mean that spiritual matters and conversations will take a front seat in the conversation of the believer.

> *Acts 1:8,* *But you will receive power when the Holy Spirit comes on you; and you will be my witnesses in Jerusalem, and in all Judea and Samaria, and to the ends of the earth.*

Third, the Spirit-controlled believer will have genuine fellowship with other believers.

> *Acts 2:43-47,* *Everyone was filled with awe at the many wonders and signs performed by the apostles. All the believers were together and had everything in common. They sold property and possessions to give to anyone who had need. Every day they continued to meet together in the temple courts. They broke bread in their homes and ate together with glad and sincere hearts, praising God and enjoying the favor of all the people. And the Lord added to their number daily those who were being saved.*

Fourth, the Spirit-controlled believer will be filled with genuine joy. The believer will know a deeper, sweeter, and greater joy that will be his or her daily possession in good times as well as bad times. This joy does not occur because the Spirit-filled believer never experiences problems or lives a life free of difficulties, but it does mean that even in the midst of trouble, the Spirit-controlled believer can rejoice in the Lord.

> *John 15:11,* *I have told you this so that my joy may be in you and that your joy may be complete.*

> *Galatians 5:22,* *But the fruit of the Spirit is love, joy, peace, forbearance, kindness, goodness, faithfulness...*

> *James 1:2,* *Consider it pure joy, my brothers and sisters, whenever you face trials of many kinds...*

Fifth, the Spirit-controlled believer continually gives thanks and manifests a grateful attitude in all things. This is because the Spirit-filled believer views every circumstance through God's eyes. The believer will understand that God allows difficulties in order to mature our joy in Him for His glory.

> *Romans 5:1-4,* *Therefore, since we have been justified through faith, we have peace with God through our Lord Jesus Christ, through whom we have gained access by faith into this grace in which we now stand. And we boast in the hope of the glory*

of God. Not only so, but we also glory in our sufferings, because we know that suffering produces perseverance; perseverance, character; and character, hope.

Finally, the Spirit-controlled believer will express mutual submission to and for others. Our attitude toward God is often revealed in our attitude toward each other. The believer will be able to practice mutual submission because he or she has reverence for the Lord and His commands. Mutual submission is truly a Christ-like characteristic. There is no room in the Church for pride or arrogance, only selfless service.

> *Philippians 2:1-6, Therefore if you have any encouragement from being united with Christ, if any comfort from his love, if any common sharing in the Spirit, if any tenderness and compassion, then make my joy complete by being like-minded, having the same love, being one in spirit and of one mind. Do nothing out of selfish ambition or vain conceit. Rather, in humility value others above yourselves, not looking to your own interests but each of you to the interests of the others. In your relationships with one another, have the same mindset as Christ Jesus: Who, being in very nature God, did not consider equality with God something to be used to his own advantage;*

In conclusion, too often the Spirit-controlled life is made out to be too mysterious a topic for one to consider. Or it is taught in a fashion that is too difficult to comprehend. Simply stated, the Holy Spirit lives in each believer and desires to control every believer. All is provided in Christ for the believer to let the Holy Spirit control our thoughts, words and actions in our daily lives. Being Spirit-filled also requires the believer to be humble and honest enough to allow the Spirit of God to change those thoughts, words and actions that do not please God, do not promote fellowship and unity in the church, or do not rightly present to Gospel to those who are lost.

Sins Against the Holy Spirit

The Bible makes it clear that the Holy Spirit can be offended and sinned against. Therefore, believers must be careful not to sin against the Spirit by suppressing His work in their lives or in the Church. What are the sins against the Spirit?

Quenching the Spirit

1 Thessalonians 5:19, Do not quench the Spirit.

Believers are warned not to "quench" the Holy Spirit. The word "quench" literally means to suppress or stifle and is used in Scripture of suppressing or extinguishing a fire. In a positive sense, believers are to quench or extinguish the fiery darts from Satan.

> *Ephesians 6:16, In addition to all this, take up the shield of faith, with which you can extinguish all the flaming arrows of the evil one.*

The Holy Spirit provides the spiritual fire in the believer's life—a fire one should not want to quench or stifle. It is impossible for the believer to completely extinguish the Holy Spirit's influence altogether, but it is possible to render the Holy Spirit functionally inoperative in the believer's life. Quenching the Holy Spirit occurs when the believer opposes or is disobedient to the Spirit's will in his or her life.

The Christian receives the call from the Holy Spirit to present himself or herself fully and unreservedly to be used by God. To do so will avail the believer of God's blessings and the results of the Spirit-controlled life discussed above. However, when believers quench the Spirit, they rob themselves of the vital power supplied by the Spirit. Quenching the Holy Spirit might also include the believer being willing to do a few things the Spirit asks, but not willing to do everything He asks.

> *Romans 6:13, Do not offer any part of yourself to sin as an instrument of wickedness, but rather offer yourselves to God as those who have been brought from death to life; and offer every part of yourself to him as an instrument of righteousness.*

The believer's greatest desire should be to fan the flame of the Holy Spirit and not limit His influence.

Grieving the Spirit

The word "grieve" informs us that the Holy Spirit has a personality and is more than just an impersonal force. The Holy Spirit is a divine person who has emotions and can be grieved by our actions just like we are grieved by the actions of others.

The Holy Spirit indwells the believer, which makes the believer's body a temple of God. Therefore, an unrepentant posture toward sin in any form grieves the Spirit. In Ephesians 4:30, the believer is exhorted not to sin and grieve the Spirit:

> *Ephesians 4:30, And do not grieve the Holy Spirit of God, with whom you were sealed for the day of redemption.*

Additionally, the Apostle Paul states that the Holy Spirit is grieved when a believer acts like a non-believer:

Ephesians 4:17-19, So I tell you this, and insist on it in the Lord, that you must no longer live as the Gentiles do, in the futility of their thinking. They are darkened in their understanding and separated from the life of God because of the ignorance that is in them due to the hardening of their hearts. Having lost all sensitivity, they have given themselves over to sensuality so as to indulge in every kind of impurity, and they are full of greed.

The Holy Spirit is grieved when the believer speaks inappropriately, lies, becomes angry, bitter, or is unforgiving:

Ephesians 4:25-32, Therefore each of you must put off falsehood and speak truthfully to your neighbor, for we are all members of one body. "In your anger do not sin": Do not let the sun go down while you are still angry, and do not give the devil a foothold. Anyone who has been stealing must steal no longer, but must work, doing something useful with their own hands, that they may have something to share with those in need. Do not let any unwholesome talk come out of your mouths, but only what is helpful for building others up according to their needs, that it may benefit those who listen. And do not grieve the Holy Spirit of God, with whom you were sealed for the day of redemption. Get rid of all bitterness, rage and anger, brawling and slander, along with every form of malice. Be kind and compassionate to one another, forgiving each other, just as in Christ God forgave you.

The Holy Spirit is grieved by sexual immorality in a believer's life:

Ephesians 5:1-3, Follow God's example, therefore, as dearly loved children and walk in the way of love, just as Christ loved us and gave himself up for us as a fragrant offering and sacrifice to God. But among you there must not be even a hint of sexual immorality, or of any kind of impurity, or of greed, because these are improper for God's holy people.

Generally speaking, grieving the Holy Spirit occurs when the Christian acts like a non-Christian in his or her thinking, words, or actions. Since we are fallen humans, we are in fact capable of grieving the Holy Spirit. However, in God's economy of living there is always a remedy for grieving the Holy Spirit—and that remedy is found in confession of sins!

1 John 1:9, If we confess our sins, he is faithful and just and will forgive us our sins and purify us from all unrighteousness.

In the above verse, believers are commanded to confess their sins to God. In confession, God is faithful and righteous to forgive sins and cleanse from all unrighteousness. Conversely, to refuse to confess and turn from sin is to bring the believer into a position of discipline from the God and seen in this passage.

Hebrews 12:5-6, And have you completely forgotten this word of encouragement that addresses you as a father addresses his son? It says, "My son, do not make light of the Lord's discipline, and do not lose heart when he rebukes you, because the Lord disciplines the one he loves, and he chastens everyone he accepts as his son."

The Christian is exhorted not to grieve the Holy Spirit of God. It is an appeal to allow nothing in our lives to remain that is contrary to holiness and the leading of the Spirit of God. It is clear that the major cause of grieving the Holy Spirit is sin which is characterized by unrepenting Christians.

Spiritual Gifts

Spiritual gifts are endowments to all members of the body of Christ. Every believer has at least one gift from the Holy Spirit.

1 Corinthians 12:12-16, Just as a body, though one, has many parts, but all its many parts form one body, so it is with Christ. For we were all baptized by one Spirit so as to form one body—whether Jews or Gentiles, slave or free—and we were all given the one Spirit to drink. Even so the body is not made up of one part but of many. Now if the foot should say, "Because I am not a hand, I do not belong to the body," it would not for that reason stop being part of the body. And if the ear should say, "Because I am not an eye, I do not belong to the body," it would not for that reason stop being part of the body.

The passage reveals: a) The body of Christ is a unit; b) The basis of the unity of one body is all believer's union with Christ; c) The reason why there is not unity in the body of Christ is because not all are fully subjected to the authority of Christ; and d) The body of Christ is the realm in which the gifts of the Spirit are to be exercised.

In the apostolic Church, there were two classifications of spiritual gifts. First, there were temporary, or sign gifts which include miraculous and revelatory gifts. These can be seen in the following passage:

1 Corinthians 12:8-10, To one there is given through the Spirit a message of wisdom, to another a message of knowledge by means of the same Spirit, to another faith by the same Spirit, to another gifts of healing by that one Spirit, to another miraculous powers, to another prophecy, to another distinguishing between spirits, to another speaking in different kinds of tongues, and to still another the interpretation of tongues.

The sign gifts are healing, working of miracles, tongues, and the interpretation of tongues. The purpose of the temporary sign gifts was to confirm the gospel message and establish the new community of faith in a pagan world. These sign gifts were the divine credentials of the Apostles. When the age of the Apostles ended, the sign gifts also ended. In these same verses, we see also that there were revelatory gifts. For example there was the word of knowledge, prophecy, and the various kinds of tongues. Through these special gifts, New Testament writers were able to instruct the believers in truth which is now recorded in the Bible. These special gifts are no longer needed because the Bible contains all of God's truth which is available to humanity.

Not only were there temporary sign gifts, but there were also service gifts which are found in Romans 12. The service gifts are prophesying or preaching, service, teaching, encouragement, giving, leadership, mercy and are still operational in today's church.

It will be of great value to spend some time defining and explaining the service gifts found in Romans 12.

> *Romans 12:6-8, We have different gifts, according to the grace given to each of us. If your gift is prophesying, then prophesy in accordance with your faith; if it is serving, then serve; if it is teaching, then teach; if it is to encourage, then give encouragement;if it is giving, then give generously; if it is to lead, do it diligently; if it is to show mercy, do it cheerfully.*

Prophecy: Notice that the gift of prophecy is distinguished from the office of the prophet. The true New Testament office of the prophet was a man who was at that particular time actually receiving the Word of God, while the gift of prophecy is the divine-given ability to preach the Word of God. Since we have the written word of God, there is no longer any need for the office of a prophet, but some do have the gift of prophecy. It should be noted that the gift of prophecy has nothing to do with the ability to tell the future. It is the divine-given ability to preach the word of God.

Service: The gift of service usually does not stand out but is essential to the church. Some people receive the greatest joy in life when they are serving others. We see this demonstrated in the church by those receive their greatest joy in simply helping or serving others and various capacities.

Teaching: There are many who have the divine ability to unfold and communicate God's revealed truth. Can you imagine the effectiveness of a Church where all those who had the gift of teaching utilized that gift? The individual who has the gift of teaching enjoys spending a great deal of time in research and has a unique desire and ability to communicate the truth of God's Word.

Encouragement: The word "encouragement" means to inspire, embolden, or comfort. The Greek word speaks of one calling another to their side for strength and comfort. God places people in the body who have the ability to inspire others to action or greater heights.

Giving: This gift involves giving of one's abilities, resources, and money. The exhortation is to give with liberality. It is the ability to make money in order to give it to God's work. Those who have the gift of giving derive great joy from exercising the gift of giving.

Leadership: The word "leadership" means the one who stands in front. There are many who have the gift of leadership, organization, or administration. These particular individuals demonstrate the ability to organize, lead, and administer the work of God. Those with the gift of leadership receive their greatest joy from leading or organizing a ministry in the church.

Mercy: The gift of mercy involves working with those who are in most need of comfort, care, and compassion. Those with the gift of mercy not only demonstrate mercy upon people with particular needs but also have genuine compassion and empathy. Those with the gift of mercy derive their greatest joy from being present with those who are suffering or struggling at the deepest level.

These seven service gifts are all given by the Holy Spirit for the work of God in the church. It is my personal conviction that every believer has at least one of the gifts listed above that should always be used in service. However, I am just as persuaded that every Spirit-filled believer can readily operate at times in all seven areas of giftedness.

Principles for Discovering and Understanding Your Gifts

One of the most exciting discoveries a believer can make is that God has graciously given him or her spiritual gifts. It is through spiritual gifts that the Spirit equips and empowers God's people for ministry in the local church. The key to discovering one's spiritual gifts if found in Romans 12:

> *Romans 12:1-2, Therefore, I urge you, brothers and sisters, in view of God's mercy, to offer your bodies as a living sacrifice, holy and pleasing to God—this is your true and proper worship. Do not conform to the pattern of this world, but be transformed by the renewing of your mind. Then you will be able to test and approve what God's will is—his good, pleasing and perfect will.*

Those verses are best understood if they are read in light of discovering God's will for your life. If you are to discover your spiritual gift, you must begin with God. Christians make a mistake when they look for a gift without first looking for the Giver of the gifts. Therefore, the starting point for discovering and determining our gifts is obedience to the God of the gospel. The word "offer," or present, speaks of a resolute consecration to God, not to some gift.

The words "holy and pleasing" speak of the nature of the sacrifice we are to make. These words mean that offering of ourselves to God must be done on God's terms not our own. After we have offered ourselves unreservedly to God, we are then aligning more with God's will for our lives. The natural result of offering oneself to God is a change in mindset and focus as seen in Colossians 3 and Ephesians 4.

> *Colossians 3:1-3, Since, then, you have been raised with Christ, set your hearts on things above, where Christ is, seated at the right hand of God. Set your minds on things above, not on earthly things. For you died, and your life is now hidden with Christ in God.*

> *Ephesians 4:17-24, So I tell you this, and insist on it in the Lord, that you must no longer live as the Gentiles do, in the futility of their thinking. They are darkened in their understanding and separated from the life of God because of the ignorance that is in them due to the hardening of their hearts. Having lost all sensitivity, they have given themselves over to sensuality so as to indulge in every kind of impurity, and they are full of greed. That, however, is not the way of life you learned when you heard about Christ and were taught in him in accordance with the truth that is in Jesus. You were taught, with regard to your former way of life, to put off your old self, which is being corrupted by its deceitful desires; to be made new in the attitude of your minds; and to put on the new self, created to be like God in true righteousness and holiness.*

Then in Romans 12, Paul says we should "renew" our minds which translates from the Greek word *anakainosis*. This word speaks of a gradual conforming of the Christian mind to the world as it truly is: the world as God sees it. This renewal of our mind becomes more and more of a spiritual renovation of thought and action in accordance with the will of God. Thus, before there can be a change in the way a believer walks, there must first be a radical, spiritual change in the believer's mindset.

Through this process of a believer's dedication and surrender, God gives him or her the ability to think spiritually and not simply naturally. Our thoughts conform more and more to God's thoughts such that we see the world as God sees it and desire that which God desires. Once our minds are controlled by the Spirit, our physical actions will follow as seen in Galatians 5:

Galatians 5:16, So I say, walk by the Spirit, and you will not gratify the desires of the flesh.

As the Spirit rules our mental faculties more and more, there is an increasing ability to discern and prove the will of God. The word "prove" means to put to the test or demonstrate. This is a simple definition, but it goes deeper than just testing something. It refers to the Holy Spirit taking over our mental processes, and as we yield to the Holy Spirit, we are saturated with truth. This can be seen in Colossians 1.

Colossians 1:9-12, For this reason, since the day we heard about you, we have not stopped praying for you. We continually ask God to fill you with the knowledge of his will through all the wisdom and understanding that the Spirit gives, so that you may live a life worthy of the Lord and please him in every way: bearing fruit in every good work, growing in the knowledge of God, being strengthened with all power according to his glorious might so that you may have great endurance and patience, and giving joyful thanks to the Father, who has qualified you to share in the inheritance of his holy people in the kingdom of light.

Once the believer comes under the control of the Holy Spirit, the Spirit uses the gifts in a believer's life for the good of the body of Christ and for the ultimate glory of God.

1 Corinthians 12:7, Now to each one the manifestation of the Spirit is given for the common good.

In conclusion, let me admonish and encourage you to diligently present yourself to God, seek His will for your life, discover your spiritual gifts, and use them for the good of the church and the glory of God!

THE DOCTRINE OF SALVATION

The need for salvation is clearly seen throughout the Bible. The fact that all mankind are sinners and consequently alienated from God is what creates that ultimate need. The Bible makes it clear that man is totally depraved. Man is not only a sinner and incapable of living a life which is pleasing to God, he is also incapable of changing his spiritual status. Therefore, if mankind is going to be in a right relationship with God and live a life that pleases God, there must be some miracle which takes place that totally transforms mankind. That miracle is called salvation. Soteriology is the study of the Doctrine of Salvation and deals with the provision of salvation by God through His Son, Jesus Christ.

The Work of Christ

The fall of man into sin had irrevocably separated man from God. Therefore, if man was to once again be in right standing with God, some provision would have to be made to take care of the issue of sin. Since man is now a fallen creature, the provisions would have to come from God. This is a fundamental point concerning the plan of salvation. The matter of salvation is purely a divine product. Salvation is not a product of man nor of the Church but is from God.

It should be understood that God was under no moral obligation to provide salvation. Some act as though God owes it to man to provide forgiveness. However, this is not the case. Man chose, and continues to choose, to disobey the commands of God. Adam did not have to sin. He did so in defiance to the divine warning. Let it be understood that

God has provided salvation as a result of His kindness and love. Salvation is a product of Divine Grace. It is a glorious privilege for fallen man to have the opportunity to know this grace by having his sins completely forgiven and the joy of being adopted into the family of God.

The Death Of Christ

The Old Testament is filled with types, symbols, and prophecies concerning the death of the Messiah. In reference to the types, there is a crimson thread which can be traced through the Old Testament that establishes a basic concept of God's dealing with man; namely, the innocent must die for the guilty. This is seen in the offerings of Cain and Abel (Genesis 4), the Passover Lamb in Egypt (Exodus 12:1-28), and the Levitical sacrifices (Leviticus 1-7), only to name a few. These, as well as many other types and symbols, point to the sacrificial offering which was to be made by Jesus Christ.

In relation to prophecies, one readily finds that the Old Testament is filled with Scriptures pointing to the death of the Messiah. We need only to list a few here. The Psalmist prophesied the betrayal of Christ (Psalm 41:9); His crucifixion (Psalm 22); and even the resurrection (Psalm 16:8-11). Indeed, we should not overlook Isaiah 53:1-6 which gives in classic detail the suffering and death of Christ.

> *Isaiah 51:1-6, Listen to me, you who pursue righteousness and who seek the Lord: Look to the rock from which you were cut and to the quarry from which you were hewn; look to Abraham, your father, and to Sarah, who gave you birth. When I called him he was only one man, and I blessed him and made him many. The Lord will surely comfort Zion and will look with compassion on all her ruins; he will make her deserts like Eden, her wastelands like the garden of the Lord. Joy and gladness will be found in her, thanksgiving and the sound of singing. Listen to me, my people; hear me, my nation: Instruction will go out from me; my justice will become a light to the nations. My righteousness draws near speedily, my salvation is on the way, and my arm will bring justice to the nations. The islands will look to me and wait in hope for my arm. Lift up your eyes to the heavens, look at the earth beneath; the heavens will vanish like smoke, the earth will wear out like a garment and its inhabitants die like flies. But my salvation will last forever, my righteousness will never fail.*

The New Testament reveals that the death of Christ is a major significance. In fact, it is repeatedly stated that His death was the very reason for His incarnation.

> *Mark 10:45, For even the Son of Man did not come to be served, but to serve, and to give his life as a ransom for many.*

Hebrews 2:9, But we do see Jesus, who was made lower than the angels for a little while, now crowned with glory and honor because he suffered death, so that by the grace of God he might taste death for everyone.

Hebrews 9:26, Otherwise Christ would have had to suffer many times since the creation of the world. But he has appeared once for all at the culmination of the ages to do away with sin by the sacrifice of himself.

The fact that Christ died for the sins of the world is the fundamental theme of the Gospel. The sacrificial death of Christ on Calvary is essential to our salvation.

1 Timothy 2:5-6, For there is one God and one mediator between God and mankind, the man Christ Jesus, who gave himself as a ransom for all people. This has now been witnessed to at the proper time.

Romans 4:25, He was delivered over to death for our sins and was raised to life for our justification.

The central meaning of the death of Christ is that it was a substitution for sin. What this means in plain language is that Christ died in the place of sinners. Saying the death of Christ is substitutionary means that He was made to be sin on our behalf (2 Corinthians 5:21); He died, the Just for the unjust (1 Peter 3:15); He came to give His life as a ransom for many (Matthew 20:28). Christ died in man's place that there might be forgiveness of sin.

2 Corinthians 5:21, God made him who had no sin to be sin for us, so that in him we might become the righteousness of God.

1 Peter 3:18, For Christ also suffered once for sins, the righteous for the unrighteous, to bring you to God. He was put to death in the body but made alive in the Spirit.

Another fact concerning the death of Christ is that it provided redemption from sin. In the New Testament, there are primarily two Greek words translated "redeem" or "redemption." The first is *exagorazo* and refers to the purchasing of a slave for the purpose of giving him freedom.

Galatians 3:13, Christ redeemed us from the curse of the law by becoming a curse for us, for it is written: "Cursed is everyone who is hung on a pole."

Galatians 4:5, to redeem those under the law, that we might receive adoption to sonship.

The second word is *lutroo* and speaks of the releasing of someone paying a ransom.

Titus 2:14, who gave himself for us to redeem us from all wickedness and to purify for himself a people that are his very own, eager to do what is good.

1 Peter 1:18, For you know that it was not with perishable things such as silver or gold that you were redeemed from the empty way of life handed down to you from your ancestors...

In the use of these words, the sacrificial death of Christ is stated as the only means of redemption.

A third value of the death of Christ is seen by the fact that it provides for reconciliation. The word translated "reconcile" is *katallasso* and means that through the substitutionary death of Christ, man's state of alienation from God is changed so that now he can be saved. Sin has separated man from God. In the fall, it was man who was changed, not God. Although God desired to bring man back into fellowship with Himself, God could not change to meet the standards of man, nor could He overlook the issue of sin.

The source of hostility between God and man is sin. Therefore, Christ died for our sins, paying the full ransom price.

1 Corinthians 6:19-20, Do you not know that your bodies are temples of the Holy Spirit, who is in you, whom you have received from God? You are not your own; you were bought at a price. Therefore honor God with your bodies.

With this matter now taken care of, God is able to invite man to be saved. When one receives Christ as his Savior, acknowledging His work on Calvary, the believer is said to be reconciled to God. When he believes, his former state of alienation from God is changed so that he becomes a child of God. Therefore, reconciliation is twofold. First, when Christ died for the sins of the world, He rendered man savable or provided a basis upon which God could forgive man. When we receive Christ as Savior, we are reconciled in the sense that we are positionally changed to meet the standards of God.

Another term which describes the death of Christ on our behalf is propitiation. Propitiation expresses the anger (wrath) which God has toward sin. The wrath of God is to be understood as personal. God hates sin and is angry with the sinner.

1 John 2:2, He Himself is the propitiation for our sins; and not for ours only, but also for those of the whole world.(NASB)

Romans 3:25, whom God displayed publicly as a propitiation in His blood through faith. This was to demonstrate His righteousness, because in the forbearance of God He passed over the sins previously committed. (NASB)

The wrath of God is said to remain on the unsaved man.

John 3:36, Whoever believes in the Son has eternal life, but whoever rejects the Son will not see life, for God's wrath remains on them.

When Christ died on the cross, He assumed the guilt which separates man from God. Hence, the work of Christ propitiated God in the sense that He satisfied the holy demands which God and His Law had against sin. Therefore Christ Himself was the source of the satisfaction. Jesus is the satisfaction not only for our sins but for the sins of the world.

1 John 2:2, He Himself is the propitiation for our sins; and not for ours only, but also for those of the whole world.(NASB)

Put it this way, once you are saved, you are in Christ, and once you are in Christ, God is satisfied with you because He is satisfied with Christ!

Other values of the death of Christ on the cross are seen in that it judged the old sinful nature. That makes it possible for the believer to live a life of victory over sin (Romans 6:1-10). This does not, however, mean that Christians don't ever sin, but it does mean that we have ultimate victory over sin both in our present state and the one to come.

Christ's death also provides a basis for the believer's daily cleansing from sin.

1 John 1:7-9, But if we walk in the light, as he is in the light, we have fellowship with one another, and the blood of Jesus, his Son, purifies us from all sin. If we claim to be without sin, we deceive ourselves and the truth is not in us. If we confess our sins, he is faithful and just and will forgive us our sins and purify us from all unrighteousness.

Christ's death on the cross is also the basis for God's final judgment on Satan and his demons.

Colossians 2:15, And having disarmed the powers and authorities, he made a public spectacle of them, triumphing over them by the cross.

His Burial And Resurrection

1 Corinthians 15:12-19, But if it is preached that Christ has been raised from the dead, how can some of you say that there is no resurrection of the dead? If there is no resurrection of the dead, then not even Christ has been raised. And if Christ has not been raised, our preaching is useless and so is your faith. More than that, we are then found to be false witnesses about God, for we have testified about God that he raised Christ from the dead. But he did not raise him if in fact the dead are not raised. For if the dead are not raised, then Christ has not been raised either. And if Christ has not been raised, your faith is futile; you are still in your sins. Then those also who have fallen asleep in Christ are lost. If only for this life we have hope in Christ, we are of all people most to be pitied.

The believer is to glory in the cross of Christ but understand that He did not remain crucified. He is a risen, glorified, exalted Savior and Lord!

<u>Galatians 6:14,</u> *May I never boast except in the cross of our Lord Jesus Christ, through which the world has been crucified to me, and I to the world.*

The literal bodily resurrection of Jesus Christ is a fundamental doctrine of Christianity. In reference to salvation, we have been reconciled to God through the death of Christ while His resurrected life perfects our salvation. The death of Jesus Christ would be of no value eternally without His resurrection.

<u>Romans 5:8-10,</u> *But God demonstrates his own love for us in this: While we were still sinners, Christ died for us. Since we have now been justified by his blood, how much more shall we be saved from God's wrath through him! For if, while we were God's enemies, we were reconciled to him through the death of his Son, how much more, having been reconciled, shall we be saved through his life!*

The Present Day Work of Christ

Today, Jesus sits at the right hand of the Father. In His position next to the Father, Jesus is anything but stationary. Jesus is our High Priest, our Advocate, the one Mediator between God and man, the Head of the Church, our intercessor, and He exercises authority over the universe.

<u>Hebrews 4:14,</u> *Therefore, since we have a great high priest who has ascended into heaven, Jesus the Son of God, let us hold firmly to the faith we profess.*

<u>1 John 2:1-2,</u> *My dear children, I write this to you so that you will not sin. But if anybody does sin, we have an advocate with the Father—Jesus Christ, the Righteous One. He is the atoning sacrifice for our sins, and not only for ours but also for the sins of the whole world.*

<u>Ephesians 1:22-23,</u> *And God placed all things under his feet and appointed him to be head over everything for the church, which is his body, the fullness of him who fills everything in every way.*

Ephesians 1:20-21, he exerted when he raised Christ from the dead and seated him at his right hand in the heavenly realms, far above all rule and authority, power and dominion, and every name that is invoked, not only in the present age but also in the one to come.

The Doctrine of Election

The Doctrine of Election has been the source of much controversy throughout church history. It is a difficult subject, to say the least. This difficulty comes primarily from the fact that no human system of interpretation will ever be able to answer all the questions or all the inquiries concerning the doctrine. This lack of fully being able to understand and explain election has everything to do with the fact that this doctrine is of purely divine origin coming from God and it is ultimately settled in the mind of eternal God and not in the mind of finite man.

Although this study is not exhaustive, there is enough light given in Scripture to at least have a working knowledge of election. Further, I do believe there is sufficient room created in the Christian faith and in biblical teaching to allow others to have a differing view when it comes to election. However, in the final say, which comes to difficult issues like election and predestination, I am always willing in my heart and mind to acknowledge that I can't limit God to what makes sense to me. God's thoughts and actions are beyond our comprehension, and with that, I affirm what God said about His own actions, thoughts, and ways in the book of Isaiah.

Isaiah 55:8-9 "For my thoughts are not your thoughts, neither are your ways my ways," declares the Lord. "As the heavens are higher than the earth, so are my ways higher than your ways and my thoughts than your thoughts."

Election is best understood as the sovereign act of God and that God was under no obligation for moral or just reason to elect or save anyone.

Ephesians 1:9, he made known to us the mystery of his will according to his good pleasure, which he purposed in Christ...

Next, it should be understood that election and predestination are topics that are purely preceded by God's foreknowledge. But what does God's foreknowledge in relation to salvation, election, and predestination mean? To be honest, that is a question of the ages, and in the following discussion I want to refer you constantly back in your mind to

Isaiah 55:8-9 which reminds us that God's thoughts and ways are so, so, so far above ours that we cannot fully comprehend them.

When it comes to foreknowledge, all Christians agree that human actions are included in God's plan, but they differ on what is the cause of those actions and what is the result. Some place greater emphasis on God's plan and election. Thus, God chooses some for salvation, and this choice of God causes man's response to salvation. These Christians rely heavily on the passages that suggest *God chose.* Other Christians have a higher view of man's freedom and response to the Gospel. These Christians point to the *whosoever will* and *all* passages. The simple fact is that both the *God chose,* and the *whosoever* passages are found throughout Scripture.

God's foreknowledge is also viewed differently by Christians as it relates to election and salvation. Some Christians see foreknowledge as God knowing beforehand what will happen because he determines what will happen and chooses who will be saved thus making God's election unconditional on man's response. Other Christians see foreknowledge as God simply knowing beforehand what will happen and who will accept salvation thus making God's election conditional on his knowledge of man's response. Millard Erickson delineates these two lines of thought as they relate to Paul's teaching in Romans.

> Romans 8:29-30, *For those God foreknew he also predestined to be conformed to the image of his Son, that he might be the firstborn among many brothers and sisters. And those he predestined, he also called; those he called, he also justified; those he justified, he also glorified.*

First, Millard Erickson said, "Calvinists believe that God's plan is logically prior and that man's decisions and actions are a consequence. With respect to the particular matter of the acceptance or rejection of salvation, God in his plan has chosen that some shall believe and thus receive the offer of eternal life. He foreknows what will happen because he has decided what is to happen." (Erickson's *Systematic Theology*)

Second, Millard Erickson wrote, "from this verse the Arminaian draws the conclusion that God's choice or determination of each individual's destiny is a result of foreknowledge. Thus, those whom God foreknew would believe are those he decided would be saved."

Millard Erickson summarizes these two views of foreknowledge and election this way, "One might, therefore, say that in the Arminian view this aspect of God's plan is conditional upon human decisions; in the Calvinistic view, on the other hand, God's plan is unconditional."

Two other passages that speak to God's foreknowledge as it relates to God's plan for salvation are:

1 Peter 1:2, *who have been chosen according to the foreknowledge of God the Father, through the sanctifying work of the Spirit, to be obedient to Jesus Christ and sprinkled with his blood: Grace and peace be yours in abundance.*

Acts 2:23, 23 *This man was handed over to you by God's deliberate plan and foreknowledge; and you, with the help of wicked men, put him to death by nailing him to the cross.*

In both of the above passages, God's foreknowledge and plan for salvation are front and center. Peter said God chose according to the "foreknowledge of God" and he said Jesus was handed over to "you by God's deliberate plan and foreknowledge." Both passages make it clear that God's foreknowledge and plan are primary in God's plan for salvation and man's actions are secondary. Beyond that, the Bible makes it abundantly clear that God chose those who would be saved not based on any merit because the Bible makes it abundantly clear that the unsaved person is totally without merit in the eyes of God.

Romans 3:10-12, *As it is written: "There is no one righteous, not even one; there is no one who understands; there is no one who seeks God. All have turned away, they have together become worthless; there is no one who does good, not even one."*

Therefore it is clear that God did not choose individuals for salvation based on their merit, but on the merit of Christ. It should be noted that some believe God's election was based on His foreknowledge of those who would receive Christ as personal Savior and Lord while others do not believe God made His election based on His foreknowledge of who would receive and who would not. To be sure, nobody knows all that was in the mind of an infinite God, but Scripture does makes it clear that His foreknowledge preceded both election and predestination in some way. Consequently, salvation is of God's grace alone.

Ephesians 2:8-9, *For it is by grace you have been saved, through faith—and this is not from yourselves, it is the gift of God— not by works, so that no one can boast.*

Regardless of one's view of the relationship of foreknowledge, election, and predestination, the Bible makes it clear that man is responsible for accepting or rejecting Jesus Christ as Savior.

John 3:18, *Whoever believes in him is not condemned, but whoever does not believe stands condemned already because they have not believed in the name of God's one and only Son.*

John 3:36, *Whoever believes in the Son has eternal life, but whoever rejects the Son will not see life, for God's wrath remains on them.*

Although man is dead in sin, God has given to him what some have called a "God consciousness" which gives man sufficient knowledge to both know what is right and wrong and be responsible for their actions. Those actions include receiving or rejecting Jesus Christ.

John 2:14-15, *Indeed, when Gentiles, who do not have the law, do by nature things required by the law, they are a law for themselves, even though they do not have the law. They show that the requirements of the law are written on their hearts, their consciences also bearing witness, and their thoughts sometimes accusing them and at other times even defending them.*

John 1:9, *The true light that gives light to everyone was coming into the world.*

In His foreknowledge, God knows what each person will do with this opportunity of salvation which has been given. Therefore, predestination and election are based on God's foreknowledge in ways that we try to understand. In the end, we merely affirm what Scripture teaches.

Romans 8:28-30, *And we know that in all things God works for the good of those who love him, who have been called according to his purpose. For those God foreknew he also predestined to be conformed to the image of his Son, that he might be the firstborn among many brothers and sisters. And those he predestined, he also called; those he called, he also justified; those he justified, he also glorified.*

It would be of value at this point to briefly consider the words "election" and "predestination." A careful study of the New Testament should reveal that the words "predestination" and "foreordination" primarily meant the same thing. When it is applied to redemption, this would mean that in election, God has decided to save those who would accept His Son and the salvation which Jesus Christ would purchase. Then in foreordination, He has determined effectively to accomplish that purpose.

Peter also mentions the foreknowledge of God in choosing believers when speaking to the exiled saints.

1 Peter 1:1-2, *Peter, an apostle of Jesus Christ, To God's elect, exiles scattered throughout the provinces of Pontus, Galatia, Cappadocia, Asia and Bithynia, who*

have been chosen according to the foreknowledge of God the Father, through the sanctifying work of the Spirit, to be obedient to Jesus Christ and sprinkled with his blood: Grace and peace be yours in abundance.

Ultimately, regardless of where one falls on trying to define the undefinable "foreknowledge" of God and how it relates to election, this much is true. Scripture makes it abundantly clear that Jesus died for the sins of the world.

<u>1 Timothy 2:6</u>, *who gave himself as a ransom for all people. This has now been witnessed to at the proper time.*

<u>2 Peter 3:9,</u> *The Lord is not slow in keeping his promise, as some understand slowness. Instead he is patient with you, not wanting anyone to perish, but everyone to come to repentance.*

<u>John 3:16</u>, *For God so loved the world that he gave his one and only Son, that whoever believes in him shall not perish but have eternal life.*

Beyond Jesus dying for the sins of the world, the offer of the Gospel is universal.

<u>John 3:16,</u> *For God so loved the world that he gave his one and only Son, that whoever believes in him shall not perish but have eternal life.*

<u>Acts 10:43</u>, *All the prophets testify about him that everyone who believes in him receives forgiveness of sins through his name.*

The words "whoever" and "everyone" are universal in nature. The word translated "whoever" is found over 100 times in the New Testament and always with the unrestricted meaning. Probably the most definitive Scripture on the relationships between election, calling, and the foreknowledge of God comes from the words of Jesus in John 6 where he alternates between people coming and believing in Him and God calling and bringing those who would be saved.

<u>John 6:35-51</u> *Then Jesus declared, "I am the bread of life. <u>Whoever comes</u> to me will never go hungry, and <u>whoever believes </u>in me will never be thirsty. But as I told you, you have seen me and still you do not believe. <u>All those the Father gives me will come to me</u>, and <u>whoever comes to me I will never drive away</u>. For I have come down from heaven not to do my will but to do the will of him who sent me. And <u>this is the will of him who sent me, that I shall lose none of all those he has given me,</u> but raise them up at the last day. For my Father's will is that <u>everyone who looks to the Son and believes in him shall have eternal life</u>, and I will raise them up at the last day." At this the Jews there began to grumble about him because he said, "I am the bread that came down from heaven." They said, "Is this not Jesus, the son of Joseph, whose father and mother we know? How can he now say, 'I came down*

from heaven'?" "Stop grumbling among yourselves," Jesus answered. "<u>No one can</u> *<u>come to me unless the Father who sent me draws them</u>, and I will raise them up at* *the last day. It is written in the Prophets: 'They will all be taught by God.' <u>Everyone</u>* *<u>who has heard the Father and learned from him comes to me.</u> No one has seen the* *Father except the one who is from God; only he has seen the Father. Very truly I tell* *you, <u>the one who believes has eternal life.</u> I am the bread of life. Your ancestors ate* *the manna in the wilderness, yet they died. But here is the bread that comes down* *from heaven,<u> which anyone may eat and not die.</u> I am the living bread that came* *down from heaven. <u>Whoever eats this bread will live forever.</u> This bread is my flesh,* *<u>which I will give for the life of the world."</u>*

In conclusion, when it comes to foreknowledge, election, and salvation several clear teachings from Jesus emerge from this passage. It is clear that anyone who comes to Jesus and believes will be saved--without exception. They will not be lost, but they will have eternal life. However, the reason they comes to Jesus is because the Father draws them.

Therefore, the believer in Christ does not and cannot fully comprehend the mind of God in salvation. Nor do we have to choose one extreme over the other. Instead, we simply say God's foreknowledge, election, and calling are God's part in salvation, and my part is to come, believe and receive. Thus the final words are nothing more than Amen and Amen!

Regeneration

When considering the subject of salvation, one may ask, How is it possible for a Holy God to save a sinful person who is marred by sin, and thus make that person holy and acceptable to God? The biblical answer is the act of regeneration. Regeneration is the communication of the divine life into the unbelieving sinner. This communication is brought about by the Holy Spirit through the power of the Word of God.

Regeneration is the door to eternal life. Without regeneration, the door between God and man is forever closed. The necessity of regeneration is seen in the sinfulness of man who is said to be dead in his sin. If man is to be acceptable to God, then one must experience some spiritual quickening which will give the individual spiritual life.

Jesus describes the act of regeneration by referring to it as a "new birth." In John 3, Jesus tells Nicodemus that unless a man is born again, he cannot see the Kingdom of God.

<u>John 3:1-7,</u> *Now there was a Pharisee, a man named Nicodemus who was a mem-* *ber of the Jewish ruling council. He came to Jesus at night and said, "Rabbi, we*

know that you are a teacher who has come from God. For no one could perform the signs you are doing if God were not with him." Jesus replied, "Very truly I tell you, no one can see the kingdom of God unless they are born again. How can someone be born when they are old?" Nicodemus asked. "Surely they cannot enter a second time into their mother's womb to be born!" Jesus answered, "Very truly I tell you, no one can enter the kingdom of God unless they are born of water and the Spirit. Flesh gives birth to flesh, but the Spirit gives birth to spirit. You should not be surprised at my saying, 'You must be born again.'"

See also Peter and James', the brother of Jesus, words:

<u>James 1:18-21,</u> *He chose to give us birth through the word of truth, that we might be a kind of firstfruits of all he created. My dear brothers and sisters, take note of this: Everyone should be quick to listen, slow to speak and slow to become angry, because human anger does not produce the righteousness that God desires. Therefore, get rid of all moral filth and the evil that is so prevalent and humbly accept the word planted in you, which can save you.*

<u>1 Peter 1:23</u>, *For you have been born again, not of perishable seed, but of imperishable, through the living and enduring word of God.*

The Apostle Paul described this divine action as making one who is dead, alive again. In these verses, we see that man being dead in his sin and trespasses must be made alive spiritually so that he might walk with God. The making alive, or spiritual resurrection, is identified as the act of regeneration.

<u>Ephesians 2:1-10:</u> *As for you, you were dead in your transgressions and sins, in which you used to live when you followed the ways of this world and of the ruler of the kingdom of the air, the spirit who is now at work in those who are disobedient. All of us also lived among them at one time, gratifying the cravings of our flesh and following its desires and thoughts. Like the rest, we were by nature deserving of wrath. But because of his great love for us, God, who is rich in mercy, made us alive with Christ even when we were dead in transgressions—it is by grace you have been saved. And God raised us up with Christ and seated us with him in the heavenly realms in Christ Jesus, in order that in the coming ages he might show the incomparable riches of his grace, expressed in his kindness to us in Christ Jesus. For it is by grace you have been saved, through faith—and this is not from yourselves, it is the gift of God—not by works, so that no one can boast. For we are God's handiwork, created in Christ Jesus to do good works, which God prepared in advance for us to do.*

Regeneration is also the impartation of the new nature. Let it be understood that in the act of regeneration, God does not awaken the old, depraved sin nature and change that nature into conformance with the will of God. Quite to the contrary, for we find that in biblical regeneration, God actually makes the believers to become partakers of a new divine nature altogether. That which makes the believer alive is the fact that God gives him His own nature. The believer receives this new life from Jesus Christ.

2 Peter 1:4, *Through these he has given us his very great and precious promises, so that through them you may participate in the divine nature, having escaped the corruption in the world caused by evil desires. In the Word of God, we find many results and benefits of the act of divine regeneration: First, the believer actually becomes a child of God.*

John 1:12, *Yet to all who did receive him, to those who believed in his name, he gave the right to become children of God...*

Second, the believer possesses eternal life once salvation has occurred.

1 John 5:11-12, *And this is the testimony: God has given us eternal life, and this life is in his Son. Whoever has the Son has life; whoever does not have the Son of God does not have life.*

Third, the believer becomes the temple of God and receives a new nature.

1 Corinthians 3:16, *Don't you know that you yourselves are God's temple and that God's Spirit dwells in your midst?*

Fourth, the regenerated person practices righteousness which means that once a person is born again, he finds that he has not only new life but a new lifestyle.

1 John 3:9, *No one who is born of God will continue to sin, because God's seed remains in them; they cannot go on sinning, because they have been born of God.*

Fifth, regeneration produces within the believer, love for God, mankind, and God's Word.

1 John 5:1-2, *Everyone who believes that Jesus is the Christ is born of God, and everyone who loves the father loves his child as well. This is how we know that we love the children of God: by loving God and carrying out his commands.*

1 Peter 2:2, *Like newborn babies, crave pure spiritual milk, so that by it you may grow up in your salvation...*

Once a believer has become a child of God and has received a love for God, God's Word, and a new lifestyle, that believer will also manifest a love for the lost.

Romans 1:16, *For I am not ashamed of the gospel, because it is the power of God that brings salvation to everyone who believes: first to the Jew, then to the Gentile.*

In thinking about regeneration, one might ask, when does this divine act of regeneration occur and how is it obtained? First of all, from a negative side, let it be stated that regeneration does not come about by good works, baptism, or joining a church.

> Ephesians 2:8-9, *For it is by grace you have been saved, through faith—and this is not from yourselves, it is the gift of God—not by works, so that no one can boast.*

The only way a person can experience regeneration is by receiving the Lord Jesus Christ as personal Savior. As to when regeneration takes place, it is the very moment a sinner receives Jesus Christ by faith as Lord and Savior the miracle of regeneration is brought about by the Holy Spirit.

Justification, Sanctification, and Eternal Security

The first part of this chapter focuses on the work of Christ in salvation, the doctrine of election, and the wonderful truth concerning regeneration. The back half of this chapter will turn our attention to the fundamental truths concerning the results of salvation which Christ purchased for mankind: Doctrine of Justification, Sanctification, the Eternal Security of the Believer, and the doctrine of Assurance.

> Romans 3:21-30, *But now apart from the law the righteousness of God has been made known, to which the Law and the Prophets testify. This righteousness is given through faith in Jesus Christ to all who believe. There is no difference between Jew and Gentile, for all have sinned and fall short of the glory of God, and all are justified freely by his grace through the redemption that came by Christ Jesus. God presented Christ as a sacrifice of atonement, through the shedding of his blood—to be received by faith. He did this to demonstrate his righteousness, because in his forbearance he had left the sins committed beforehand unpunished—he did it to demonstrate his righteousness at the present time, so as to be just and the one who justifies those who have faith in Jesus. Where, then, is boasting? It is excluded. Because of what law? The law that requires works? No, because of the law that requires faith. For we maintain that a person is justified by faith apart from the works of the law. Or is God the God of Jews only? Is he not the God of Gentiles too? Yes, of Gentiles too, since there is only one God, who will justify the circumcised by faith and the uncircumcised through that same faith.*

Justification

Justification is a legal term which refers to the judicial act of God, who on account of Christ declares the believing sinner no longer to be exposed to the penalty of the Law, but has been eternally restored to God's divine favor. Simply stated, justification is the act of God bringing man into a legal and right-standing with God.

When the sinner receives Jesus Christ as personal Savior, the Bible teaches that God actually imputes to that person God's own righteousness, and declares the believer to be acceptable and in right standing with Himself. Let it be thoroughly understood that justification is not based on the goodness or righteousness of the one who is justified, but relies on the goodness and righteousness of the one who is doing the justifying. Therefore, justification is based on the reality and fact that God actually attributes His righteousness to the sinner.

When God looks at the believer, He sees Himself, beholds His own righteousness and the work of Christ on Calvary, and is satisfied with what has been done on behalf of the sinner. In salvation, the believer is just identifying himself with that which God has done on his behalf through the process of divine grace.

The first aspect, one must understand about justification and all truths of salvation is that it is done in accordance with the grace of God. Grace is the unmerited or unearned favor of God. The believer does not and cannot earn God's grace, for there is nothing the believer can do to earn the favors of God. Thus, justification is an unmerited favor which is bestowed on the believer through the process of God's grace.

Ephesians 2:8-9, *For it is by grace you have been saved, through faith—and this is not from yourselves, it is the gift of God—not by works, so that no one can boast.*

Romans 3:24, *and all are justified freely by his grace through the redemption that came by Christ Jesus.*

Second, justification should be understood as being based on the redeeming and atoning death of Jesus Christ as stated in Romans 3:24. As we looked at earlier, the doctrine of propitiation stated that Jesus Christ died for the purpose of satisfying God's holy law and God's righteous demands on the sinner. When the death of Christ was completed, God looked upon Christ's sacrifice and was satisfied. Note careful that the work which Jesus performed at Calvary was not for Himself, but was on behalf of the sinner. Therefore, when the sinner through the preaching of the Word of God and ministry of the Holy Spirit recognizes that Christ died on his behalf, and through faith receives Christ as personal Savior, then God is able to justify him based upon what Christ has done for all sinners on Calvary.

Romans 10:17, *and all are justified freely by his grace through the redemption that came by Christ Jesus.*

Romans 3:24 states that justification came as a free gift of grace "through the redemption which is in Jesus Christ." Note again that justification came about as an act of God's grace and not human works. The grace which is demonstrated to the believer is made possible by the redemption which is in Jesus Christ. The word "redemption" comes from the Greek *apolutroseos* and means to redeem or to pay the redemption price. The redemption price of sin was the blood of Jesus Christ. Through the blood of Christ, the believer is purchased from the slave market of sin and set free to live a new life that is pleasing to God.

> 1 Corinthians 6:19-20, *Do you not know that your bodies are temples of the Holy Spirit, who is in you, whom you have received from God? You are not your own; you were bought at a price. Therefore honor God with your bodies.*

> Titus 2:14, *who gave himself for us to redeem us from all wickedness and to purify for himself a people that are his very own, eager to do what is good.*

> 1 Peter 1:18-19, *For you know that it was not with perishable things such as silver or gold that you were redeemed from the empty way of life handed down to you from your ancestors, but with the precious blood of Christ, a lamb without blemish or defect.*

It took the death of Christ on Calvary in order for God to provide salvation to man, for this is the only way that God could remain just and still be the Justifier of the unjust. The way in which God did this was by publicly displaying Jesus Christ as our propitiation or atoning sacrifice for sins.

> Romans 3:25, *God presented Christ as a sacrifice of atonement, through the shedding of his blood—to be received by faith. He did this to demonstrate his righteousness, because in his forbearance he had left the sins committed beforehand unpunished...*

The word "propitiation" comes from the Greek word *hilasterion* and means "to satisfy." That means that Christ, through His blood, has met and satisfied all the just demands of the Law and a Holy God which have been placed upon the sinner because of his or her sinfulness. When the sinner receives Jesus Christ as Savior, then the satisfactory work of Christ on the cross is attributed to that sinner who then becomes identified with Christ. Since God is satisfied with Christ, God is also satisfied with the new believer.

Thirdly, let us note that justification comes through the process of *faith alone*. Justification is not secured by an ordinance of the Church, nor is it attained through human works. Justification comes through *faith alone.*

Romans 3:28, *For we maintain that a person is justified by faith apart from the works of the law.*

Once genuine faith has arrived in the heart of an individual, God gives or imputes His own righteousness to the new believer which results in the forgiveness of sin and the removal of guilt and punishment.

Romans 3:21-22, *But now apart from the law the righteousness of God has been made known, to which the Law and the Prophets testify. This righteousness is given through faith in Jesus Christ to all who believe. There is no difference between Jew and Gentile...*

Romans 5:1, *Therefore, since we have been justified through faith, we have peace with God through our Lord Jesus Christ...*

Justification does not come as a result of good works or the works of the Law but through faith in the person and work of the Lord Jesus Christ. First, Justification is an act that only God can perform and the Bible explicitly rejects the idea that justification ever has or ever will be accomplished by human works. Justification does not make one righteous or holy, but it accounts one as righteousness or holy. The only true righteousness which the believer has is a product of God's work in his or her life. Justification is not a change brought about by God in us, but a change of our relationship to God. Clarifying statement: Regeneration (new birth) brings a change in us, while justification is a judicial act of accounting which changes our standing with God.

Sanctification

One of the most misunderstood doctrines in the Bible is that of Sanctification. In the beginning of this study, we first would like to approach the subject of sanctification from the negative aspect by stating what sanctification is not. First, sanctification is not, the eradication of the sinful nature. Secondly, sanctification does not constitute moral perfection. There are some who teach that when a believer receives the Lord Jesus Christ as his personal Savior that his old sinful nature is eradicated, the result being that he now has the capacity to move into a state of moral perfection. Similarly, some have referred to sanctification as a so-called "second blessing." Some have taught that if we would pray hard enough and seek God long enough that we could come into a state of having a second blessing from God, and in so doing, we could move into a condition of spiritual perfection which they call sanctification. Both of these ideas of moral perfection or spiritual perfection violate the clear teaching of God's Word.

> 1 John 1:8, *If we claim to be without sin, we deceive ourselves and the truth is not in us.*

The primary idea of the word "sanctification" is to be set apart. It comes from a Greek term which had reference to the Greek gods. When a temple was built for the purpose of serving a Greek idol, it was said to have been sanctified. That temple was set apart for the purpose of worshipping that particular idol or false god. Therefore, the primary meaning is that something is "set apart" for a specific purpose or design.

The Bible teaches us that sanctification actually is in three phases. First, the believer is set apart to God through the acts of salvation. When the believer receives the Lord Jesus Christ as personal savior, God sets that believer apart to Himself for all eternity. This is called "positional sanctification," and is an eternal condition brought about by God. Positional sanctification is a permanent condition which can never be removed or lost.

> 1 Peter 1:1-2, *Peter, an apostle of Jesus Christ, To God's elect, exiles scattered throughout the provinces of Pontus, Galatia, Cappadocia, Asia and Bithynia, ²who have been chosen according to the foreknowledge of God the Father, through the sanctifying work of the Spirit, to be obedient to Jesus Christ and sprinkled with his blood: Grace and peace be yours in abundance.*

The second part of sanctification has to do with the ministry of the Holy Spirit in the daily life of the believer. It is the state of maturing in Christ where the Holy Spirit reveals sin to the believer, and the believer becomes more yielded and obedient to the Holy Spirit's leading. This is described by the term *"practical or progressive sanctification."*

> 1 Thessalonians 4:3, *It is God's will that you should be sanctified: that you should avoid sexual immorality...*

> 2 Corinthians 7:1, *Therefore, since we have these promises, dear friends, let us purify ourselves from everything that contaminates body and spirit, perfecting holiness out of reverence for God.*

The primary difference between positional sanctification and progressive or practical sanctification can be seen in the fact that positional sanctification is the act of God setting the believer apart to Himself, while progressive sanctification is the act of the believer through the Holy Spirit's leading setting himself apart for the service of God. The need for progressive sanctification is seen the biblical commands given to the believer to grow spiritually. If sanctification was a sinless perfection, then there would be no need to grow. Real spiritual growth comes through the accurate handling of God's Word.

> 2 Timothy 2:15, *Do your best to present yourself to God as one approved, a worker who does not need to be ashamed and who correctly handles the word of truth.*

> 2 Timothy 3:16-17, *All Scripture is God-breathed and is useful for teaching, rebuking, correcting and training in righteousness, so that the servant of God may be thoroughly equipped for every good work.*

The third aspect of sanctification can be described by terms of *perfect, complete, or ultimate sanctification*. Perfect and complete sanctification will occur at physical death when the believer is translated and shall remain forever in a glorified state. The Bible teaches that once Jesus Christ comes and brings the believer into His presence that they believe will undergo such a change that there will be no possibility of sinning. The Body of the believer shall be glorified and made like unto the glorious body of the Lord Jesus Christ.

> 1 Thessalonians 3:12-13, *May the Lord make your love increase and overflow for each other and for everyone else, just as ours does for you. May he strengthen your hearts so that you will be blameless and holy in the presence of our God and Father when our Lord Jesus comes with all his holy ones.*

> Philippians 3:20-21, *But our citizenship is in heaven. And we eagerly await a Savior from there, the Lord Jesus Christ, who, by the power that enables him to bring everything under his control, will transform our lowly bodies so that they will be like his glorious body.*

> Romans 8:23, *But our citizenship is in heaven. And we eagerly await a Savior from there, the Lord Jesus Christ, who, by the power that enables him to bring everything under his control, will transform our lowly bodies so that they will be like his glorious body.*

The biblical understanding of sanctification is a paramount doctrine that must be understood correctly. The three phases of sanctification should be seen clearly and understood in order not to venture into error. Those who hold that a believer can lose salvation, do not believe in a positional sanctification. Everything is practical, and the believer must continue to "be good or do good," or salvation will be lost. Those who believe in sinless perfection confuse positional sanctification with ultimate sanctification, thus leading one to erroneously believe that he can experience the benefits of ultimate sanctification here on earth.

In conclusion, we see that steps of sanctification offer us a threefold revelation concerning salvation: *we have been saved through positional sanctification; we are being saved through practical sanctification, and we will ultimately be saved by our final or perfect sanctification.*

Just how does the process of sanctification come about? First, we are told that it is the process which is affected by God the Father. God sanctifies the believer in that he reckons or attributes the righteousness of Christ to him.

> <u>1 Corinthians 1:2,</u> *To the church of God that is in Corinth, to those sanctified in Christ Jesus, called to be saints together with all those who in every place call upon the name of our Lord Jesus Christ, both their Lord and ours.*

Secondly, we are told that Christ sanctifies the believer through His death.

> <u>Hebrews 10:10,</u> *And by that will we have been sanctified through the offering of the body of Jesus Christ once for all.*

Finally, the Holy Spirit sanctifies the believer through His own power.

> <u>Romans 8:2</u>, *For the law of the Spirit of life has set you free in Christ Jesus from the law of sin and death.*

Eternal Security

The doctrine of Eternal security is one of the most beautiful, as well as most mis-understood, truths in the Bible. Controversy has raged over this doctrine throughout Christian history. However, there is no greater subject to bring into consideration, for it is a blessed thing for a person to realize they are not only saved but also secure in Christ.

Baptists believe that once a person has been regenerated by the Holy Spirit and has become a child of God through Jesus Christ, that person can never fall away from Christ and be lost again. This does not imply that the believer does not sin again, because all people sin, including believers. It does mean that the believer can never lapse into such a condition of such spiritual degradation that will result in his complete separation from God. In the previous chapter, the discussion of Positional Sanctification dealt with this issue. Positional sanctification is a work of God and never changes. Eternal security is based on this positional sanctifying work of God.

Those who oppose the doctrine of eternal security will argue against his concept based on an a philosophical argument. They argue that if we believe in the doctrine of eternal security, then it appears that we are actually giving license to sin to the children of God. However, in considering the actual reality of any doctrine, the Bible must be the final authority for all that we believe and practice. The question then is, Does the Bible teach eternal security of the believer? The answer to this question is found in Scripture alone and not philosophy.

First, we see that through His Word, God has promised to save and to keep us saved through all eternity. Consider first of all this scripture:

> John 5:24, *Truly, truly, I say to you, whoever hears my word and believes him who sent me has eternal life. He does not come into judgment, but has passed from death to life.*

In this verse, Jesus promises that those who hear the word and believe on Him who has sent Him: a) have eternal life; b) will not come into judgment and c) have passed from death to life. Here we find an unconditional eternal promise from Jesus himself that if a person receives and believes, that person at the point of belief possesses eternal life. The words "has eternal life" mean that the believer possess eternal life the minute he believed and that he will have eternal life forever. If a person has eternal life and then were to lose it in the future somehow regardless of the reason, then it could be clearly stated that the individual never really had eternal life because it clearly was not eternal. Thus, the believer can know that they are saved now and forevermore.

In addition to this Scripture, let us look carefully at the words of Jesus In John 6.

> John 6:37, *All that the Father gives me will come to me, and whoever comes to me I will never cast out.*

Is this a promise of eternal security? If Jesus Christ has promised to receive all those who come to Him and to never cast them out, then it certainly reveals the glorious truth of eternal security.

Look at the words of Jesus found in John 10.

> John 10:28, *I give them eternal life, and they will never perish, and no one will snatch them out of my hand.*

First, note carefully that this verse says that eternal life is a gift of the Lord Jesus Christ. It is not something that is earned. It stands to reason then if eternal life is a gift which is given to us by God and is not earned by man, then in order for a believer to keep salvation, he does not have to perform a certain amount of works to keep from losing the gift.

Taken together, those two verses emphasize the truth that Jesus will never cast out one of his followers and no one can snatch them out of his hand. How secure we are to know that once we are in the hand of Christ, we can't be snatched away or thrown away—that is eternal security. Look also to Peter's words on the subject of eternal security.

> 1 Peter 1:5, *who by God's power are being guarded through faith for a salvation ready to be revealed in the last time.*

Peter is talking about the matter of salvation and the believer in relation to God. Peter says the reason why the believer cannot be snatched from the hand of the Lord is because they are protected by the power of God. Accordingly, Paul gives further evidence that the believer cannot lose salvation.

> Colossians 3:1-3, *If then you have been raised with Christ, seek the things that are above, where Christ is, seated at the right hand of God. Set your minds on things that are above, not on things that are on earth. For you have died, and your life is hidden with Christ in God.*

Now, if the believer could lose his salvation, there would have to be some force, some individual in the universe which possesses greater power than God. We know that this is an impossibility. Therefore, we see the glorious truth of eternal security of the believer again. Paul adds even more weight to the doctrine of eternal security in Romans.

> Romans 8:38-39, *For I am sure that neither death nor life, nor angels nor rulers, nor things present nor things to come, nor powers, nor height nor depth, nor anything else in all creation, will be able to separate us from the love of God in Christ Jesus our Lord.*

In the above verse, Paul affirms that nothing can separate the believer from the love of God, and Jude says that God is able to keep us from stumbling.

> Jude 24, *To him who is able to keep you from stumbling and to present you before his glorious presence without fault and with great joy...*

Thus, those who would refute the Doctrine of Eternal Security offer a threefold argument: 1) God casts away the constant sinner; 2) a believer who turns his life over to sin and Satan is stolen from God; 3) the believer stumbles away from the faith.

First of all, when a believer sins, God casts him away. We have already seen in John 6:37 that this is not possible according the words of Jesus. Secondly, those who oppose the doctrine of eternal security would say, "well, if a believer sins and turns his life over to the devil he is able to snatch them out of the hand of God." Jesus said in John 10 this also is impossible because of the power of God. Finally, the last argument opposing eternal security is that it is possible for a believer to stumble on his own and fall away from the grace of God. However, we are told in Jude 24 that God is able to keep us from stumbling. It is the Lord who will not allow the believer to come to such a state that he would totally apostatize and completely and ultimately fall away from the grace of God.

We are not only kept by the power of God, but He is able also to keep us from stumbling. Not only does He do that, but we find that He is able to make us stand in the presence of His glory blameless with great joy.

Nowhere in the Bible are we commanded to keep ourselves saved. The word of God plainly declares that eternal security rests purely on God's power and ability to keep one saved.

> John 10:29, *My Father, who has given them to me, is greater than all, and no one is able to snatch them out of the Father's hand.*

> Romans 4:21, *fully convinced that God was able to do what he had promised.*

> Philippians 1:6, *And I am sure of this, that he who began a good work in you will bring it to completion at the day of Jesus Christ.*

> Hebrews 7:25, *Consequently, he is able to save to the uttermost those who draw near to God through him, since he always lives to make intercession for them.*

In considering the matter of believer's being kept by the power of God, take note of the phrases listed above regarding God's power to keep us: "no one is able to snatch them out of the Father's hand"; "God was able to do what he had promised"; "he who began a good work in you will bring it to completion at the day of Jesus Christ"; "he is able to guard until that Day what has been entrusted to me; he is able to save to the uttermost." If those simple phrases were not enough, Peter's words add more clarity to the position of eternal security. Peter says,

> 1 Peter 1:5, *who by God's power are being guarded through faith for a salvation ready to be revealed in the last time.*

Beyond God's power in our Eternal Security, we also can see the believer's hiding place after salvation. When one receives Jesus Christ as his personal Savior, the Bible teaches us that the Holy Triune Godhead actually comes and takes residence in the believer.

Colossians 3:1-3, *For you have died, and your life is hidden with Christ in God.*

So Paul states clearly, that once a person is saved, he/she is hidden with Christ in God. However, Paul even goes further than that by stating not only are we hidden with Christ in God, but God gives every believer His Holy Spirit which makes us the temple of God.

1 Corinthians 6:19-20, *Or do you not know that your body is a temple of the Holy Spirit within you, whom you have from God? You are not your own, for you were bought with a price. So glorify God in your body.*

What a supreme comfort it is to know that no one has the ability or power to remove the believer from the hand of Jesus Christ.

What would need to happen for a believer to lose his or her salvation? There would have to be some power or force that can overcome God, that can overcome Jesus, and remove Jesus out of the hand of God and then remove the believer out of the hand of Jesus Christ. The Bible teaches us that if this were a possibility (which it is not), would be only half the battle. Not only would this force or power have to be able to remove us out of the hand of God and the believer out of the hand of Jesus, but then the same force or power would have to be able to remove the Holy Spirit from living inside the believer. This is what must occur in order for a true child of God to lose salvation, but the power of almighty God says, "No!"

The fact of eternal security also depends on the sacrifice and merit of the Son of God. Through his sacrificial death on the cross, we find that Jesus Christ removed all condemnation forever from the believer.

John 3:18, *Whoever believes in him is not condemned, but whoever does not believe is condemned already, because he has not believed in the name of the only Son of God.*

John 5:24, *Truly, truly, I say to you, whoever hears my word and believes him who sent me has eternal life. He does not come into judgment, but has passed from death to life.*

In these verses, Jesus gave explicit promises to believers that they will not be condemned. Through the substitutionary death of Jesus Christ, He has assumed all of the divine punishment which was due the sinner and has removed any possibility of the believer ever experiencing divine judgment. For Christ to have been our substitute and taken upon himself the divine punishment due to the sinner, and then for the believer to somehow be able to lose his salvation and experience the wrath and judgment, would amount to theological double jeopardy and God making his son a liar. Thus, the apostle Paul states the obvious that there is no condemnation for those who are in Christ.

> Romans 8:1, *There is therefore now no condemnation for those who are in Christ Jesus.*

The Bible tells us that the work of Christ on behalf of the Christian is perpetual. In the Bible, we find that one of the strongest reasons for eternal security of the believer is that Jesus Christ is in constant contact with the believer, ministering before God on their behalf. Further, Jesus Christ paid the full price for our salvation, but it is His life today as He is seated at the right hand of the Father which assures our eternal security. Therefore contact between God and the believer can never be broken because the Bible teaches that Jesus Christ lives forever, and He is constantly in the process of making intercession between the believer and God.

> Hebrews 7:25, *Consequently, he is able to save to the uttermost those who draw near to God through him, since he always lives to make intercession for them.*

The purity of God's grace is also a strong argument in favor of eternal security. Salvation is all of God, and the works of man have absolutely nothing to do with the question of being saved as Scripture clearly attests.

> Romans 11:5-6, *So too at the present time there is a remnant, chosen by grace. But if it is by grace, it is no longer on the basis of works; otherwise grace would no longer be grace.*

> Ephesians 2:8-9, *For by grace you have been saved through faith. And this is not your own doing; it is the gift of God, not a result of works, so that no one may boast.*

The Bible plainly teaches that we can do nothing in order to obtain salvation. Therefore if we can do nothing in order to be saved, we can certainly do nothing in order to be unsaved. If works did not play a part in our initial salvation, how can they play a part in our losing salvation?

> Titus 3:5-7, *he saved us, not because of works done by us in righteousness, but according to his own mercy, by the washing of regeneration and renewal of the Holy Spirit, whom he poured out on us richly through Jesus Christ our Savior, so*

that being justified by his grace we might become heirs according to the hope of eternal life.

It should be noted, that many who teach that a believer can lose salvation also must believe in some form of works based salvation which is completely unbiblical. If a person can earn salvation, then it is reasonable to believe that he or she can lose salvation as well. However, salvation from beginning to end is entirely a work of God and never a work of man. Once a person is truly saved, they cannot lose salvation, and God could not condemn them. Thus, salvation is entirely based on the purity and perfection of God's grace and never at any point contingent on the works of an individual either to gain or lose salvation.

The believer's eternal security is also based on the person and ministry of the Holy Spirit. The Bible teaches that it is through the work of the Holy Spirit that the believer experiences divine regeneration and the divine life.

> 1 Peter 3:18, *For Christ also suffered once for sins, the righteous for the unrighteous, that he might bring us to God, being put to death in the flesh but made alive in the spirit...*

> Romans 8:11, *If the Spirit of him who raised Jesus from the dead dwells in you, he who raised Christ Jesus from the dead will also give life to your mortal bodies through his Spirit who dwells in you.*

The Holy Spirit is also the one who places the believer into the body of Christ. The Apostle Paul speaks of the fact that all believers are baptized in one body by the one Spirit. The ministry of the Holy Spirit to place the believer into the body of Christ as the moment of salvation. This places the believer in a divine union with Christ. If a believer would lose salvation, this union with Christ and the body of Christ would be broken, tearing one from the body of Christ.

> 1 Corinthians 12:13, *For in one Spirit we were all baptized into one body—Jews or Greeks, slaves or free—and all were made to drink of one Spirit.*

Not only does the Holy Spirit place a new believer into the body of Christ, but the Holy Spirit puts Himself into the believer for the purpose of keeping the believer eternally saved. We are told in John that the Holy Spirit will never leave the believer. For the believer to lose his salvation, the Holy Spirit would have to leave him, which the Bible says will not happen.

John 14:16, *And I will ask the Father, and he will give you another advocate to help you and be with you forever...*

Before we leave the subject, we must not forget to point out that it is also the ministry of the Holy Spirit to seal the believer until the day of redemption. In ancient times, the seal was a critical matter. When something was sealed by the king or emperor, then it could only be broken by those who had the authority to do so. The Bible tells us that when the believer receives Jesus Christ as Savior, He is sealed unto the day of Redemption.

Ephesians 4:30, *And do not grieve the Holy Spirit of God, with whom you were sealed for the day of redemption.*

2 Corinthians 1:22, *set his seal of ownership on us, and put his Spirit in our hearts as a deposit, guaranteeing what is to come.*

That means that the Holy Spirit Himself seals the new believer on the day of salvation and that seal will not be opened until the day of redemption. The day of redemption is the day the believer stands in the presence of Eternal God and the presence of the Holy Spirit in the believer's life guarantees that delivery. So the Holy Spirit also ensures eternal security.

The doctrine of Eternal Security is therefore based on

- The Promises of God
- The Power of God
- The Substitutionary Death of Jesus Christ
- The Mediatorship of Jesus Christ
- The Purity of God's Grace
- The work of the Holy Spirit.

But what about the sinning saint? It is not uncommon for someone who disagrees with the doctrine of eternal security to pose a hypothetical example of a sinning saint: They will say, "So you are saying that someone can be saved, live an irresponsible life that never shows any fruit of repentance or godly sorrow, never demonstrate the fruit of the spirit in their lives, and still not lose their salvation?"

Are they saved? Are they eternally secure? My response is pretty simple to that person. No, that person can never lose anything they never had to begin with. I believe if a person says they are a Christian but never demonstrate any fruits that prove that they were a believer, they were never saved. The one exception to this would be a person who accepted Christ just before death like the example of the thief on the cross. A true believer becomes a new Creature in Christ and has been transferred from the kingdom of darkness into the kingdom of light.

Scripture also teaches that the grace of God in our lives leads the believer towards living a holy and separated life.

2 Corinthians 5:17, *Therefore, if anyone is in Christ, he is a new creation. The old has passed away; behold, the new has come.*

1 John 1:6, *If we say we have fellowship with him while we walk in darkness, we lie and do not practice the truth.*

1 John 2:15-16, *Do not love the world or the things in the world. If anyone loves the world, the love of the Father is not in him. For all that is in the world—the desires of the flesh and the desires of the eyes and pride of life—is not from the Father but is from the world.*

Yes, it is true that Christians still sin, which is why John speaks of confession of sins. However, a true believer will experience a godly guilt and conviction of when sin occurs.

1 John 1:9, *If we confess our sins, he is faithful and just and will forgive us our sins and purify us from all unrighteousness.*

Beyond that, the true child of God will have a Holy Spirit given desire to honor God more and more in life. Yes, believers sin and stumble all the time, but a true believer will never have the attitude that sinful actions against God are not a problem. Even further, a true believer would never willfully and completely abandon the faith. Thus, the sinner who only *says* he was saved, but never demonstrates any Christlike activity didn't lose his salvation, he never had it to begin with. Salvation will always be supported by fruit!

Assurance

So many today contend that we cannot really know if we are saved. They say all we can do is work and pray and do the best we can, and hope that God will decide to save us in the end. However, the Bible teaches that we can know that we are saved.

Why do so many people lack assurance of their salvation? Anyone who has spent any time at all in the Christian life, knows there are times when people demonstrate no assurance of salvation. The *first* and obvious reason that many do not have assurance of salvation is that they have never actually been saved. The solution to their problem is the confession of sin and receiving Jesus Christ as Savior.

Another reason why some people have no assurance is because they have a tendency to place too much attention on their own works and begin to doubt their commitment to Christ. Too much emphasis is based on emotions and not simply on faith. For example, an individual who received the Lord Jesus Christ at a very young age would not have experienced lots of emotion, nor would there have been a dynamic change in lifestyle or thinking. However that individual may listen to the testimony of a person who was saved at an older age, and during the course of this testimony, this individual who was saved at an older age will speak of glowing experiences and dynamic changes in life. The ones sitting there who had been saved at an early age may begin to doubt the fact that they were saved because they lack some dynamic experience.

It should be stated again that we often place too much emphasis on the matter of emotions and not on faith. The cure to this issue of doubt is to realize that salvation is not a matter of feelings or emotions, but a matter of faith.

Another cause of doubting is questioning the faithfulness of God to save and keep us. The cure to this problem is a better understanding of God and His word. We must never forget that one of the leading causes of loss of assurance is personal sin. We should realize that when a believer begins to activate or allow sin to be activated in their lives, a distance develops between them and God. Since it is the person of the Holy Spirit who bears witness that we are children of God, when the Holy spirit ceases to be able to operate in the believer, then a natural result would be to lose assurance of salvation.

This doesn't mean that the Holy Spirit has left the believer, but it does mean the Holy Spirit has ceased operating in the believer's life because of disobedient sinfulness. The cure for all personal sin is genuine confessions of sins and renewing our fellowship with God. John assures us of our forgiveness when we confess.

1 John 1:9, *If we confess our sins, he is faithful and just to forgive us our sins and to cleanse us from all unrighteousness.*

A good illustration of this option would be the Prodigal Son that Jesus spoke about in Luke 15. When the Son left the father, he had no conversation with the father nor did he have any fellowship with the father. However, at no point did the son cease to be the father's child. Sin is that way in our lives. If we want to renew our fellowship with God, we must do as the son did and repent and return. That repentance, confession, and returning is what allows the believer to regain the assurance of salvation and ongoing fellowship and conversation with the father.

In closing, we should point out that assurance of salvation may be lost through the failure on the believer's part to practice communion with God. Jesus Christ is not real to many people because they do not daily communicate with Him through worship, bible study, and prayer. Someone has said that absence makes the heart grow fonder. Actually, it can cause the heart to grow forgetful. The Christian faith is a practiced faith just like a good marriage is a practiced, experienced, and daily marriage.

Assurance of salvation can never be based on feelings and emotions. There are times when the believer may not feel as though they are saved. Too much emphasis is based on the matter of feeling. Salvation is a fact not a feeling! Salvation is a matter of faith! It is a matter of trust in God and his Word. Therefore one of the surest ways of having assurance of salvation is to see what the bible actually teaches concerning your relationship with God. Look first at what the Apostle John writes about assurance.

> 1 John 5:13, *I write these things to you who believe in the name of the Son of God that you may know that you have eternal life.*

John is saying that the purpose of writing the book of 1 John was so that the believer in Jesus Christ may know and have absolute assurance of salvation and eternal life. It must be noted that the reason John would write this is because surely there were some who were believers but struggled with salvation just as many believers do today.

Next, let's see what Jesus has to say about our assurance. We are told believers do not have to wait to find out if they are saved or not, but that we are saved and possess eternal life the very minute of receiving Jesus Christ as Savior. Read what Jesus said.

> John 5:24, *Truly, truly, I say to you, whoever hears my word and believes him who sent me has eternal life. He does not come into judgment, but has passed from death to life.*

The emphasis is placed on the statement "**has** eternal life." What Jesus means is the very minute a person receives Jesus Christ as personal savior, he/she possesses eternal life. They don't have to wait to find out whether he is going to get it from God at some point in the future. The believer has it for all eternity from that moment on.

Let's see what the Apostle Paul has to say about assurance. Paul, in his address to Timothy, declared that he knew for a fact that he has been saved.

> 2 Timothy 1:12, *which is why I suffer as I do. But I am not ashamed, for I know whom I have believed, and I am convinced that he is able to guard until that Day what has been entrusted to me.*

The Bible makes it exceedingly clear that those who believe in Jesus Christ can know for absolute certainty they have salvation. God is not the author of confusion and does not want the believer to doubt salvation but wants the believer to walk in full assurance of salvation. However, many Christians miss assurance because they do not read the word of God daily, nor do they live in community with other believers through the life and the ministry of the church.

The following is a list of experiences which may come about as the result of the believer knowing that he is saved. First, the relationships which the believer has with God will become more real and more personal. Certainly the process of prayer will be more real and more personal. Prayer will become viable part of the believer's life. When the believer begins to walk in assurance, the Word of God will be desired. There will be a hunger and thirst for the study and the knowledge of the Word of God.

In addition to these truths, the believer will also become concerned about the unsaved. One of the reasons why more believers are not soul winners is because their personal salvation is not exceedingly real to them. Once the believer truly understands how glorious it is to be a child of God and what Christ has done on their behalf, they will truly realize God has saved the unworthy and they will have the same concern for their friends, neighbors, and relatives. The assured believer will begin to demonstrate a greater concern for the unsaved. Surely, when a believer starts to walk in assurance of salvation, there will be a new understanding and appreciation for the great fellowship which all believers enjoy in the family of God.

> 1 John 1:1-4, *That which was from the beginning, which we have heard, which we have seen with our eyes, which we have looked at and our hands have touched— this we proclaim concerning the Word of life. The life appeared; we have seen it and testify to it, and we proclaim to you the eternal life, which was with the Father and has appeared to us. We proclaim to you what we have seen and heard, so that you also may have fellowship with us. And our fellowship is with the Father and with his Son, Jesus Christ. We write this to make our joy complete.*

How wonderful it is to know that we can have fellowship with God personally and daily, and how truly marvelous it is to know that we have the joy of having fellowship with God's children. There is no greater honor in this world that a person can have than to be a child of God and walk daily in fellowship with his children in the church.

THE DOCTRINE OF THE CHURCH

Matthew 16:18, *And I tell you that you are Peter, and on this rock I will build my church, and the gates of Hades will not overcome it.*

When people today hear the word church, they naturally tend to think of a building or a denomination, but those are not the church biblically speaking. The Greek word translated "church" is *ekklesia* and means "an assembly" or "called-out ones." So at its core, the church is about people, not buildings. *Ekklesia* is used in Scripture at least three different ways: it refers to any group of people who have been called together; it refers to the body of Christ universally; and finally, it refers to a local body of believers.

The universal church is made up of all those who have accepted Jesus Christ as their Lord and Savior regardless of location, denomination, race, or gender. The local church is a group of believers gathered in a particular location. Therefore, the Church is not a building or a denomination, it is the body of Christ made up of all believers (Universally), and exercised in specific places (Local).

The Church is a Living Organism

The church is a living organism consisting of every true believer from every race, country, and denomination. Thus everyone who has received Jesus Christ as Lord and Savior is a member of the Church, which is also referred to synonymously as the Body

137

of Christ. When salvation occurs in an individual's life, Scripture teaches that that new believer is placed into the body of Christ through the baptizing work of the Holy Spirit.

The Bible declares that Christ is the Head of His body, the Church. The Church Universal had its birth on the Day of Pentecost when the Holy Spirit came to form the body of Christ on earth through Salvation and Spirit-baptism.

> 1 Corinthians 12:13, *For we were all baptized by one Spirit so as to form one body—whether Jews or Gentiles, slave or free—and we were all given the one Spirit to drink.*

> Ephesians 1:22-23, *And God placed all things under his feet and appointed him to be head over everything for the church, which is his body, the fullness of him who fills everything in every way.*

The Church As An Organization

Some Christians today de-emphasize the importance of local church and stress only the universal body of Christ. While it is possible to be a member of the Church Universal and not be a member of a local church, that is not the biblical model for a New Testament believer. God's clear pattern for the believer was that a follower of Jesus Christ would be a member of the universal church through salvation and a local church through association.

At the birth of the church, new believers were added to the local church and the importance of the local church is seen throughout the New Testament.

> Acts 2:41, *Those who accepted his message were baptized, and about three thousand were added to their number that day.*

To what were they added? Certainly to the body of Christ, but they were also added to the local body of believers in Jerusalem. That is what led to the establishment of a local Church in Jerusalem.

> Acts 15:2-4, *This brought Paul and Barnabas into sharp dispute and debate with them. So Paul and Barnabas were appointed, along with some other believers, to go up to Jerusalem to see the apostles and elders about this question. The church sent them on their way, and as they traveled through Phoenicia and Samaria, they told how the Gentiles had been converted. This news made all the believers very glad. When they came to Jerusalem, they were welcomed by the church and the apostles and elders, to whom they reported everything God had done through them.*

Paul and Barnabas were called to be the first Christian missionaries and were sent out by the local church in Antioch.

> Acts 13:1-3, *Now in the church at Antioch there were prophets and teachers: Barnabas, Simeon called Niger, Lucius of Cyrene, Manaen (who had been brought up with Herod the tetrarch) and Saul. While they were worshiping the Lord and fasting, the Holy Spirit said, "Set apart for me Barnabas and Saul for the work to which I have called them." So after they had fasted and prayed, they placed their hands on them and sent them off.*

Everywhere they went, these first missionaries preached the Gospel and established local Churches. The purpose of Paul's second missionary journey was to strengthen the Church which had been planted on his first missionary journey.

> Acts 15:36, *Some time later Paul said to Barnabas, "Let us go back and visit the believers in all the towns where we preached the word of the Lord and see how they are doing.*

> Acts 16:4-5, *As they traveled from town to town, they delivered the decisions reached by the apostles and elders in Jerusalem for the people to obey. So the churches were strengthened in the faith and grew daily in numbers.*

The majority of Paul's epistles were either written directly to a local body of believers or were written concerning the organization and doctrine of the local church.

Purpose of the Church

What is the purpose of the church? Many answers are given to that question today. Some see the church as a place for social action; others see it as a place for political influence. Still, others see the church as a place that takes care of the poor or feeds the hungry. While those things are certainly part of the overall ministry of the church, none of those are the purpose of the church. In the Great Commission, Jesus said:

> Matthew 28:19-20, *Therefore go and make disciples of all nations, baptizing them in the name of the Father and of the Son and of the Holy Spirit, and teaching them to obey everything I have commanded you. And surely I am with you always, to the very end of the age.*

In those words, Jesus gives us the explicit purposes of the church which are: to *make* disciples by sharing the Gospel, to *mark* disciples through baptism, and finally, *mold* disciples through teaching them to obey the Word of God.

Evangelism-The Gospel

The Bible is very clear that God loves the lost and gave His Son that all people could receive forgiveness of sin and the gift of eternal life. A healthy church just like a healthy believer will constantly be sharing the Gospel. In His last words to His disciples, Jesus told them that the Holy Spirit would empower them for evangelism and sharing their faith. Thus, one of the evidences of salvation and the Holy Spirit is witnessing for Christ. Jesus said that when the Holy Spirit takes over, His disciples would be witnesses of Him. The Church has the good news of Jesus Christ and the hope of the world, thus every believer should be busy spreading the good news. Perhaps the most cruel thing a person can do is to have the good news of salvation and refuse to share it with those who are lost.

John 3:16, *For God so loved the world that he gave his one and only Son, that whoever believes in him shall not perish but have eternal life.*

Acts 1:8, *But you will receive power when the Holy Spirit comes on you; and you will be my witnesses in Jerusalem, and in all Judea and Samaria, and to the ends of the earth.*

Acts 4:19-20, *But Peter and John replied, "Which is right in God's eyes: to listen to you, or to him? You be the judges! As for us, we cannot help speaking about what we have seen and heard."*

Peter declared that he was a witness by the Holy Spirit of Jesus Christ. When new deacons were appointed in the early church, the result was the salvation of many. The Holy Spirit took Philip out into the desert to witness to an Ethiopian eunuch. Immediately upon his salvation, Paul became a witness of Christ. God wants the lost of the world to be saved, and He wants every believer and every church to evangelize and share the Gospel actively.

Acts 5:29-32, *Peter and the other apostles replied: "We must obey God rather than human beings! The God of our ancestors raised Jesus from the dead—whom you killed by hanging him on a cross. God exalted him to his own right hand as Prince and Savior that he might bring Israel to repentance and forgive their sins. We are witnesses of these things, and so is the Holy Spirit, whom God has given to those who obey him."*

Acts 6:1-4,7, *In those days when the number of disciples was increasing, the Hellenistic Jews among them complained against the Hebraic Jews because their widows were being overlooked in the daily distribution of food. So the Twelve gathered all the disciples together and said, "It would not be right for us to neglect the ministry of the word of God in order to wait on tables. Brothers and sisters, choose seven men from among you who are known to be full of the Spirit and wisdom. We will turn this responsibility over to them and will give our attention to prayer and the ministry of the word...." So the word of God spread. The number of disciples in Jerusalem increased rapidly, and a large number of priests became obedient to the faith.*

Spiritual Training

Not only does God want the Church to proclaim the Gospel and bring the lost to Christ, but He also desires the Church teach the Word of God so that all believers may become mature believers. God wants every child of His to grow in grace and knowledge of Jesus Christ. The only way a believer can truly grow spiritually is through the study of God's Word either by hearing it, reading it, discussing it, or practicing it.

<u>2 Peter 3:18,</u> *But grow in the grace and knowledge of our Lord and Savior Jesus Christ. To him be glory both now and forever! Amen.*

<u>2 Timothy 2:15,</u> *Do your best to present yourself to God as one approved, a worker who does not need to be ashamed and who correctly handles the word of truth.*

<u>2 Timothy 3:16-17,</u> *All Scripture is God-breathed and is useful for teaching, rebuking, correcting and training in righteousness, so that the servant of God may be thoroughly equipped for every good work.*

God in his infinite wisdom has given gifted people to the Church for the purpose of teaching, training, and equipping the saints for the work of service. The Bible is the textbook of the church. Many good books have been written by many people throughout the ages, but none compare or even come close to the Scriptures. For only the Scriptures are "God-breathed and useful for teaching, rebuking, correcting and training in righteousness." With that in mind, the Bible above and beyond any other book is what must be taught, read, and studied in every church and by every Christian everywhere at all times—there is no substitute!

<u>Ephesians 4:11-16,</u> *So Christ himself gave the apostles, the prophets, the evangelists, the pastors and teachers, to equip his people for works of service, so that the body of Christ may be built up until we all reach unity in the faith and in the knowledge of the Son of God and become mature, attaining to the whole measure of the fullness of Christ. Then we will no longer be infants, tossed back and forth by the waves, and blown here and there by every wind of teaching and by the cunning*

and craftiness of people in their deceitful scheming. Instead, speaking the truth in love, we will grow to become in every respect the mature body of him who is the head, that is, Christ. From him the whole body, joined and held together by every supporting ligament, grows and builds itself up in love, as each part does its work.

Membership in the Church

It bears repeating again, that one does not have to be a member of a local Church in order to be saved. However, it should also be noted that a true believer will want to become a member of a local body of believers.

<u>Hebrews 10:25</u>, *…not giving up meeting together, as some are in the habit of doing, but encouraging one another—and all the more as you see the Day approaching.*

Since the Church is a divine organization founded upon divine truth and revelation of salvation through Jesus Christ, God's only Son, then it naturally follows that the primary qualification for membership in the local body is a personal regeneration.

Salvation: That is, only those who have personally received Jesus Christ as personal Saviour are eligible for Church membership. It must be noted with humility that the earthly church with earthly members cannot completely guarantee that only Christians join a local church. However, the church should make the effort to clearly communicate the gospel with each individual who desires membership in the church. To fail to share the gospel with all who express a desire to join the church might give some the false hope that by joining the church they are automatically eternally saved.

Confession of Faith: Before the Church can receive an individual into its fellowship, that individual should at least make a personal confession of his or her faith. This confession of faith is necessary because it is that shared confession that binds believers together through the death, burial, and resurrection of Jesus Christ. Jesus made it clear that true believers will find great joy in making their relationship with Christ public, and Jesus also made it clear that the church's primary objective is the share the gospel.

<u>1 John 1:1-3,</u> *That which was from the beginning, which we have heard, which we have seen with our eyes, which we have looked at and our hands have touched—this we proclaim concerning the Word of life. The life appeared; we have seen it and testify to it, and we proclaim to you the eternal life, which was with the Father and has appeared to us. We proclaim to you what we have seen and heard, so that you also may have fellowship with us. And our fellowship is with the Father and with his Son, Jesus Christ.*

Matthew 10:32-33, *Whoever acknowledges me before others, I will also acknowledge before my Father in heaven. But whoever disowns me before others, I will disown before my Father in heaven.*

Baptism: Another condition of church members is biblical baptism. The biblical pattern of baptism is after salvation and by immersion. According to Paul, Baptism is a visible picture of the death, burial, and resurrection of Jesus Christ.

Romans 6:4, *We were therefore buried with him through baptism into death in order that, just as Christ was raised from the dead through the glory of the Father, we too may live a new life.*

When a person is buried, they are not laid out on the ground, and a little dirt sprinkled on them. No, they are buried beneath the surface of the ground, and true baptism consists of the believer being placed beneath the surface of the water. When Jesus was placed in the tomb, He was placed fully in the tomb. As such, if baptism is symbolic of the death of Jesus Christ it naturally flows that the water would completely entomb the individual.

Lifestyle: Another condition of Church membership is Christian behavior or lifestyle. Scripture makes it clear that the believer is required by God to live a life which is in keeping with his or her profession of faith. Church membership should be recognized as a holy obligation to both God and the other church members. Paul tells us that the behavior of individual members should be a matter of concern for the local church.

Ephesians 4:1, *As a prisoner for the Lord, then, I urge you to live a life worthy of the calling you have received.*

Colossians 1:10, *...so that you may live a life worthy of the Lord and please him in every way: bearing fruit in every good work, growing in the knowledge of God...*

1 Corinthians 5:1-5, *It is actually reported that there is sexual immorality among you, and of a kind that even pagans do not tolerate: A man is sleeping with his father's wife. And you are proud! Shouldn't you rather have gone into mourning and have put out of your fellowship the man who has been doing this? For my part, even though I am not physically present, I am with you in spirit. As one who is present with you in this way, I have already passed judgment in the name of our Lord Jesus on the one who has been doing this. So when you are assembled and I am with you in spirit, and the power of our Lord Jesus is present, hand this man over to Satan for the destruction of the flesh, so that his spirit may be saved on the day of the Lord.*

In summation, as best as the local body can manage, church membership is for saved individuals who have confessed their faith, have been biblically baptized, and who are seeking to live a godly and growing lifestyle.

Typically, evangelical church membership in a local church can be achieved in one of three ways: First, a person can make a profession of faith in Jesus Christ and be biblically baptized; Second, an individual can transfer a letter of membership from one like-minded congregation to another; Third, a person can make a personal statement of faith by stating that they have been saved and biblically baptized at a previous time.

Responsibility of Church Membership

Each and every member of the local body of Christ should recognize that it is a high and holy thing to be a Church member. We are to recall that Jesus Christ loves the Church and gave Himself for it. Therefore, every individual Church member must recognize that there are certain responsibilities which are incumbent upon every member.

The Apostle Paul exhorts Christians to be diligent to preserve the unity of the Spirit in the bond of peace. It is the desire of the Holy Spirit that unity prevail among believers, and if allowed to do His work, the Holy Spirit will bring about spiritual unity. The believer is to be careful and delighted to preserve this unity.

Ephesians 4:3, *Make every effort to keep the unity of the Spirit through the bond of peace.*

Philippians 2:1-5, *Therefore if you have any encouragement from being united with Christ, if any comfort from his love, if any common sharing in the Spirit, if any tenderness and compassion, then make my joy complete by being like-minded, having the same love, being one in spirit and of one mind. Do nothing out of selfish ambition or vain conceit. Rather, in humility value others above yourselves, not looking to your own interests but each of you to the interests of the others. In your relationships with one another, have the same mindset as Christ Jesus.*

It should be noted from the passage above that believers in Christ do not create unity in the church or among other believers—that is the work and ministry of the Holy Spirit. All a believer can do is either preserve that unity by living in harmony or destroy it by living in disharmony or acting in a disunifying way. So it is the responsibility of every believer in Christ to preserve the unity in the local body of believers, i.e., the church.

Another important responsibility of every member in the church is service and working. The Apostle Paul said that part of what holds the church together is when believers join together in supporting each other and growing with each person doing their work. Too often in churches, much of the work is done by too few of the members. This was never God's design or plan for the church. When God designed the church, every member had a part to play. The church is like our body—every part of our body needs to work for us to function in a fully healthy manner. If a large part of our physical body stopped working, we would immediately go to the doctor. However, too often the church strives to function with most of the body not participating in the work of the church.

> Ephesians 4:11-16, *So Christ himself gave the apostles, the prophets, the evangelists, the pastors and teachers, to equip his people for works of service, so that the body of Christ may be built up until we all reach unity in the faith and in the knowledge of the Son of God and become mature, attaining to the whole measure of the fullness of Christ. Then we will no longer be infants, tossed back and forth by the waves, and blown here and there by every wind of teaching and by the cunning and craftiness of people in their deceitful scheming. Instead, speaking the truth in love, we will grow to become in every respect the mature body of him who is the head, that is, Christ. From him the whole body, joined and held together by every supporting ligament, grows and builds itself up in love, as each part does its work.*

When Jesus began His earthly ministry, He did not establish a board of advisors. Instead, He called disciples. If there is anything that is explicitly taught in the Bible about the New Testament Church, it is this: There are no bystanders in the kingdom of God. There are no grandstands in the arena of faith. The Word of God makes it clear that God's will is that every believer be involved in working in the local church. Notice again the words that the church grows and builds itself up as "each part does its work." While every member's work may differ a little in function, the working will always involve serving, giving, loving, and sharing with others. As such the church grows and is built up.

> Hebrews 4:14-16, *Therefore, since we have a great high priest who has ascended into heaven, Jesus the Son of God, let us hold firmly to the faith we profess. For we do not have a high priest who is unable to empathize with our weaknesses, but we have one who has been tempted in every way, just as we are—yet he did not sin. Let us then approach God's throne of grace with confidence, so that we may receive mercy and find grace to help us in our time of need.*

Fellowship in the Church

What do you think of when you hear the word fellowship? Most people believe that it means getting together or hanging out. When the New Testament talks about fellowship, it is discussed in two parts: positional fellowship and practical fellowship.

In the New Testament, every believer is placed into the body of Christ by the Holy

Spirit, and as a result, all believers are members of one another. The Church body is compared to the human body where the tissues are connected—muscles, bones, ligaments, and organs. Each part of an individual's body has a position in the same body—this is similar to positional fellowship.

Similarly, all members of a church are united in a positional relationship with the Lord Jesus Christ. The health and welfare of the body of Christ, its witness and testimony are dependent upon the faithful ministering of every member to each other. For a more detailed description of the work of each member in the church, please refer back to the chapter on the Holy Spirit and the discussion of Spiritual Gifts and their value to individual believers and the body of Christ.

> I Corinthians 12:13, *For we were all baptized by one Spirit so as to form one body—whether Jews or Gentiles, slave or free—and we were all given the one Spirit to drink.*

The Greek word used in the New Testament for fellowship is *koinonia,* meaning communion, fellowship, or agreement. Actually, it speaks of a basis of agreement. God never intended for the church to simply be a building. The church is a communion, fellowship, and agreement of individual members. Fellowship speaks of a common ground of beliefs, words, behaviors, and actions. The purpose of the church goes well beyond a simple social organization as seen in 1 John 1:3. In that passage, we see the biblical basis for common ground. John tells his readers they have fellowship with the Father and the Son, Jesus Christ. Therefore the basis for true Christian fellowship is found in the person of God and His Son Jesus Christ. There can be no true spiritual fellowship apart from a close walk with God the Father, God the Son, and God the Holy Spirit. This is the common ground which every believer has with one another.

Certainly, there are times when believers get together and go out to eat or play games and fellowship in some way. Those are good and healthy expressions of true fellowship. However, the basis of that true fellowship is a relationship with Jesus Christ.

> 1 John 1:3, *We proclaim to you what we have seen and heard, so that you also may have fellowship with us. And our fellowship is with the Father and with his Son, Jesus Christ.*

True fellowship is a great deal more spiritual and significant than most believers realize. It is communion which we have with God which is the basis for the strength and fellowship of the local Church. Much damage has been brought into the local Church and the cause of Christ because many Christians do not understand the true significance of

Christian fellowship.

Jesus Christ lives within every believer through the Holy Spirit. When the church and its members realize the basis for their fellowship, the impact of the Christian Church could and should be far greater than it is in most cases. Jesus made it clear that the world will take notice to the power of genuine fellowship among believers when we rightly demonstrate our love for each other.

> John 13:34-35, *A new command I give you: Love one another. As I have loved you, so you must love one another. By this everyone will know that you are my disciples, if you love one another.*

As Jesus stated, the practical outworking of our fellowship with one another is love, and the visible manifestation of our love for other believers will let everyone know we are a Christian. The positional fellowship, communion, and agreement we have with God affect the practical fellowship we have with God's children. Because God loves us, we not only love Him, but we love those God loves.

> 1 John 4:7-9, *Dear friends, let us love one another, for love comes from God. Everyone who loves has been born of God and knows God. Whoever does not love does not know God, because God is love. This is how God showed his love among us: He sent his one and only Son into the world that we might live through him.*

Ordinances of the Church

Baptism and the Lord's Supper are correctly called ordinances of the church because they have been ordained or instituted by Christ Himself. They are not considered sacraments because there is no sacrificial value in them. The reason for the term ordinance in relation to baptism and the Lord's supper is because the use of these terms helps to define their nature, making them simple ceremonies performed as a symbol of loyalty or obedience to the commands of Jesus Christ.

Baptism

Biblical baptism or Christian baptism is by immersion in water in the name of the Father, the Son, and the Holy Spirit. For those who believe and practice baptism by immersion, it is firmly stated that the ordinance of Christian baptism follows the pattern and teaching of John the Baptist.

> Mark 1:4-8, *And so John the Baptist appeared in the wilderness, preaching a baptism of repentance for the forgiveness of sins. The whole Judean countryside and all the people of Jerusalem went out to him. Confessing their sins, they were baptized by him in the Jordan River. John wore clothing made of camel's hair, with a leather belt around his waist, and he ate locusts and wild honey. And this was his message: "After me comes the one more powerful than I, the straps of whose sandals I am not worthy to stoop down and untie. I baptize you with water, but he will baptize you with the Holy Spirit.*

The manner of biblical baptism is noted throughout the New Testament and was submitted to by the Lord Jesus Christ Himself when he was baptized by John. Subsequently, Christ commanded His followers to teach all men His commandments and to baptize them for the purpose of revealing their faith in Jesus Christ to the world. Therefore, the ordinance of baptism is practiced and taught from the authority and example of Christ.

> Mark 1: 9-11, *At that time Jesus came from Nazareth in Galilee and was baptized by John in the Jordan. Just as Jesus was coming up out of the water, he saw heaven being torn open and the Spirit descending on him like a dove. And a voice came from heaven: "You are my Son, whom I love; with you I am well pleased."*

> Matthew 28:19-20, *Therefore go and make disciples of all nations, baptizing them in the name of the Father and of the Son and of the Holy Spirit, and teaching them to obey everything I have commanded you. And surely I am with you always, to the very end of the age.*

One of the primary questions about Christian baptism relates to method. What is the New Testament method of baptism? It can be clearly stated that the means of baptism recorded in the New Testament was always by immersion. There cannot be found one single account in the New Testament where anyone was sprinkled for Christian baptism.

The New Testament accounts of baptism, clearly show the implication that the people who went to John the Baptist for baptism went down into the the Jordan river to be baptized. In the baptism of Jesus, we are told that Jesus was baptized in the Jordan river and after His baptism, Jesus went up out of the water. Two facts seem evident from these passages: Jesus was baptized by immersion, and if the believer desires to follow the Lord in baptism, going down into the water and coming out of the water is the biblical model.

> Matthew 3:4-6, *John's clothes were made of camel's hair, and he had a leather belt around his waist. His food was locusts and wild honey. People went out to him from*

Jerusalem and all Judea and the whole region of the Jordan. Confessing their sins, they were baptized by him in the Jordan River.

Matthew 3:16, *As soon as Jesus was baptized, he went up out of the water. At that moment heaven was opened, and he saw the Spirit of God descending like a dove and alighting on him.*

In the book of Acts, when Philip prepared the newly converted eunuch for baptism, the Scriptures record that they both went down into the water. If Philip was merely going to sprinkle the eunuch, why was it necessary for them both to go down into the water? Surely, the eunuch was carrying enough drinking water in his carriage to perform the task of sprinkling. The only logical answer is that both went down into the water so Philip could immerse the eunuch.

Acts 8:39, *When they came up out of the water, the Spirit of the Lord suddenly took Philip away, and the eunuch did not see him again, but went on his way rejoicing.*

In addition to scriptural argument, we find that the very meaning of the word "baptism" indicates immersion. *Bapto* is the Greek word which means to dip, dip in, or immerse, and is the root word of *baptizo* which is translated "baptize." The word literally means to dunk or immerse. The verb can be seen where Jesus dipped a piece of bread in the sop and in Revelation where the robe is dipped in blood.

John 13:26, *Jesus answered, "It is the one to whom I will give this piece of bread when I have dipped it in the dish." Then, dipping the piece of bread, he gave it to Judas, the son of Simon Iscariot.*

Revelation 19:13, *He is dressed in a robe dipped in blood, and his name is the Word of God.*

The fact is the English word "baptism" that we see in Scripture was a transliteration instead of a translation. The reason for this is simple. When the King James Version of the Bible was translated, the Church of England held to the erroneous, but historical, position of baptism by sprinkling. The translators certainly did not want to offend the Church of England in their translation of the Bible; therefore, instead of calling John the Immerser, they called him John the Baptizer or John the Baptist. Instead of translating the Greek word to say immerse they translated the Greek word into Baptist. If we had an accurate translation of the word "baptism" in that first Bible, we would always find the word immersion.

Therefore, the only method of baptism used in the New Testament was immersion.

There has been no change in God's Word; thus, the only method of baptism which has biblical support is immersion. It should be noted here that many Churches practice sprinkling because they feel that the church has the authority to decide how the individual is to be baptized. However, the Church does not have authority over Jesus and the Word of God; rather, the Word of God and Jesus have authority over the church.

When did sprinkling enter the history of the church as a form of baptism? The earliest known deviation from the scriptural teaching concerning baptism by immersion is found in 250 A.D. when a man name Novation was baptized on his deathbed. Since he was physically unable to be immersed, it was decided that he would be sprinkled or have baptismal waters brought to him and poured on him. It should also be noted that those who performed the act of this deathbed baptism did so with the hopes that this sprinkling would help assure the dying man's salvation. However, baptism is an act of obedience and has nothing to do with a person's salvation; it is not necessary that a person have a deathbed baptism.

Many who argue for sprinkling as opposed to immersion say the method or mode of baptism is insignificant as long as a genuine spirit of the ordinance is maintained. While this may be true to some extent, it should be our priority to uphold the Word of God to its highest standard and form whenever possible. It has also been stated that immersion was changed for those who were ill and unable to be immersed.

Who is to be baptized?

In the New Testament, baptism was only administered to those who consciously placed their trust and faith in Jesus Christ and confessed their sins. As we look at Scripture, without exception, every person who was baptized in the New Testament had previously expressed a belief in Christ as Savior before they were baptized.

Acts 8:36-39 *As they traveled along the road, they came to some water and the eunuch said, "Look, here is water. What can stand in the way of my being baptized?" And he gave orders to stop the chariot. Then both Philip and the eunuch went down into the water and Philip baptized him. When they came up out of the water, the Spirit of the Lord suddenly took Philip away, and the eunuch did not see him again, but went on his way rejoicing.*

Acts 9:17-18 *Then Ananias went to the house and entered it. Placing his hands on Saul, he said, "Brother Saul, the Lord—Jesus, who appeared to you on the road as you were coming here—has sent me so that you may see again and be filled with* *the Holy Spirit." Immediately, something like scales fell from Saul's eyes, and he could see again. He got up and was baptized.*

It should be noted that there is not one account in the New Testament of an infant being baptized. Some have argued that the practice of infant baptism can be surmised from the account of the Philippian Jailer. While it is true from this account that the jailer's entire family was baptized, the ages of his children were not given. However, the Apostle clearly states that the prerequisite for salvation was "believing in the Lord Jesus." Then it says they spoke the word of the Lord to Him (the Jailer) and all the others in his household (his family and children). The clear insinuation is that all who were in his household were of the age where they could hear the message and respond to the message of faith thus leading to their baptism.

Acts 16:30-33, He then brought them out and asked, "Sirs, what must I do to be saved? They replied, "Believe in the Lord Jesus, and you will be saved—you and your household." Then they spoke the word of the Lord to him and to all the others in his house. At that hour of the night the jailer took them and washed their wounds; then immediately he and all his household were baptized.

Not only does the word baptism mean to immerse or dip, and the method of baptism seen throughout the New Testament is immersion, but also baptism by immersion is the method which best portrays the death, burial, and resurrection of Jesus Christ.

Romans 6:3-5, Or don't you know that all of us who were baptized into Christ Jesus were baptized into his death? We were therefore buried with him through baptism into death in order that, just as Christ was raised from the dead through the glory of the Father, we too may live a new life. For if we have been united with him in a death like his, we will certainly also be united with him in a resurrection like his.

When a person accepts Jesus as Savior, they are considering themselves dead and buried to sin and raised to live a new life that is pleasing to God. Immersion then is the only method of baptism which gives full expression to the idea of dying and being buried to sin and raised to walk in the new life of Christ.

Romans 6:12-14, Therefore do not let sin reign in your mortal body so that you obey its evil desires. Do not offer any part of yourself to sin as an instrument of wickedness, but rather offer yourselves to God as those who have been brought from death to life; and offer every part of yourself to him as an instrument of righteousness. For sin shall no longer be your master, because you are not under the law, but under grace.

Why don't we believe that baptism is essential for salvation? First, because of the thief on the cross. Although the man had no opportunity to be baptized, Jesus still promised him that he would go with Him to Paradise. Second, salvation is by grace alone and no works are needed or required. Third, the only place in Scripture where a person directly asked "what must I do to be saved" in Scripture is found in Acts 16. If baptism was a requirement of salvation, this would have been the perfect place to add it as a necessity. Finally, the Apostle Paul, who was specifically sent by God as a messenger of the gospel to the Gentiles, declared he was not sent to baptize but to preach the Gospel.

> _Luke 23:39-43,_ One of the criminals who hung there hurled insults at him: "Aren't you the Messiah? Save yourself and us!" But the other criminal rebuked him. "Don't you fear God," he said, "since you are under the same sentence? We are punished justly, for we are getting what our deeds deserve. But this man has done nothing wrong." Then he said, "Jesus, remember me when you come into your kingdom." Jesus answered him, "Truly I tell you, today you will be with me in paradise."

> _Titus 3:5-7,_ He saved us, not because of righteous things we had done, but because of his mercy. He saved us through the washing of rebirth and renewal by the Holy Spirit, whom he poured out on us generously through Jesus Christ our Savior, so that, having been justified by his grace, we might become heirs having the hope of eternal life.

> _Ephesians 2:8-9,_ For it is by grace you have been saved, through faith—and this is not from yourselves, it is the gift of God—not by works, so that no one can boast.

> _Acts 16:30-31,_ He then brought them out and asked, "Sirs, what must I do to be saved?" They replied, "Believe in the Lord Jesus, and you will be saved—you and your household."

> _1 Corinthians 1:17,_ For Christ did not send me to baptize, but to preach the gospel—not with wisdom and eloquence, lest the cross of Christ be emptied of its power.

The most difficult passage to deal with as it relates to the idea of salvation and baptism is found in Acts 2:28.

> _Acts 2:38,_ Peter replied, "Repent and be baptized, every one of you, in the name of Jesus Christ for the forgiveness of your sins. And you will receive the gift of the Holy Spirit.

In that verse, the Apostle Peter declares "repent and be baptized." The proponents of baptismal regeneration have made much out of this verse claiming that here Peter is teaching that baptism is necessary for salvation. This idea is problematic for two reasons. First, is the Greek word _eis_ which is translated "for" in the passage. The word _eis_ can be rendered in one of two ways. It can be understood as meaning "for" or it can be understood as meaning "because." Both are equally acceptable in the Greek. If it is understood as "for the forgiveness of your sins" then one can rightly say Peter is saying that repentance and baptism lead to salvation. However, if it Greek word *eis* is understood as "because" then it can be stated that people can be baptized because their repentance has already led to forgiveness and salvation.

Further leading to the translation that "baptism" is because of their repentance and salvation is that in the next two chapters when Peter is still preaching about salvation he mentions repentance for salvation, but he does not mention baptism.

Acts 3:19, Repent, then, and turn to God, so that your sins may be wiped out, that times of refreshing may come from the Lord,

Another grammatical reason to say with assurance that Peter was not teaching baptismal regeneration can be found in the original Greek which changes from singular to plural and from second person to third person, which is not perceptible in the English translation. The verb "repent" is in the second person plural and the phrase "for the forgiveness of your sins" is also in the second person plural. So repent and forgiveness of your sins clearly flow together in the original language. However, the verb "be baptized" is in the third person singular. The result of this change in person and plurality leads to a more accurate way of understanding Peter's words as "you all (plural) repent for the forgiveness of all of your(plural) sins, and let each one of you(singular) be baptized (singular)."

The teaching of baptismal regeneration can be rejected by the fact that baptism is not mentioned in the three most commonly agreed upon salvation passages in the New Testament.

John 3:16, For God so loved the world that he gave his one and only Son, that whoever believes in him shall not perish but have eternal life.

Romans 10:9-13, If you declare with your mouth, "Jesus is Lord," and believe in your heart that God raised him from the dead, you will be saved. For it is with your heart that you believe and are justified, and it is with your mouth that you profess your faith and are saved. As Scripture says, "Anyone who believes in him will never be put to shame." For there is no difference between Jew and Gentile—the same Lord is Lord of all and richly blesses all who call on him, for, "Everyone who calls on the name of the Lord will be saved."

Ephesians 2:8-9, For it is by grace you have been saved, through faith—and this is not from yourselves, it is the gift of God—not by works, so that no one can boast. For we are God's handiwork, created in Christ Jesus to do good works, which God prepared in advance for us to do.

In conclusion, biblical baptism is best understood as an ordinance of the church that is practiced by a believer after the point of salvation. The biblical mode of baptism is by immersion, representing the death, burial, and resurrection of Jesus and does not complete nor is it necessary for salvation. Baptism is an important act of obedience for every Christian just like church membership, but it is not a necessary part of salvation.

The Lord's Supper

The Lord's Supper is the other ordinance of the New Testament Church. It was originated by the Lord Jesus Christ with His disciples prior to His death. Jesus instituted the Lord's Supper as an ordinance to remember His death on the cross and the fact that His blood would be shed for the forgiveness of sins. Jesus tells the disciples that the Lord's Supper is a way for them to remember His sacrifice. The bread symbolizes His body that would be beaten and nailed to a cross, and the wine symbolizes His blood that would be shed for the sins of the world.

> *Luke 22:17-20,* After taking the cup, he gave thanks and said, "Take this and divide it among you. For I tell you I will not drink again from the fruit of the vine until the kingdom of God comes." And he took bread, gave thanks and broke it, and gave it to them, saying, "This is my body given for you; do this in remembrance of me." In the same way, after the supper he took the cup, saying, "This cup is the new covenant in my blood, which is poured out for you."

The Apostle Paul also led the Corinthians believers to practice the Lord's Supper and used the same idea of "remembrance" as Jesus himself did as it relates to the Lord's Supper. Thus, when the church gathers for the Lord's Supper, the elements of bread and wine serve as reminders of the real sacrifice of Jesus on the cross.

> *1 Corinthians 11:23-26,* For I received from the Lord what I also passed on to you: The Lord Jesus, on the night he was betrayed, took bread, and when he had given thanks, he broke it and said, "This is my body, which is for you; do this in remembrance of me." In the same way, after supper he took the cup, saying, "This cup is the new covenant in my blood; do this, whenever you drink it, in remembrance of me." For whenever you eat this bread and drink this cup, you proclaim the Lord's death until he comes.

There are two primary views of the Lord's Supper that try to add more meaning and significance to the elements of the bread and the wine that are not biblical. The first is called "transubstantiation" which means "a change of substance" and is taught and believed by the Roman Catholic Church. The Roman Catholic Church teaches that when the Priest consecrates the elements, the bread and wine actually change into the literal body and blood of Jesus. As such, the Catholic Church teaches that when a person receives the Lord's Supper, they are actually receiving more saving and sanctifying grace from God.

Another less extreme unbiblical view of the Lord's Supper is called "consubstantiation." At the time of the Reformation, Martin Luther rejected many teachings of the Roman Catholic Church including teaching "transubstantiation." In its place, Martin Luther developed the idea of "consubstantiation" which teaches that the elements of bread and wine don't actually change as the Roman Catholics taught, but upon their blessing as spiritual combining of the body and blood and actually bring grace to the recipient. This view of the Lord's Supper also has no biblical support.

The proper view of the Lord's Supper is the bread and the wine are symbols of Christ's body and blood which were offered upon Calvary's cross for our sins. The Lord's Supper does not impart any special or added grace to the life of the believer or the unbeliever. However, the Lord's Supper does serve as a special time for believers to remember and look back to the sacrificial death of Jesus Christ on the cross.

Romans 5:8, But God demonstrates his own love for us in this: While we were still sinners, Christ died for us.

Thus the Lord's Supper is a reminder to the believer of the high-cost Jesus paid on the cross for the forgiveness of our sins. For the unbeliever viewing believers partaking the Lord's Supper, the ordinance is a proclamation that only the death of Jesus Christ was the sufficient payment for sinfulness and is the only hope of forgiveness and salvation.

1 Corinthians 11:26, For whenever you eat this bread and drink this cup, you proclaim the Lord's death until he comes.

How often should the church practice the ordinance of the Lord's Supper? It is not uncommon for the question of timing to come up in relationship to the Lord's Supper. Some denominations practice the Lord's Supper every week, others observe it monthly, and still others quarterly. What does Scripture say? The Bible does not tell us when or how often the church is to commemorate the Lord's Supper. The only instruction we are given in Scripture about the timing of the Lord's Supper is found in Paul's words to the

Corinthians where he says, "whenever you eat the bread or drink the cup." Thus, there is no set frequency in Scripture that the church is given to receive the Lord's Supper; therefore, it is best to leave that up to each individual congregation.

Spiritual Authority in the Church

Every agency or organization that God has established on earth has an authority or organizational structure. God has created an authority structure in the government, on the job, and in the home, and God has also given us spiritual authority in the Church.

The Bible delineates several types of authority. First, there is Divine Authority. The Bible Tells us that all authority is of God, and there is no authority except from God. God is the absolute authority in everything, and He is the creator of all authority structures.

> _Romans 13:1, Let everyone be subject to the governing authorities, for there is no authority except that which God has established. The authorities that exist have been established by God._

Second, there is Delegated Authority. Delegated authority means that God, in certain situations and organizations, appointed or delegated His authority to another individual or entity for the purpose of overseeing an organizational structure from a human perspective. This delegated authority structure is seen in earthly governments, in the home, and we also see it in the church. Delegated authority was given by God to mankind because the sinfulness of all mankind, if left unchecked, would cause significant harm to societies, the home, and even in the church.

> _Romans 13:4, For the one in authority is God's servant for your good. But if you do wrong, be afraid, for rulers do not bear the sword for no reason. They are God's servants, agents of wrath to bring punishment on the wrongdoer. Therefore, it is necessary to submit to the authorities, not only because of possible punishment but also as a matter of conscience._

It must also be noted that because of sinfulness, we are prone to reject or abuse authority. Government authorities and leaders are not perfect and sometimes inflict great harm on the citizenry they are supposed to serve, protect, and care for. Family structures also breakdown when authority figures in the home abuse or abdicate their authority and cause great harm within the family. The church also has a delegated authority structure which is meant to help the church function as God has designed for the benefit of members and the spreading of the Gospel.

Where does delegated authority in the church lie? What does the authority structure in the church look like? The Bible makes it plain that all things have been created by God's authority, and all physical, as well as spiritual laws of the universe, are maintained by His authority.

> *Hebrews 1:3, The Son is the radiance of God's glory and the exact representation of his being, sustaining all things by his powerful word.*

God set His church in a divine and perfect order. The problem today within the Church is that humanity has taken God's delegated authority and dismantled it, or reconstructed it, according to human principles or practices. In the church, Jesus is the undisputed head of the church. This means that Jesus is the head of both the universal church as well as each individual local church.

> *Colossians 1:17-18, And he is before all things, and in him all things hold together. And he is the head of the body, the church...*

> *Ephesians 5:23-24, Christ is the head of the church, his body, and is himself its Savior. Now as the church submits to Christ,*

So Jesus is the undisputed head of the church and the ultimate authority in the church. However, God has chosen to structure the church in such a way that each church also has a delegated earthly authority structure. This means that church leaders' ultimate authority and love go to the Lord Jesus Christ. Jesus determines the practice and order in the church, and church leaders should also always operate with a sense of humility and surrender to the will of Christ for the church.

As one surveys that landscape of church leadership, many different models can be found. Some churches operate with one individual as head over. Other churches work with a group of people leading the church. Still, other churches operate by a committee structure. Some believe that delegated authority is to be found in the deacon body.

Which one is biblical?

Before we discuss the biblical model of leadership in the church, it bears noting that there are two models of leadership in the church that are seen today that are unscriptural. The first unscriptural model of church leadership is that of a "one person" rule in the church. This one person is considered a dictator and rules over the congregation or group with a heavy hand and with unquestioned power. This dictator form of church leadership is unscriptural.

The second unscriptural form of church leadership is full "congregational-rule." This "congregational-rule" gives everyone an equal vote and gives no specific leadership authority to the pastor or elders. This is also an unscriptural model of church leadership because it fails to acknowledge the reality that not all church members are at the same level spiritually.

What is the biblical model of authority in the church? The legitimate position of authority found in the Bible is with the Pastor and elders. Notice two things about that statement before we dig deeper into the roles of the pastor and elders in the church. First, by definition Pastor and Elders are a group of individuals who lead the church, not an individual. Second, this also means that there is an authority structure within the church where certain spiritual individuals are set above the rest of the congregation to provide spiritual and organizational leadership to the church.

Three word studies will help us determine the matters of spiritual authority and leadership in the church. First is the word "pastor" and it is found in Ephesians 4:11. It is a translation of the Greek word *poimen* and literally means shepherd. Second is the word "elder" and is a translation of the Greek word *presbuteros.* Third is the word *"overseer"* and is the translation of the Greek word *episkopos.*

Concerning the words "elders" and "overseer," we find in Scripture that these two terms are sometimes used interchangeably. Elders and overseers are not just any individual in the church. They are first to be tested before they are appointed, so they can serve and lead the congregation well.

1 Timothy 3:1-7, Here is a trustworthy saying: Whoever aspires to be an overseer desires a noble task. Now the overseer is to be above reproach, faithful to his wife, temperate, self-controlled, respectable, hospitable, able to teach, not given to drunkenness, not violent but gentle, not quarrelsome, not a lover of money. He must manage his own family well and see that his children obey him, and he must do so in a manner worthy of full respect. (If anyone does not know how to manage his own family, how can he take care of God's church?) He must not be a recent convert, or he may become conceited and fall under the same judgment as the devil. He must also have a good reputation with outsiders, so that he will not fall into disgrace and into the devil's trap.

Titus 1:5-7, The reason I left you in Crete was that you might put in order what was left unfinished and appoint elders in every town, as I directed you. An elder must be blameless, faithful to his wife, a man whose children believe and are not open to the charge of being wild and disobedient. Since an overseer manages God's household, he must be blameless—not overbearing, not quick-tempered, not given to drunkenness, not violent, not pursuing dishonest gain. Rather, he must be hospitable, one who loves what is good, who is self-controlled, upright, holy and disciplined.

The term elder is used a number of times in Scripture to refer to those individuals who served in church leadership, and the word is always found in the plural which means that every New Testament church had more than one. Although not perfect individuals, these elders were spiritually tested and qualified to lead the church.

Acts 14:23, Paul and Barnabas appointed elders for them in each church and, with prayer and fasting, committed them to the Lord, in whom they had put their trust.

Acts 15:6, The apostles and elders met to consider this question.

Acts 15:22-23, Then the apostles and elders, with the whole church, decided to choose some of their own men and send them to Antioch with Paul and Barnabas. They chose Judas (called Barabbas) and Silas, men who were leaders among the believers. With them they sent the following letter: The apostles and elders, your brothers, To the Gentile believers in Antioch, Syria and Cilicia: Greetings.

James 5:14, Is anyone among you sick? Let them call the elders of the church to pray over them and anoint them with oil in the name of the Lord.

It seems best to understand the term "elder" as the position or office and the term "overseer" as the practice or duties the elders perform. Several of the functions of elders/overseers are specifically mentioned in scripture and include: taking care of the church (1 Timothy 5:17); guarding the church against false doctrine or error (Titus 1:9); overseeing the Church as a shepherd does a flock (Acts 20:28, John 21:16, Hebrews 13:17, 1 Peter 5:2); oversee the finances of the church (Acts 11:30), and making decisions in the church (Acts 16:4).

Acts 16:4, As they traveled from town to town, they delivered the decisions reached by the apostles and elders in Jerusalem for the people to obey.

Acts 20:28, Keep watch over yourselves and all the flock of which the Holy Spirit has made you overseers. Be shepherds of the church of God[j] which he bought with his own blood.

1 Peter 5:1-5, To the elders among you, I appeal as a fellow elder and a witness of Christ's sufferings who also will share in the glory to be revealed: Be shepherds of God's flock that is under your care, watching over them—not because you must, but because you are willing, as God wants you to be; not pursuing dishonest gain, but eager to serve; not lording it over those entrusted to you, but being examples to the flock. And when the Chief Shepherd appears, you will receive the crown of glory that will never fade away. In the same way, you who are younger, submit yourselves to your elders. All of you, clothe yourselves with humility toward one another, because, "God opposes the proud but shows favor to the humble."

1 Timothy 5:17, The elders who direct the affairs of the church well are worthy of double honor, especially those whose work is preaching and teaching.

Hebrews 13:17, Have confidence in your leaders and submit to their authority, because they keep watch over you as those who must give an account. Do this so that their work will be a joy, not a burden, for that would be of no benefit to you.

As stated earlier, the term "Pastor" means shepherd and is connected to the word teacher. This leads many to refer to the role of the Pastor as the Pastor-Teacher. This Pastor-Teacher would be one of the elders in the church and serve as the spiritual leader and shepherd for a local congregation or a church. This Pastor-Teacher would also serve in the primary teaching role among the other elders or leaders of the congregation.

Ephesians 4:11, So Christ himself gave the apostles, the prophets, the evangelists, the pastors and teachers,

Another position within the church that deserves mention is that of "deacon," which comes from the Greek word *diakonos.* Deacons are different from Pastor-Teachers and elders as can be seen in their initial call to serve the needs of the congregation. The qualifications of a deacon are also listed in Scripture, and they serve a vital and indispensable function of service within the church but are not the same as elders or overseers.

Acts 6:1-7, In those days when the number of disciples was increasing, the Hellenistic Jews among them complained against the Hebraic Jews because their widows were being overlooked in the daily distribution of food. So the Twelve gathered all the disciples together and said, "It would not be right for us to neglect the ministry of the word of God in order to wait on tables. Brothers and sisters, choose seven men from among you who are known to be full of the Spirit and wisdom. We will turn this responsibility over to them and will give our attention to prayer and the ministry of the word." This proposal pleased the whole group. They chose Stephen, a man full of faith and of the Holy Spirit; also Philip, Procorus, Nicanor, Timon, Parmenas, and Nicolas from Antioch, a convert to Judaism. They presented these men to the apostles, who prayed and laid their hands on them. So the word of God spread. The number of disciples in Jerusalem increased rapidly, and a large number of priests became obedient to the faith.

1 Timothy 3:8-13, In the same way, deacons are to be worthy of respect, sincere, not indulging in much wine, and not pursuing dishonest gain. They must keep hold of the deep truths of the faith with a clear conscience. They must first be tested; and then if there is nothing against them, let them serve as deacons. In the same way, the women are to be worthy of respect, not malicious talkers but temperate and trustworthy in everything. A deacon must be faithful to his wife and must manage his children and his household well. Those who have served well gain an excellent standing and great assurance in their faith in Christ Jesus.

In conclusion, we can see several clear guidelines for the authority and leadership in the church. Biblical leadership in the church is best done by a plurality or group of elders overseeing and leading the affairs of the church. The Pastor-Teacher serves as the primary or major teaching role among the elders. Deacons are a group of servants who meet specific needs within the church. Those who serve in the positions of Elders, Pastor-Teacher, or Deacons are first to be tested, and while never being found perfect they are to be above reproach as to character and Christian commitment. As such, leaders within the church need to serve the church well, and those within the church should honor and follow their leaders according to Scripture.

Hebrews 13:7, Remember your leaders, who spoke the word of God to you. Consider the outcome of their way of life and imitate their faith.

Hebrews 13:17, Have confidence in your leaders and submit to their authority, because they keep watch over you as those who must give an account. Do this so that their work will be a joy, not a burden, for that would be of no benefit to you.

161

THE DOCTRINE OF THE SECOND COMING OF JESUS CHRIST

The Second Coming of Jesus Christ or the End Times is probably the most difficult of all the main doctrinal topics to discuss. Eschatology is the word used to describe the study of the last things. Eschatology deals with the consummation of human history and the ultimate completion or end of God's work in the world.

Eschatology is so exceedingly difficult to discuss and write about because of a number of reasons: 1) there is much disagreement about the end times among many who were strong believers throughout history, 2) there are multiple plausible ways that many eschatological ideas and verses of Scripture can be interpreted, 3) God has specifically left much about His end time activities unclear, and 4) God is God, and we are not. What takes place during the End Times is God's plan, and He will bring all things to completion in His time and in His way.

When we approach the topic of Eschatology, it is best to do so with a sense of humility. Remember what God said through the prophet Isaiah:

Isaiah 55:8-9, *"For My thoughts are not your thoughts, neither are your ways My ways," declares the Lord. "As the heavens are higher than the earth, so are My ways higher than your ways and My thoughts than your thoughts."*

We would also do well to remember the words our Lord Jesus spoke to his followers when they asked Jesus when God would restore the Kingdom.

Acts 1:7-8, He said to them: "It is not for you to know the times or dates the Father has set by His own authority. But you will receive power when the Holy Spirit comes upon you, and you will be My witnesses in Jerusalem, and in all Judea and Samaria, and to the ends of the earth."

Jesus' response was clear that our focus should never be on the return of the Lord or specific dates and times, but instead, our focus should be on being a witness to the world of the saving grace of Jesus Christ. With the above idea in mind, I will humbly set out to explain with wide latitude and grace the major themes, concepts, and theological positions as they relate to the End Times.

The word "millennium" comes from two Latin words which mean a thousand years or an extended period of time and refers to the reign of Jesus Christ on the earth. There are three major theological positions of the Second Coming of Jesus Christ.

First, there is the **Postmillennial** View. The Postmillennial View holds that through the preaching of the Gospel of Jesus Christ, the world will be converted to salvation. Over the years, things will get better to the extent that after a period of 1,000 years of peace, the Lord Jesus Christ will return to earth. According to the Postmillennial View, Jesus Christ will come to the earth after the 1,000 year period of peace.

The second major position is **Amillennialism**. The Amillennialist view holds that there is no literal Millennial at all. Those who hold to this view maintain that there will be no literal reign of Jesus Christ here upon the earth at all.

The third position is **Premillennialism**. The Premillennialist position teaches that Jesus Christ is going to come and rapture, or remove the Church from the earth. Then Christ will return to the earth in all His glory and establish His kingdom and reign here upon the earth for a period of 1,000 years according to Scripture.

Revelation 20:4, I saw thrones on which were seated those who had been given authority to judge. And I saw the souls of those who had been beheaded because of their testimony about Jesus and because of the word of God. They had not worshiped the beast or its image and had not received its mark on their foreheads or their hands. They came to life and reigned with Christ a thousand years.

The Rapture of the Church

The word rapture does not appear in Scripture. Rapture comes from the Latin word meaning "to carry off, snatch away, or transport." Even though the word rapture is not found in Scripture, it is clearly taught in Scripture.

> *1 Thessalonians 4:13,* Brothers and sisters, we do not want you to be uninformed about those who sleep in death, so that you do not grieve like the rest of mankind, who have no hope. For we believe that Jesus died and rose again, and so we believe that God will bring with Jesus those who have fallen asleep in him. According to the Lord's word, we tell you that we who are still alive, who are left until the coming of the Lord, will certainly not precede those who have fallen asleep. For the Lord himself will come down from heaven, with a loud command, with the voice of the archangel and with the trumpet call of God, and the dead in Christ will rise first. After that, we who are still alive and are left will be caught up together with them in the clouds to meet the Lord in the air. And so we will be with the Lord forever. Therefore encourage one another with these words.

> *1 Corinthians 15:52,* in a flash, in the twinkling of an eye, at the last trumpet. For the trumpet will sound, the dead will be raised imperishable, and we will be changed. For the perishable must clothe itself with the imperishable, and the mortal with immortality. When the perishable has been clothed with the imperishable, and the mortal with immortality, then the saying that is written will come true: "Death has been swallowed up in victory." "Where, O death, is your victory? Where, O death, is your sting?" The sting of death is sin, and the power of sin is the law. But thanks be to God! He gives us the victory through our Lord Jesus Christ. Therefore, my dear brothers and sisters, stand firm. Let nothing move you. Always give yourselves fully to the work of the Lord, because you know that your labor in the Lord is not in vain.

The return of Jesus Christ for the believers is referred to most commonly as the Rapture of the Church. Those who deny the Doctrine of the Rapture argue that the word rapture cannot be found in the Bible. While this is true, it is just as true that such words as "Trinity" and "Theology" are not found in the Bible either, but are accepted terms throughout Christianity to describe specific biblical teachings.

The word rapture has been used to describe or designate an event which is foreshadowed in Scripture. It is a descriptive word which speaks of the catching away of the saints which Christ returns. Therefore rapture is the word which expresses that event when Christ will come again according to His promise to take away His Church. This will be done to prepare the Church for His return and reign upon the earth. The word comes from the Latin word *rapio* which means to snatch away suddenly.

One of the questions which is often asked concerns those who will be taken at the rapture. When we speak of the rapture of the Church, to what group of people are we referring? It is to be remembered that the Church had its beginning on the day of Pentecost (Acts 2) when the Holy Spirit came to baptize all believers into the Body of Christ. That event formed the body of Christ. The Church as the body of Christ is, therefore, a new entity, created from both unsaved Jews and unsaved Gentiles.

> *Ephesians 2:11,* Therefore, remember that formerly you who are Gentiles by birth and called "uncircumcised" by those who call themselves "the circumcision" (which is done in the body by human hands)— remember that at that time you were separate from Christ, excluded from citizenship in Israel and foreigners to the covenants of the promise, without hope and without God in the world. But now in Christ Jesus you who once were far away have been brought near by the blood of Christ. For he himself is our peace, who has made the two groups one and has destroyed the barrier, the dividing wall of hostility, by setting aside in his flesh the law with its commands and regulations. His purpose was to create in himself one new humanity out of the two, thus making peace, and in one body to reconcile both of them to God through the cross, by which he put to death their hostility.

The Church had its beginning on the day of Pentecost and is made up only of those who have received Jesus Christ as Savior and have been placed in the body of Christ by the Holy Spirit. When Christ comes to rapture the Church, He will call out those who have been saved.

There are three major views concerning the rapture of the Church. The first is referred to as **Post-Tribulation** Theory of the Rapture. Those who hold to this view believe that the Church will go through the Great Tribulation but that God will preserve and protect His Church in spite of great distress and wrath upon the earth. This view states that the rapture of the Church will happen in connection with Christ's return to the earth to establish His kingdom. This theory holds that the Church will continue on the earth going through the Tribulation until the Second Coming at the end of the present age. At that time the Church will be caught up into the cloud to meet the Lord who has come in the air on His way from heaven to earth for the Second Advent to return immediately to the earth. This would require the Church to go through the tribulation.

The second major view of the rapture is referred to as the **Mid-Tribulation** Theory. This theory holds that the rapture of the church will take place in the middle of the Tribulation thus allowing the Church to avoid the worst of the wrath of God that is to come during the great tribulation.

The third view is the **Pretribulational** Theory of the rapture. The Pre-Tribulation interpretation means that the coming of Jesus Christ and the translation of the Church precedes the tribulation period. The Lord has given the church a specific promise that it will not go through the period of the Tribulation. Not only is there no mention of the Church in any eschatological passage describing the future tribulation, but there are definite promises given to the Church that deliverance from that period is assured.

Revelation 3:10, Since you have kept My command to endure patiently, I will also keep you from the hour of trial that is going to come on the whole world to test the inhabitants of the earth.

1 Thessalonians 5:9, For God did not appoint us to suffer wrath but to receive salvation through our Lord Jesus Christ.

Rapture And Resurrection

Two major events take place here on this earth when Jesus returns. The first is the resurrection of the dead saints. Jesus Christ will not only remove all of the living saints from the earth, but He will also resurrect all the dead saints of old. Again, this resurrection is only for the Church and will involve only those who have died in the Lord Jesus since the establishment of the Church on the day of Pentecost.

1 Thessalonians 4:13, Brothers and sisters, we do not want you to be uninformed about those who sleep in death, so that you do not grieve like the rest of mankind, who have no hope. For we believe that Jesus died and rose again, and so we believe that God will bring with Jesus those who have fallen asleep in Him. According to the Lord's word, we tell you that we who are still alive, who are left until the coming of the Lord, will certainly not precede those who have fallen asleep. For the Lord Himself will come down from heaven, with a loud command, with the voice of the archangel and with the trumpet call of God, and the dead in Christ will rise first. After that, we who are still alive and are left will be caught up together with them in the clouds to meet the Lord in the air. And so we will be with the Lord forever. Therefore encourage one another with these words.

Secondly, Jesus will remove every living Christian from the earth. The translation of the saints will be instantaneous. There will be no time to repent, for it will occur in a moment, in the twinkling of an eye.

Thus, two events will take place at the rapture: the dead in Christ shall rise first, then the living believers will be translated. One of the glorious things which will occur in the life of those who are raptured or resurrected will be that every believer will receive a new body.

1 Corinthians 15:52, in a flash, in the twinkling of an eye, at the last trumpet. For the trumpet will sound, the dead will be raised imperishable, and we will be changed.

Philippians 3:21, who, by the power that enables Him to bring everything under His control, will transform our lowly bodies so that they will be like His glorious body.

We cannot even imagine how amazing this will be. When considering the excitement brought on by a stunning new outfit, a whole new body free from sin, sin's nature, pain, disease, and death far surpass the thought of earthly clothing.

Judgment Seat Of Christ

When the Church is removed from the earth at the rapture, the Church will face Jesus Christ at the Judgment Seat. The Judgment Seat of Christ will occur immediately following the rapture of Christians.

> *1 Corinthians 3:10-15, By the grace God has given me, I laid a foundation as a wise builder, and someone else is building on it. But each one should build with care. For no one can lay any foundation other than the one already laid, which is Jesus Christ. If anyone builds on this foundation using gold, silver, costly stones, wood, hay or straw, their work will be shown for what it is, because the Day will bring it to light. It will be revealed with fire, and the fire will test the quality of each person's work. If what has been built survives, the builder will receive a reward. If it is burned up, the builder will suffer loss but yet will be saved—even though only as one escaping through the flames.*

> *2 Corinthians 5:10, For we must all appear before the judgment seat of Christ, so that each of us may receive what is due us for the things done while in the body, whether good or bad.*

The Judgement Seat of Christ is reserved for Christians only. The pronoun "we" occurs twenty-six times in this chapter and in every instance refers to the believer. It is clear that this judgment has to do only with Christians. It is a sobering thought to realize that the believer's life is being built upon the foundation of Christ and that some day every believer will be brought before Christ and examined as to the quality of his or her life.

> *1 Corinthians 3:12-13, If anyone builds on this foundation using gold, silver, costly stones, wood, hay or straw, their work will be shown for what it is, because the Day will bring it to light. It will be revealed with fire, and the fire will test the quality of each person's work.*

The quality of the believer's life can be seen in materials discussed. The gold, silver, and precious stones speak of actions in the life of the believer that are pleasing to the Lord and worthy of reward, but the wood, hay, and straw speak of a life built on temporal values, and is, therefore, of no lasting value.

It must also be noted that at the Judgment Seat of Christ, the salvation or loss of salvation does not come up at all. There are rewards for acceptable service, and there is loss for poor service, but even those who suffer almost complete loss of their rewards, are said to be saved as though by fire.

> *John 5:24,* Very truly I tell you, whoever hears my word and believes him who sent me has eternal life and will not be judged but has crossed over from death to life.

> *1 Corinthians 3:15,* If it is burned up, the builder will suffer loss but yet will be saved—even though only as one escaping through the flames.

In this judgment, all the judged are saved but not rewarded at the same level. The actual basis of this judgment will not be that of condemnation but will deal with the believer's service and faithfulness to Christ. The Greek word *Bema* used in Romans does not speak of condemnation but has reference to Grecian games in Athens. In the arena, there was a raised platform on which the president or umpire of the arena sat. From this place, he rewarded all the contestants. It was designated as the *Bema* Seat or the seat of rewards. This judgment seat was never a judicial bench. The nature of this judgment is to be seen more clearly in the word *Bema* which is translated "Judgment Seat."

> *Romans 14:10,* You, then, why do you judge your brother or sister? Or why do you treat them with contempt? For we will all stand before God's judgment seat.

The Christian life is a race, and the Divine Umpire or Judge is watching every contestant. After the Church has run its course, Christ will gather every member before the *Bema* seat for the purpose of examining each one and giving the proper reward for the way the race was run.

Scripture delineates five awards or crowns which will be given out by Jesus at the *Bema* Seat: 1) there will be the *Incorruptible Crown,* which will be given to the Christian who exercises self-control in her personal and moral life (1 Corinthians 9:24-27); 2) there will be the *Crown of Exultation,* which will be given to the Christian who has been a faithful witness for Jesus Christ. This has been called the evangelist crown (1 Thessalonians 2:19-20); 3). There will be the *Crown of Righteousness,* which is given to the Christian who loves and looks for the second coming of Jesus Christ (2 Timothy 4:5-8); 4). There will be the *Crown of Life,* which will be given to those who are faithful to Christ under trials and tribulation. This crown goes to the individual who has been faithful even unto death (Revelation 2:10); and 5). There is the *Crown of Glory,* which will be given to the faithful pastor who has faithfully fed the followers of Christ (1 Peter 5:1-4).

> *1 Corinthians 9:24-27,* Do you not know that in a race all the runners run, but only one gets the prize? Run in such a way as to get the prize. Everyone who competes

in the games goes into strict training. They do it to get a crown that will not last, but we do it to get a crown that will last forever. Therefore I do not run like someone running aimlessly; I do not fight like a boxer beating the air. No, I strike a blow to my body and make it my slave so that after I have preached to others, I myself will not be disqualified for the prize.

1 Thessalonians 2:19-20, For what is our hope, our joy, or the crown in which we will glory in the presence of our Lord Jesus when He comes? Is it not you? Indeed, you are our glory and joy.

2 Timothy 4:5-8, But you, keep your head in all situations, endure hardship, do the work of an evangelist, discharge all the duties of your ministry. For I am already being poured out like a drink offering, and the time for my departure is near. I have fought the good fight, I have finished the race, I have kept the faith. Now there is in store for me the crown of righteousness, which the Lord, the righteous Judge, will award to me on that day—and not only to me, but also to all who have longed for His appearing.

Revelation 2:10, Do not be afraid of what you are about to suffer. I tell you, the devil will put some of you in prison to test you, and you will suffer persecution for ten days. Be faithful, even to the point of death, and I will give you life as your victor's crown.

1 Peter 5:1-4, To the elders among you, I appeal as a fellow elder and a witness of Christ's sufferings who also will share in the glory to be revealed: Be shepherds of God's flock that is under your care, watching over them—not because you must, but because you are willing, as God wants you to be; not pursuing dishonest gain, but eager to serve; not lording it over those entrusted to you, but being examples to the flock. And when the Chief Shepherd appears, you will receive the crown of glory that will never fade away.

The purpose of this judgment is so that every believer can be presented to Jesus as His bride beautifully adorned in white garments. At the Judgment Seat of Christ, the fire or holiness of God will actually burn away the dross out of each believer's life, and every believer will be brought into complete harmony with God and with one another. We must state again that this judgment is based on the believer's service, not salvation. To receive the crown from His pierced hand will be a blessing indeed, but still, more of a blessing will be the privilege of taking those same crowns and placing them before Him who bought our salvation and is worthy of all glory, honor, and rewards.

Revelation 4:9-11, Whenever the living creatures give glory, honor and thanks to Him who sits on the throne and who lives for ever and ever, the twenty-four elders fall down before Him who sits on the throne and worship Him who lives for ever and ever. They lay their crowns before the throne and say: "You are worthy, our Lord and God, to receive glory and honor and power, for you created all things, and by your will they were created and have their being."

Marriage Feast Of The Lamb

At the end of the tribulation, prior to the return of Jesus Christ to the earth, there will occur an event which is described as the *Marriage Feast of the Lamb.* The Marriage Feast of the Lamb is illustrated by the Oriental marriage custom.

In the days of Christ, there were three stages to the Oriental marriage. First, there was a marriage contract or the betrothal. This marriage contract was often forged by one or both of the fathers and was legally binding. Second, there was the actual marriage when the couple had reached the marriage age. Note carefully that this ceremony was consummated by the bridegroom going with his friends to receive the bride to himself and to escort the bride to his home. Thirdly, after the bridegroom went to get the bride himself and escorted her to his father's home, they would enter the bed chambers which he had built for them, and for seven days, they would consummate their marriage after which they would enjoy the marriage feast. At the marriage feast, all of the bridegroom's friends were invited to the supper. At this time, the bridegroom would proudly show his bride to his friends, and they would rejoice together. The length of the supper depended upon the financial status of the bridegroom.

> *Revelation 19:1-10, After this I heard what sounded like the roar of a great multitude in heaven shouting: "Hallelujah! Salvation and glory and power belong to our God, for true and just are his judgments. He has condemned the great prostitute who corrupted the earth by her adulteries. He has avenged on her the blood of his servants." And again they shouted: "Hallelujah! The smoke from her goes up for ever and ever." The twenty-four elders and the four living creatures fell down and worshiped God, who was seated on the throne. And they cried: "Amen, Hallelujah!" Then a voice came from the throne, saying: "Praise our God, all you His servants, you who fear him, both great and small!" Then I heard what sounded like a great multitude, like the roar of rushing waters and like loud peals of thunder, shouting: "Hallelujah! For our Lord God Almighty reigns. Let us rejoice and be glad and give him glory! For the wedding of the Lamb has come, and His bride has made herself ready. Fine linen, bright and clean, was given her to wear." (Fine linen stands for the righteous acts of God's holy people.) Then the angel said to me, "Write this: Blessed are those who are invited to the wedding supper of the Lamb!" And he added, "These are the true words of God." At this I fell at his feet to worship Him. But He said to me, "Don't do that! I am a fellow servant with you and with your brothers*

and sisters who hold to the testimony of Jesus. Worship God! For it is the Spirit of prophecy who bears testimony to Jesus."

Ephesians 5:25-27, Husbands, love your wives, just as Christ loved the church and gave himself up for her to make her holy, cleansing her by the washing with water through the word, and to present her to himself as a radiant church, without stain or wrinkle or any other blemish, but holy and blameless.

There is an obvious parallel between the Oriental wedding ceremony and the Second Coming of Christ and the Marriage Feast of the Lamb. First, the wedding contract is sealed at the time the Church is redeemed. When a person receives Jesus Christ as personal Saviour, they are betrothed to Christ to become His bride. This is a legal, binding contract on the part of parties. Christ is bound to keep His promise to carry out the marriage contract, and the believer is responsible for remaining a true and chaste bride of Christ. The pledge which is given to the believer by the Lord Jesus Christ concerning the redemption is the person of the Holy Spirit.

> *Ephesians 1:13-14, And you also were included in Christ when you heard the message of truth, the gospel of your salvation. When you believed, you were marked in Him with a seal, the promised Holy Spirit, who is a deposit guaranteeing our inheritance until the redemption of those who are God's possession—to the praise of His glory.*

Secondly, the actual marriage will take place when Christ comes back to receive His bride and to escort her to His home in the sky personally. In the Oriental marriage process, after the betrothal, the bridegroom was responsible for building a wedding chamber at his father's house. This is what the Lord Jesus Christ is doing today when He says that He is going to prepare a place for us. Christ is going to come again and receive us to Himself. When preparations are complete, the Bridegroom (Christ) will take His bride (The Church/Believers) to be with Him forever.

> *John 14:1-6, "Do not let your hearts be troubled. You believe in God; believe also in Me. My Father's house has many rooms; if that were not so, would I have told you that I am going there to prepare a place for you? And if I go and prepare a place for you, I will come back and take you to be with Me that you also may be where I am. You know the way to the place where I am going." Thomas said to Him, "Lord, we don't know where You are going, so how can we know the way?" Jesus answered, "I am the way and the truth and the life. No one comes to the Father except through Me."*

Finally, the Marriage Supper of the Lamb is the wedding feast. This is the time when Christ will present the bride to Himself. This is also the time when Jesus will present His bride to His Father with great joy, rejoicing, celebrating, and eternal fellowship between Christ and His followers.

> *Revelation 19:7,* Let us rejoice and be glad and give Him glory! For the wedding of the Lamb has come, and his bride has made herself ready.

> *Jude 24,* To Him who is able to keep you from stumbling and to present you before His glorious presence without fault and with great joy.

The Tribulation

The Tribulation or Great Tribulation is a time on earth of unparalleled trouble. The Tribulation will occur at some future time when God will finish disciplining Israel for her disobedience, and He will judge unbelievers on the earth. The Tribulation is described in Revelation chapters 6-19. The Tribulation will last seven years and is divided into two equal parts of three and a half years each. The last three and a half years is more accurately referred to as the Great Tribulation but often times Tribulation and the Great Tribulation are used synonymously. The last part of the Tribulation as denoted in Scripture is the time of the Antichrist and increasing intensity of the wrath of God.

Will the Church go through the Tribulation? Those who believe in a post-tribulation rapture believe the church will go through the Tribulation. Those who believe in a mid-tribulation rapture believe the church will go through the first part of the Tribulation but be raptured out before the worst part of the Tribulation. Those who believe in the pretribulation view of the rapture believe the Church will be rejoicing with Jesus Christ in glory while the earth is experiencing a time of chaos known as the Tribulation.

Pre-tribulationists believe the Church will not go through the Tribulation for the following reasons: 1) during the period of the tribulation, the Church will be in the air with Jesus (1 Thessalonians 4:17; Revelation 3:10, 4:1-2); 2) The Church has been promised deliverance (Revelation 3:10); 3) the Holy Spirit will be removed from the earth during the period of the Tribulation. Since every believer is sealed by the Holy Spirit unto redemption, if the Holy Spirit leaves, then believers must also be removed from the earth. (2 Thessalonians 2:7; Ephesians 1:13-14).

1 Thessalonians 4:17, After that, we who are still alive and are left will be caught up together with them in the clouds to meet the Lord in the air. And so we will be with the Lord forever.

Revelation 3:10, Since you have kept my command to endure patiently, I will also keep you from the hour of trial that is going to come on the whole world to test the inhabitants of the earth.

2 Thessalonians 2:7, For the secret power of lawlessness is already at work; but the one who now holds it back will continue to do so till he is taken out of the way.

Another reason cited for the Church not going through the Tribulation is that the Church is not mentioned during the Tribulation. The only mention of the Church in Revelation 6-19 has to do with the "false" church and not the true Church in Revelation 17. It is interesting to note that the word "church" is last used in Revelation 3:14. The word "churches" is last used in Revelation 3:6, and is not used again until Revelation 22:16.

In Revelation 21 & 22 the true Church is referred to as the "bride" and the "wife" of the Lamb. Thus the true Church is not mentioned in Revelation during the time of the Tribulation at all.

The Antichrist And The False Prophet

The term "antichrist" means "against Christ." John writes that the spirit of the antichrist denies the Father and the Son, does not acknowledge Jesus Christ, is already in the world, and does not acknowledge that Jesus came in the flesh.

1 John 2:22, Who is the liar? It is whoever denies that Jesus is the Christ. Such a person is the antichrist—denying the Father and the Son.

1 John 4:3, but every spirit that does not acknowledge Jesus is not from God. This is the spirit of the antichrist, which you have heard is coming and even now is already in the world.

2 John 7, I say this because many deceivers, who do not acknowledge Jesus Christ as coming in the flesh, have gone out into the world. Any such person is the deceiver and the antichrist.

1 John 2:18, Dear children, this is the last hour; and as you have heard that the antichrist is coming, even now many antichrists have come. This is how we know it is the last hour.

When speaking of the end times, there is coming one who is referred to as "The Antichrist." This ultimate Antichrist will demonstrate what it means to be completely against Christ in every way. Most scholars of the end times believe that this ultimate and final Antichrist will oppose Christ and His followers in ways never seen before in the history of the world. This final Antichrist will claim to be the true Messiah and will attempt to rule over the world and destroy Israel and the faithful followers of Jesus Christ.

From the beginning, Satan's desire has been to supplant the work of God in every possible way. Satan wants to be like the Most High and be worshipped instead of God. His primary plan has been to receive worship and reverence from humanity since the day he tempted Eve in the garden. Although Satan has been successful to some degree, the Bible tell us that his work has been hindered by the work of the Spirit of God.

The main desire of Satan through the ages has been to receive praise and glory from man; therefore, the purpose of the Antichrist is to centralize and focus humanity's worship of Satan. The Antichrist is the final false messiah who will someday attain world domination in order to destroy Israel and the followers of the true Messiah, Jesus Christ.

The Antichrist will work and speak more than any other person in history against Jesus Christ and God's plan for this world. The Antichrist will do everything within his power to usurp the laws of God. He will succeed in having himself worshipped by all inhabitants of the earth except those who are truly saved.

> 2 Thessalonians 2:3, *Don't let anyone deceive you in any way, for that day will not come until the rebellion occurs and the man of lawlessness is revealed, the man doomed to destruction.*

The Antichrist will successfully establish a system that could truly be called anti-Christianity. The work of the Antichrist is very religious, seeking worship and complete devotion to himself and ultimately Satan.

The Bible tells us that the Antichrist: establishes and then breaks a seven-year covenant with Israel (Daniel 9), sets up the abomination of desolation (Mark 13:14), is the man of lawlessness; rides a white horse claiming to be a man of peace (Revelation 6:2), receives power from the dragon(Satan) to wage war against God's holy people. The number 666 is associated with him. The Antichrist will ultimately be thrown into the lake of fire for eternity.

> Mark 13:14, *"When you see 'the abomination that causes desolation' standing where it does not belong—let the reader understand—then let those who are in Judea flee to the mountains.*

2 Thessalonians 2:4, He will oppose and will exalt himself over everything that is called God or is worshiped, so that he sets himself up in God's temple, proclaiming himself to be God.

Revelation 6:2, I looked, and there before me was a white horse! Its rider held a bow, and he was given a crown, and he rode out as a conqueror bent on conquest.

Revelation 13:4-8, People worshiped the dragon because he had given authority to the beast, and they also worshiped the beast and asked, "Who is like the beast? Who can wage war against it?" The beast was given a mouth to utter proud words and blasphemies and to exercise its authority for forty-two months. It opened its mouth to blaspheme God, and to slander his name and his dwelling place and those who live in heaven. It was given power to wage war against God's holy people and to conquer them. And it was given authority over every tribe, people, language and nation. All inhabitants of the earth will worship the beast—all whose names have not been written in the Lamb's Book of Life, the Lamb who was slain from the creation of the world.

Revelation 13:16-17, It also forced all people, great and small, rich and poor, free and slave, to receive a mark on their right hands or on their foreheads, so that they could not buy or sell unless they had the mark, which is the name of the beast or the number of its name.

Revelations 13:18, This calls for wisdom. Let the person who has insight calculate the number of the beast, for it is the number of a man. That number is 666.

Revelations 19:20, But the beast was captured, and with it the false prophet who had performed the signs on its behalf. With these signs he had deluded those who had received the mark of the beast and worshiped its image. The two of them were thrown alive into the fiery lake of burning sulfur.

As a side note, since the number 666 is somehow related to the Antichrist, many have tried to use numerology to identify the Antichrist. Over the years, this has led to many false designations of individuals throughout history who were supposedly the Antichrist because of the spelling of their name. It is probably best to remember that John said calculating the number of the beast "calls for wisdom."

Perhaps the best wisdom one can employ is to acknowledge that the number 666 is associated with the Antichrist. The number 6 is the number of man for it was the 6th day that man was created. The number 6 falls short of the number 7 which is the number of God and perfection. So, the number 666, while it may designate the power of the Antichrist, has no ultimate power over the Child of God because the Antichrist will meet his destruction at the hands of almighty God.

The Revelation

The Second Coming of Christ is actually a twofold event. First, Christ will return for His followers, an event which is called the Rapture. At the Rapture, Christ will remove all believers, both living and dead from the earth. Second, Christ will return with His Church which is called the Revelation and shall take place immediately after the tribulation. At that point, Christ will set up His earthly kingdom.

Revelation 19:11-21, *I saw heaven standing open and there before me was a white horse, whose rider is called Faithful and True. With justice He judges and wages war. His eyes are like blazing fire, and on His head are many crowns. He has a name written on Him that no one knows but He Himself. He is dressed in a robe dipped in blood, and His name is the Word of God. The armies of heaven were following Him, riding on white horses and dressed in fine linen, white and clean. Coming out of His mouth is a sharp sword with which to strike down the nations. "He will rule them with an iron scepter." He treads the winepress of the fury of the wrath of God Almighty. On His robe and on His thigh He has this name written: And I saw an angel standing in the sun, who cried in a loud voice to all the birds flying in mid-air, "Come, gather together for the great supper of God, so that you may eat the flesh of kings, generals, and the mighty, of horses and their riders, and the flesh of all people, free and slave, great and small." Then I saw the beast and the kings of the earth and their armies gathered together to wage war against the rider on the horse and his army. But the beast was captured, and with it the false prophet who had performed the signs on its behalf. With these signs he had deluded those who had received the mark of the beast and worshiped its image. The two of them were thrown alive into the fiery lake of burning sulfur. The rest were killed with the sword coming out of the mouth of the rider on the horse, and all the birds gorged themselves on their flesh.*

1 Thessalonians 4:13-18, *Brothers and sisters, we do not want you to be uninformed about those who sleep in death, so that you do not grieve like the rest of mankind, who have no hope. For we believe that Jesus died and rose again, and so we believe that God will bring with Jesus those who have fallen asleep in Him. According to the Lord's word, we tell you that we who are still alive, who are left until the coming of the Lord, will certainly not precede those who have fallen asleep. For the Lord Himself will come down from heaven, with a loud command, with the voice of the archangel and with the trumpet call of God, and the dead in Christ will rise first. After that, we who are still alive and are left will be caught up together with them in the clouds to meet the Lord in the air. And so we will be with the Lord forever. Therefore encourage one another with these words.*

The Appearance Of Christ

Faithful and true: In verse 11 above, we find that Christ rides a "white horse." The white horse speaks of the purity and holiness of Christ and is a sign of victory. In addition, the one who is riding the white horse is called "Faithful and True." Faithful in contrast to the unfaithfulness displayed on the earth during the Tribulation. True is in contrast to the satanic era which has been perpetrated upon mankind.

His eyes are a flame of fire: We are told that Christ's eyes are a "flame of Fire." This speaks to His divine omniscience—the all seeing and all knowing divine judgment. No sin is hidden from His view, for He knows everything.

Revelation 19:11, *I saw heaven standing open and there before me was a white horse, whose rider is called Faithful and True. With justice he judges and wages war.*

Revelation 2:18, *To the angel of the church in Thyatira write: These are the words of the Son of God, whose eyes are like blazing fire and whose feet are like burnished bronze.*

Revelation 19:12, *His eyes are like blazing fire, and on His head are many crowns. He has a name written on Him that no one knows but He Himself.*

Upon His head are many diadems: This is in contrast to the crown of thorns which He wore at His crucifixion and speaks of His right as King of Kings and Lord of Lords to rule over the earth. The many diadems speak of the absolute authority of Christ to possess and rule the world.

Dipped in Blood: His robe is dipped in blood and speaks of His own blood which was shed for humanity's redemption. The blood, which is offered to all men for cleansing from sin, now becomes the basis upon which Christ will exercise righteous vengeance upon those who have rejected Him. His coming will be personal, visible, glorious, and sudden.

Luke 21:27, *At that time they will see the Son of Man coming in a cloud with power and great glory.*

Matthew 24:27-30, *For as lightning that comes from the east is visible even in the west, so will be the coming of the Son of Man. Wherever there is a carcass, there the vultures will gather. "Immediately after the distress of those days "'the sun will be darkened, and the moon will not give its light; the stars will fall from the sky, and the heavenly bodies will be shaken.' "Then will appear the sign of the Son of Man in heaven. And then all the peoples of the earth will mourn when they see the Son of Man coming on the clouds of heaven, with power and great glory.*

The Purpose Of Christ Coming To The Earth

Why is Jesus returning to the earth? Jesus is returning for both negative and positive reasons. Negatively, Jesus is coming to strike the nations, destroy earthly governments, rule the world with a rod of iron, and judge the Antichrist and False Prophet. Also, Jesus is also coming to bind Satan. Positively, Jesus is coming to save Israel, deliver and bless creation, and set up His earthly kingdom.

Jesus came the first time in humility as a baby in a manger and a lamb led to the slaughter. He will come the second time as a King, the Lion of Judah, triumphant and with great exaltation. The first-time Jesus was born of a virgin, worked as a carpenter, died on a Roman cross, and was buried in a borrowed tomb. However, when He returns, Jesus will come in all His glory and reign as the King of Kings and the Lord of Lords.

Revelations 19:15, *Coming out of His mouth is a sharp sword with which to strike down the nations. "He will rule them with an iron scepter." He treads the winepress of the fury of the wrath of God Almighty.*

Daniel 2:31-35, *Your Majesty looked, and there before you stood a large statue—an enormous, dazzling statue, awesome in appearance. The head of the statue was made of pure gold, its chest and arms of silver, its belly and thighs of bronze, its legs of iron, its feet partly of iron and partly of baked clay. While you were watching, a rock was cut out, but not by human hands. It struck the statue on its feet of iron and clay and smashed them. Then the iron, the clay, the bronze, the silver and the gold were all broken to pieces and became like chaff on a threshing floor in the summer. The wind swept them away without leaving a trace. But the rock that struck the statue became a huge mountain and filled the whole earth.*

Revelation 19:19-21, *Then I saw the beast and the kings of the earth and their armies gathered together to wage war against the rider on the horse and his army. But the beast was captured, and with it the false prophet who had performed the signs on its behalf. With these signs he had deluded those who had received the mark of the beast and worshiped its image. The two of them were thrown alive into the fiery lake of burning sulfur. The rest were killed with the sword coming out of the mouth of the rider on the horse, and all the birds gorged themselves on their flesh.*

2 Thessalonians 1:7-10, *and give relief to you who are troubled, and to us as well. This will happen when the Lord Jesus is revealed from heaven in blazing fire with His powerful angels. He will punish those who do not know God and do not obey the gospel of our Lord Jesus. They will be punished with everlasting destruction and shut out from the presence of the Lord and from the glory of His might on the day He comes to be glorified in His holy people and to be marveled at among all those who have believed. This includes you, because you believed our testimony to you.*

Revelation 20:1-2, *And I saw an angel coming down out of heaven, having the key to the Abyss and holding in his hand a great chain. He seized the dragon, that ancient serpent, who is the devil, or Satan, and bound him for a thousand years.*

Romans 11:1, *I ask then: Did God reject his people? By no means! I am an Israelite myself, a descendant of Abraham, from the tribe of Benjamin.*

Matthew 24:27-31, *For as lightning that comes from the east is visible even in the west, so will be the coming of the Son of Man. Wherever there is a carcass, there the vultures will gather. "Immediately after the distress of those days "'the sun will be darkened, and the moon will not give its light; the stars will fall from the sky, and the heavenly bodies will be shaken.' "Then will appear the sign of the Son of Man in heaven. And then all the peoples of the earth will mourn when they see the Son of Man coming on the clouds of heaven, with power and great glory. And He will send His angels with a loud trumpet call, and they will gather His elect from the four winds, from one end of the heavens to the other.*

Matthew 25:31-34, *"When the Son of Man comes in His glory, and all the angels with Him, He will sit on his glorious throne. All the nations will be gathered before Him, and He will separate the people one from another as a shepherd separates the sheep from the goats. He will put the sheep on His right and the goats on his left. "Then the King will say to those on His right, 'Come, you who are blessed by my Father; take your inheritance, the kingdom prepared for you since the creation of the world."*

The Millennium

The Bible declares that there is yet in the future a Golden Age of Peace here upon the earth. The Millennium is used to describe this period because it carries the meaning of a thousand years or a long period of time. The word comes from the Latin *mille* and *annus* meaning a thousand years. In its plain interpretive sense, the Bible asserts that Jesus will literally, not figuratively, return to earth and rule and reign on the earth. Properly speaking the word "millennium" does not occur in the Bible, but a thousand years is mentioned six times in Revelation 20:2-7.

> Revelation 20:2-7, *He seized the dragon, that ancient serpent, who is the devil, or Satan, and bound Him for a thousand years. He threw him into the Abyss, and locked and sealed it over him, to keep him from deceiving the nations anymore until the thousand years were ended. After that, he must be set free for a short time. I saw thrones on which were seated those who had been given authority to judge. And I saw the souls of those who had been beheaded because of their testimony about Jesus and because of the word of God. They had not worshiped the beast or its image and had not received its mark on their foreheads or their hands. They came to life and reigned with Christ a thousand years. (The rest of the dead did not come to life until the thousand years were ended.) This is the first resurrection. Blessed and holy are those who share in the first resurrection. The second death has no power over them, but they will be priests of God and of Christ and will reign with him for a thousand years. When the thousand years are over, Satan will be released from his prison.*

The Scriptures are not silent concerning the Golden Age. The Bible student can find multitudes of Scriptures dealing with the subject of the Millennium. While not an exhaustive list of the topic of the Millennium, there are some key characteristics of this period of time.

Jesus in the Millennium

Christ will be personally present on earth and sit on the throne of His Father David. He will reign over all the earth. Two things will characterize Christ's kingdom on earth: universal peace and righteousness.

> Zechariah 14:9, *The LORD will be king over the whole earth. On that day there will be one LORD, and his name the only name.*

> Isaiah 11:3-4, *and he will delight in the fear of the LORD. He will not judge by what he sees with his eyes, or decide by what he hears with his ears; but with righteousness he will judge the needy, with justice he will give decisions for the poor of the earth. He will strike the earth with the rod of his mouth; with the breath of his lips he will slay the wicked.*

The Church and the Millennium

Although the Millennium is the blessing promised especially to Israel, do not overlook the fact that God has provided a unique place for the Church during this period. The church will reign with Christ over the Gentile world. The Church as the bride of Christ will sit with Christ on His throne.

> 1 Corinthians 6:2, *Or do you not know that the Lord's people will judge the world? And if you are to judge the world, are you not competent to judge trivial cases?*

> Revelation 20:4-6, *I saw thrones on which were seated those who had been given authority to judge. And I saw the souls of those who had been beheaded because of their testimony about Jesus and because of the word of God. They had not worshiped the beast or its image and had not received its mark on their foreheads or their hands. They came to life and reigned with Christ a thousand years. (The rest of the dead did not come to life until the thousand years were ended.) This is the first resurrection. Blessed and holy are those who share in the first resurrection. The second death has no power over them, but they will be priests of God and of Christ and will reign with him for a thousand years.*

> 2 Timothy 2:12, *if we endure, we will also reign with him. If we disown him, he will also disown us;*

The Character Of The Millennium As Regard To Israel

In contrast to the present age in which Jews and Gentiles are on an equal plane of privilege, the Millennium is clearly a period of time in which Israel is in prominence and blessing. Though many passages speak of Gentile blessings as well, Christ will reign as the Son of David, and Israel as a nation will be exalted. In the Old Testament, the regathering of Israel is a prominent theme through the prophets. During the Millennium that ultimate regathering, blessings, and restoration will take place.

> Isaiah 35:1-10, *The desert and the parched land will be glad; the wilderness will rejoice and blossom. Like the crocus, it will burst into bloom; it will rejoice greatly and shout for joy. The glory of Lebanon will be given to it, the splendor of Carmel and Sharon; they will see the glory of the Lord, the splendor of our God. Strengthen the feeble hands, steady the knees that give way; say to those with fearful hearts, "Be strong, do not fear; your God will come, he will come with vengeance; with divine retribution he will come to save you." Then will the eyes of the blind be opened and the ears of the deaf unstopped. Then will the lame leap like a deer, and the mute tongue shout for joy. Water will gush forth in the wilderness and streams in the desert. The burning sand will become a pool, the thirsty ground bubbling springs. In the haunts where jackals once lay, grass and reeds and papyrus will grow. And a highway will be there; it will be called the Way of Holiness; it will be for those who walk on that Way. The unclean will not journey on it; wicked fools will not go about on it. No lion will be there, nor any ravenous beast; they will not be found there. But*

only the redeemed will walk there, and those the Lord has rescued will return. They will enter Zion with singing; everlasting joy will crown their heads. Gladness and joy will overtake them, and sorrow and sighing will flee away.

Satan and the Millennium

The Bible declares that prior to setting up His earthly Kingdom, Christ will send an angel from heaven to cast Satan into the bottomless pit, where he shall remain during the entire period of the Millennium. During this time of the incarceration, Satan will be powerless to tempt the nations. Satan will continue to be immobile in the pit for 1,000 years, but at the end of the Millennium, he shall once again be turned loose for a short period of time. This is called the second coming of Satan.

> Revelation 20:1-3, *And I saw an angel coming down out of heaven, having the key to the Abyss and holding in his hand a great chain. He seized the dragon, that ancient serpent, who is the devil, or Satan, and bound him for a thousand years. He threw him into the Abyss, and locked and sealed it over him, to keep him from deceiving the nations anymore until the thousand years were ended. After that, he must be set free for a short time.*

The Mllennium and Nature

The Millennium will be a virtual paradise when the curse upon the earth will be lifted. One of the great changes that will take place at the millennium will be that ferocious animals will be altered. There will also be widespread topographical changes as well.

> Romans 8:19-22, *For the creation waits in eager expectation for the children of God to be revealed. For the creation was subjected to frustration, not by its own choice, but by the will of the one who subjected it, in hope that the creation itself will be liberated from its bondage to decay and brought into the freedom and glory of the children of God. We know that the whole creation has been groaning as in the pains of childbirth right up to the present time.*

> Isaiah 11:6-9, *The wolf will live with the lamb, the leopard will lie down with the goat, the calf and the lion and the yearling together; and a little child will lead them. The cow will feed with the bear, their young will lie down together, and the lion will eat straw like the ox. The infant will play near the cobra's den, and the young child will put its hand into the viper's nest. They will neither harm nor destroy on all my holy mountain, for the earth will be filled with the knowledge of the LORD as the waters cover the sea.*

General Conditions During The Millennium

The Bible presents the period as one of great personal joy and happiness. Physical healing will be granted to many. The Millennial Period will be one which will be void of threats of life. Sorrow will not be a threat, and joy will be experienced beyond our comprehension. Perhaps greatest of all will be a universal knowledge of the Lord.

> Isaiah 35:5-6 *Then will the eyes of the blind be opened and the ears of the deaf unstopped. Then will the lame leap like a deer, and the mute tongue shout for joy. Water will gush forth in the wilderness and streams in the desert.*

> Isaiah 35:10, *and those the LORD has rescued will return. They will enter Zion with singing; everlasting joy will crown their heads. Gladness and joy will overtake them, and sorrow and sighing will flee away.*

The Final Judgment

The final judgment is the last of seven judgments found in the book of Revelation. Jesus is the judge who sits on the throne for this final judgment. Those who are judged at this final judgment are those who have rejected Jesus Christ as Savior; therefore, they will stand face to face with Christ and give an account of their unbelief. However, Christ will not appear at this judgment as Savior but will appear as Judge. Those who are being judged are the dead both great and small. The term dead should be taken both physically and spiritually. The designations of "great and small" indicates that those who stand at this judgment come from all walks and stratum of life.

> Revelation 20:11-15, *Then I saw a great white throne and him who was seated on it. The earth and the heavens fled from his presence, and there was no place for them. And I saw the dead, great and small, standing before the throne, and books were opened. Another book was opened, which is the book of life. The dead were judged according to what they had done as recorded in the books. The sea gave up the dead that were in it, and death and Hades gave up the dead that were in them, and each person was judged according to what they had done. Then death and Hades were thrown into the lake of fire. The lake of fire is the second death. Anyone whose name was not found written in the book of life was thrown into the lake of fire.*

> Revelation 20:12, *And I saw the dead, great and small, standing before the throne, and books were opened. Another book was opened, which is the book of life. The dead were judged according to what they had done as recorded in the books.*

The condition of those who stand at this final judgment is that they are: Dead in sin (Eph. 2:1); under the wrath of God (John 3:36); already condemned (John 3:18); sinners (Romans 3:23); and enemies of God (Romans 5:10). The outcome of this Final Judgment will be the condemnation of the unregenerate sinners and the glorification of God.

The Eternal State of the Saved and Unsaved

When God's plan for humanity and the earth has been completed, and the eternal battle of good and evil has ceased, what is the final state of the unsaved and saved? When the judgments of both the saved and unsaved have ended, each of those groups will spend eternity somewhere.

First, let's look at the final condition of the unsaved or those who have rejected Jesus Christ as Savior and have died in trespasses and sin. If heaven is a definite place where the saved spend eternity, then there must also be an exact place where those who are lost spend eternity. This place is called the Lake of Fire, and Scripture makes it abundantly clear that it is a definite eternal place.

While not a popular topic, the doctrine of eternal death is clearly stated in Scripture. While many passages could be referenced here, let me just point out a few of them. In chapter 12, Daniel clearly states that everyone who dies will awake to either everlasting life or everlasting contempt. If we are willing to accept that everlasting means everlasting as it relates to "life," we must also be willing to agree that everlasting also means everlasting as it relates to the negative or "eternal contempt."

> Daniel 12:2, *Multitudes who sleep in the dust of the earth will awake: some to everlasting life, others to shame and everlasting contempt.*

Throughout His earthly ministry, Jesus spoke and taught some of the most comforting, loving, and encouraging words ever spoken. Many who reference the teachings of Jesus only focus on these loving and gracious words. However, on many occasions, Jesus also warned of the eternal punishment awaiting those who rejected Him and die in their sins. On several occasions, Jesus clearly pointed out that those who are righteous or saved will be rewarded with eternal life and joy while those who reject him will suffer eternal punishment.

> Matthew 25:41, *"Then he will say to those on his left, 'Depart from me, you who are cursed, into the eternal fire prepared for the devil and his angels.'"*

Matthew 25:46, *"Then they will go away to eternal punishment, but the righteous to eternal life."*

Mark 9:43, *If your hand causes you to stumble, cut it off. It is better for you to enter life maimed than with two hands to go into hell, where the fire never goes out.*

On numerous occasions, the book of Revelation explicitly states that the punishment of the unsaved will be eternal. This eternal punishment is referred to variously as the eternal torment, second death, or eternal punishment. The reason for this eternal punishment is that unbelievers' names are not found in the Book of Life which contains all the names of those who are saved. The place of this second death or eternal punishment is the Lake of Fire.

Revelation 14:11, *And the smoke of their torment will rise for ever and ever. There will be no rest day or night for those who worship the beast and its image, or for anyone who receives the mark of its name."*

Revelation 20:13-15, *The sea gave up the dead that were in it, and death and Hades gave up the dead that were in them, and each person was judged according to what they had done. Then death and Hades were thrown into the lake of fire. The lake of fire is the second death. Anyone whose name was not found written in the book of life was thrown into the lake of fire.*

Revelation 21:8, *But the cowardly, the unbelieving, the vile, the murderers, the sexually immoral, those who practice magic arts, the idolaters and all liars—they will be consigned to the fiery lake of burning sulfur. This is the second death."*

While the eternal state of unbelievers is sealed for eternal punishment, the eternal state of believers is completely different. The believer will experience the New Heaven eternally. This eternal experience will be free from pain, death, sin, and tears. Beyond that, it will even be free from all the bad memories of a life of difficulty regardless of how bad things were for the individual in this sinful and broken world. As much as the believer would like to think we can imagine how beautiful and magnificent this eternal life of joy will be with God in heaven, the Bible makes it clear we cannot even conceive of heaven's beauty and our eternal life with God.

Revelation 21:1-4, *Then I saw "a new heaven and a new earth," for the first heaven and the first earth had passed away, and there was no longer any sea. I saw the Holy City, the new Jerusalem, coming down out of heaven from God, prepared as a bride beautifully dressed for her husband. And I heard a loud voice from the throne saying, "Look! God's dwelling place is now among the people, and he will dwell with them. They will be his people, and God himself will be with them and be their God. 'He will wipe every tear from their eyes. There will be no more death' or mourning or crying or pain, for the old order of things has passed away."*

Isaiah 65:17, *See, I will create new heavens and a new earth. The former things will not be remembered, nor will they come to mind.*

1 Corinthians 2:9, *However, as it is written: "What no eye has seen, what no ear has heard, and what no human mind has conceived"—the things God has prepared for those who love him...*

Even beyond the above-mentioned glories for the believer, the Word of God also states that believers will eternally experience salvation, selflessness, association with God, perfect spiritual knowledge, fullness of glory and joy, no more sickness, and the very presence of the one we serve and worship, Jesus.

One of the most asked questions concerning our eternal future has to do with our heavenly bodies. What kind of body will we have eternally? While it is impossible to know exactly what these God given bodies will be like, the Word of God does provide some detail of the differences between our heavenly and earthly bodies. Our heavenly bodies are spiritual, imperishable and filled with glory and power. Our earthly bodies are perishable, weak, natural, and sown in dishonor. Our current bodies are fragile and susceptible to disease, deformity, and death. Our heavenly bodies are not.

1 Corinthians 15:42-44, *So will it be with the resurrection of the dead. The body that is sown is perishable, it is raised imperishable; it is sown in dishonor, it is raised in glory; it is sown in weakness, it is raised in power; it is sown a natural body, it is raised a spiritual body. If there is a natural body, there is also a spiritual body.*

1 Corinthians 15:53-55, *For the perishable must clothe itself with the imperishable, and the mortal with immortality. When the perishable has been clothed with the imperishable, and the mortal with immortality, then the saying that is written will come true: "Death has been swallowed up in victory." "Where, O death, is your victory? Where, O death, is your sting?"*

While we do not understand what our resurrected bodies will be like, we can take note of what Jesus' resurrected body was like. After His resurrection, Jesus could be physically touched, but he could also move through walls and doors. Jesus also ate, drank, sat, and talked with His disciples. Thus, just as Jesus' resurrected body was freed from physical limitations, so will our resurrected body be free from sin and limitations. Thus, we celebrate with the apostle Paul that through God's power, our lowly bodies will be transformed to be like Christ glorious body.

Philippians 3:20-21, 20, But our citizenship is in heaven. And we eagerly await a Savior from there, the Lord Jesus Christ, who, by the power that enables him to bring everything under his control, will transform our lowly bodies so that they will be like his glorious body.

Conclusion

What is a correct response to the study of the end times? As we examine the doctrine of the end times and glean insight about the Millennium, Tribulation, Rapture, eternal punishment of unbelievers and the eternal blessing of believers, we miss the point if all we come away with is more knowledge to discuss with other believers. No, the study of the end times should serve as motivation to share our faith more, witness more, worship more, and seek to grow the church more. Every Sunday when we sit in worship and see an empty seat, we should pray that God would bring us across someone's path this next week to invite to church or share the Gospel. The Gospel is good news for sure, but in reality, it is the only news that matters eternally. Let us consecrate ourselves to share it daily in order to see another soul make that transition from eternal death to eternal life. That is the message of the end times.

> 2 Corinthians 5:17-21, *Therefore, if anyone is in Christ, the new creation has come: The old has gone, the new is here! All this is from God, who reconciled us to himself through Christ and gave us the ministry of reconciliation: that God was reconciling the world to himself in Christ, not counting people's sins against them. And he has committed to us the message of reconciliation. We are therefore Christ's ambassadors, as though God were making his appeal through us. We implore you on Christ's behalf: Be reconciled to God. God made him who had no sin to be sin for us, so that in him we might become the righteousness of God.*

Glossary of Eschatological Terms

- Allegorical Interpretation: A method of interpretation which finds a sense higher than the literal sense in otherwise apparently historical statements.

- Amillennialism: The belief that there is no millennial reign of Christ on earth. The prefix "a" in Amillennialism means that this system of belief holds that there will be no literal millennium or 1,000-year reign of Christ.

- <u>Apocalupsis/Apocalypse</u>: Unveiling, uncovering or manifestation. Apocalypse is the most accurate title for the book of Revelation.

- <u>Bema Seat</u>: The judgment seat or reward seat before which each Christian must appear.

- <u>Cilia</u>: Greek word for one thousand (1,000).

- <u>Chiliasm:</u> A better term for the school of thought usually designated millenarianism.

- <u>Epiphaneia</u>: Revelation or appearance.

- <u>Eschatology</u>: The study of last things.

- <u>Gehenna:</u> Place of eternal suffering which is accurately translated "hell" in the New Testament.

- <u>Hades</u>: The abode of the dead (Greek), or the grave.

- <u>Harpazo:</u> To catch up or snatch away. This word is used of the translation of believers at the Lord's coming.

- <u>Kingdom:</u> May refer to (1) the reign of Christ in man's hearts, (2) the heavenly kingdom, or (3) the earthly kingdom of Christ.

- <u>Israel:</u> Except in rare instances, reference to the literal nation group designated Israel.

- <u>Mid-tribulational Rapture</u>: The Rapture will occur at the midpoint of the Tribulation.

- <u>Millennium</u>: Latin word for one thousand (1,000) years and specifically speaks to the reign of Jesus Christ.

- <u>Natural Interpretation:</u> The interpretation of Scripture which takes the natural sense of the word to be the right one.

- <u>Parousia</u>: Presence, and hence, the coming of the Lord to be with His own.

- <u>Postmillennialism</u>: The belief that Christ will return at the conclusion of the millennial age. The Second Coming of Jesus Christ comes after the "millennium" or after a golden age or era of Christian prosperity and dominance on the earth for good.

- <u>Post-tribulational Rapture</u>: The Rapture will occur at the end of the Tribulation.

- <u>Premillennialism</u>: The belief that Christ will return prior to the millennial age. The Second Coming of Jesus Christ will occur prior to His millennial kingdom, and that the millennial kingdom will be a "literal" 1000-year reign of Christ on earth.

- <u>Pre-tribulational Rapture:</u> The Rapture will occur before the Tribulation begins.

- <u>Rapture</u>: From Latin *ratio*, meaning "to snatch or seize." Rapture is a non-Biblical word used for the removal of Christians from the world at the appearance of Christ.

- <u>Sheol</u>: The abode of the dead (Hebrew).

- <u>Tribulation</u>: Seven-year period of unparalleled distress and judgment on earth. This future seven year period of distress on the earth is also referred to as the Great Tribulation although biblically speaking the Great Tribulation specifically references the last half of the Tribulation which is also the worst half of the Tribulation.

- <u>Scriptural References For The Harpazo/Rapture:</u>

Matthew 24:30-31, 24:32-44; John 14:2-3; 1 Corinthians 15:51-57; Colossians 3:4; 1 Thessalonians 4:13-18; Revelation. 20:6

- <u>Scriptural References For The Tribulation:</u>
  Isaiah 2:19, 24:1, 3, 6, 24:19-21; Jeremiah 30:7; Daniel 9:24-27, 12:1; Joel 2:1-2; Amos 5:18, 20; Zephaniah 1:14-18; Matthew 24:21-22; Luke 21:25-26; 1 Thessalonians 5:3; Rev. 6:15-17.

- <u>Scriptural References For The Millennium:</u>
  Isaiah 11:1-9, 2:1-5; Jeremiah 31:31-34; Joel 3:17-21; Amos 9:11-16; Micah 4:1-5; Luke 1:31-33; 1 Corinthians 15:24-28; Revelation 20:1-3.